THOMAS-ROBERT BUGEAUD

France and Algeria, 1784-1849:
Politics, Power, and the Good Society

Antony Thrall Sullivan

ARCHON BOOKS
1983

First published 1983 as an Archon Book,
an imprint of The Shoe String Press, Inc.
Hamden, Connecticut 06514

Printed in the United States of America

Library of Congress Cataloging in Publication Data

Sullivan, Antony Thrall.
    Thomas-Robert Bugeaud, France and Algeria, 1784-1849.
    Bibliography: p.
    Includes index.
    1. Bugeaud, Thomas Robert, duc d'Isly, 1784-1849.
2. Algeria—Governors—Biography.   3. Soldiers—
France—Biography.   I. Title.
DT294.B94S94   1983   965'.02'0924   [B]   82-18448
ISBN 0-208-01969-3

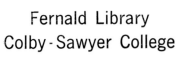

THOMAS-ROBERT BUGEAUD

To Marjory, Sandra and David
for whom Bugeaud
is a familiar companion

Contents

Acknowledgments

Among the pleasures of scholarly research are the guidance, encouragement, and counsel one receives. The debts that I incurred during preparation of this book are legion. Here, I can attempt partially to repay only a few. John Bowditch, Raymond Grew, and William Schorger helped greatly early on. J. Clayburn La Force and Dennis Showalter assisted at later stages. Pierre Boyer and Charles Uthéza in the Archives d'Outre-Mer in Aix-en-Provence went beyond the call of duty in placing their staffs and microfilm and copyflow capabilities at my disposal. Equally supportive were Noel Becquart, Jacqueline Faure, and their associates in the Archives du Département de la Dordogne (Perigueux). The advice of M. F. Dousset in the Archives de France in Paris made what once seemed an intimidating research project more manageable. Sonja Page did yeoman service as typist of two drafts of the manuscript. And to Jacques and Françoise Moiroux, Parisians and Perigordans extraordinary, goes my heartfelt appreciation for their unstinting hospitality.

Special thanks are due three individuals. Without the encouragement of Stephen Tonsor, this book would never have been begun. Without that of Melvin Richter, it might not have been completed. And without the support and patient understanding of my wife, who shares my fascination with the Mediterranean's several shores, the whole enterprise would have been far less satisfying. Of course, I alone am responsible for whatever defects may exist in this study.

9

Introduction

This analytical biography of Thomas-Robert Bugeaud attempts to integrate the European and metropolitan aspects of his career with the values, policies, and accomplishments evidenced during his sojourns in Algeria. Unlike all previous studies of Bugeaud or Algeria, it argues that much of what Bugeaud attempted or achieved in Africa after 1835 was foreshadowed in his earlier career in Spain or elsewhere in Europe or outlined in his speeches in the Chamber of Deputies during the 1830s. Similarly, the policies that Bugeaud advocated in France after 1846 grew out of personal and societal values which he acquired or validated overseas after 1841. The key to understanding Bugeaud's development during the final ten years of his life, I maintain, is an awareness of his encouragement and substitution of the violence of colonial warfare for that political *juste milieu* which he had once defended in France. Alienation and *durcissement*, both personal and collective, are fundamental to an appreciation of Bugeaud, the Algerian army, and French society in the decade prior to 1850. Hopefully, this book will prove useful to students of both French and North African history during the first half of the 19th century.

Few scholarly or interpretative studies of Bugeaud and his world exist. Indeed, the lack of serious attention to one of France's most outspoken agrarian ideologues and successful military commanders is surprising. Little scrutiny has been given to Bugeaud's career before 1841, or after 1847. The dearth of scholarship on his agricultural reforms, military ideas, and evolving political philosophy is particularly noteworthy. Thus, it may be useful to state briefly what

11

is "known" about Bugeaud, and highlight the major themes of this book.

Bugeaud is perhaps best known as the conqueror of Algeria and father of French rule in North Africa. He is considered the first of the great nineteenth and early twentieth century French empire builders. Unfortunately, the violence of war in Algeria during the 1840s endowed him with a reputation as an eternal and ferocious Rightist. William Langer, for example, describes Bugeaud as a "fire-eating" militarist "itching to put 'the rabble' in its place."[1] Langer's description of him is accurate for 1848, on the far side of the great Algerian divide. However, before 1841 Bugeaud was a different individual with rather different priorities. Nonetheless, Langer's description rests on a firm body of received opinion. As early as 1834, events in Paris helped Bugeaud gain a reputation as an incorrigible reactionary and extremist.

In mid-April 1834, riots broke out near the Hotel de Ville and were put down with considerable bloodshed. In the Rue Transnonain, national guardsmen and soldiers invaded one building from which they believed shots had been fired and massacred fourteen of the inhabitants. A famous lithograph by Daumier, depicting the riddled corpses of men, women, and children, memorialized the action, constituting a powerful political statement. Immediately, rumors spread that Bugeaud had directed the slaughter, and the press denounced him as "butcher of the Rue Transnonain." In reality, troops commanded by Bugeaud never entered the street, and he knew nothing of the massacre until hours later. A misplaced sense of loyalty kept him from denouncing General de Lascours, the officer responsible. Thereafter, Bugeaud grimly accepted the abuse heaped upon him. From 1834 on, the legend of "butcher of the Rue Transnonain" shaped writing and commentary on Bugeaud. In fact, then and later Bugeaud remained a defender of political Centrism. Before 1841, his principal political objective was to maintain the juste milieu. For purposes of this book, I use the term juste milieu as both a political definition and a moral category.

One of the least subtle of juste milieu theorists, Bugeaud during the quarter century after 1815 belonged to the parliamentary and intellectual party led by Francois Guizot and Pierre Paul Royer-Collard, a party that also included Camille Jordan, de Barante, de Broglie, and de Serre, with Pasquier and de Rémusat as occasional members. These exponents of "middlingness" were known as *doctrinaires*, not because of ideological inflexibility, but because of their professorial manner in parliamentary debate. That manner Bugeaud most emphatically did not share. However, he did faithfully advocate most of the school's principal beliefs. Although one biographer comments briefly on his commitment to the juste milieu, Bugeaud is not mentioned as a doctrinaire in either of the two best studies of post-Napoleonic political philosophy.[2]

Contrary to general belief, Bugeaud worried more about the Right than he did about the Left prior to 1835. Before 1841, his most violent combat experience was in Spain after 1807, where French troops struggled to repress Catholic, anti-Revolutionary conservatives. Never committed to the Jacobin ideology of territorial aggrandizement, Bugeaud rallied to the restored Monarchy in 1814. The following year, he attempted to defend the king by blocking Napoleon's march on Paris. Still, he accepted the restored Empire and fought brilliantly in Savoy in June 1815 against an Austro-Sardinian invasion force. During the next several years, he condemned Ultra extremism in the Midi, and warned against a possible Rightist coup d'etat. Throughout the two decades before 1835, Bugeaud continued to defend the political system established in 1815 against various Rightist conspiracies. He was a logical appointee as overseer of the imprisoned Duchesse de Berry in 1832 and 1833. At the same time, fear of the Right never drove him into alliance with the Left. Always, the juste milieu, that posture of political moderation between the competing claims of Left and Right, constituted his ideological lodestar.

As victor over the Arab chieftain Abdel Qadir and Duc d'Isly, Bugeaud long has occupied an important place in French history. Little understood, however, is the significance of that extremism which he and other *Algériens* imported into France from North Africa. That violence worked itself out in the streets of Paris during 1848, and again, even more savagely, twenty-three years later, during the civil war of 1871. To veterans of North Africa, it became ever more difficult to draw distinctions between foreign and domestic "savages". After 1848, alienation of the colonial army from European values continued to deepen, and it remained for several decades an active threat to maintenance of the metropolitan juste milieu.

Although there are detailed studies of aspects of Bugeaud's rule in Algeria, no work heretofore has tied his policies together into a consistent whole. The present study, by contrast, gives special attention to the French and indigenous hierarchy which Bugeaud attempted to create, the commercial policies which he favored, and the various benefits which he anticipated from European and native colonization. Among other purposes, Bugeaud designed these initiatives to render Algeria forever French, and to protect France itself from all European dangers. To date, few if any have been aware of the connection Bugeaud perceived between peace in North Africa and prosperity in the Dordogne. Below, we will show how Bugeaud negotiated with Abdel Qadir in order to secure subsidies for highway construction in Perigord. Especially during the late 1830s, Bugeaud's objectives as a French agrarian reformer had a significant impact on his conduct as a military commander and negotiator. This is another demonstration of the importance of adopting a trans-Mediterranean perspective in order to understand his career.

Agriculture was always one of Bugeaud's ruling passions. In an uncritical way, many books extol his commitment to the soil. However, no serious study has yet dealt with precisely what he was attempting to accomplish in the Perigordin countryside, and to what degree he was successful. Furthermore, links between his agrarianism and his wider world view remain obscure. Here, I have tried to elucidate connections between Bugeaud's agricultural reforms, his commitment to societal holism, and his general antimodernism. Agrarian traditionalism and rejection of politics as a means to material and moral improvement never ceased to animate his thought. When he died from cholera on June 10, 1849, Bugeaud already was well established as a prominent spokesman of French "peasantism."

Historians usually have discussed Bugeaud's military theories only in connection with his campaigns in Algeria, but this book attempts to paint a larger picture. It highlights the contributions of the Peninsular Campaign and of that desultory guerrilla warfare, or *chouannerie*, in the Vendée to his North African strategy, and underscores the importance of the idea of élan to Bugeaud and the significance of the notion of morale to subsequent French military thought.

Other aspects of Bugeaud's life remain largely unknown. His long-standing opposition to foreign adventures and territorial acquisitions (Algeria ultimately being an exception) has never been adequately discussed. No attention has been given to how his concern with preserving Centrism in France consistently shaped his recommendations on foreign affairs. Contrary to popular impression, moderation and prudence characterized his foreign policy, and continentalism provided its tone. In fact, even in Algeria something of this was apparent. Despite his sanction of generalized violence there, Bugeaud's desire to accelerate the conquest and thereby free France to respond to European dangers led him staunchly to defend Muslims who had surrendered. Paternalism, which he manifested earlier in the Dordogne was also apparent in his policies in North Africa. Unlike most French settlers, Bugeaud and the military came near to becoming Muslim advocates, attempting to restrict European colonization to specified zones, and providing native Algerians with improved hygiene and medical care. Here as elsewhere, Bugeaud's thought and action demonstrate a fine web of complexities.

Needless to say, this book does not purport to be a history of France and North Africa in the post-Napoleonic period. It was conceived as a monograph, and I have attempted to limit its focus primarily to Bugeaud. I have also tried to keep it as compact as possible, a general knowledge of French and Algerian history being assumed. All translations from the French (except where noted) are my own. Thus, let us begin.

1

The Sword and the Plow
Retrospect and Prospect

The youngest of seven surviving children, Thomas-Robert Bugeaud was born on October 15, 1784, to Jean-Ambroise and Françoise Sutton Bugeaud in Limoges, near the brow of the climatological divide between the northern European and Mediterranean worlds and the medieval marches between Christianity and Islam. Fortune apparently favored him. The wealthy Françoise Sutton de Clonard, of Irish Jacobite lineage, had contributed a dowry of 40,000 *livres* to the Bugeaud family coffers at the time of her marriage in 1771. Jean-Ambroise owned an estate west of Lanouaille, in Perigord, valued at 268,000 livres in 1781, and possessed a patent of nobility purchased in the early eighteenth century. During the 1780s, the Bugeauds were among the wealthier landed families in southwestern France. However, their wealth did not survive the revolutionary upheaval which began at decade's end.

In 1790 the National Assembly first extracted a loan of 110,000 livres from Jean-Ambroise Bugeaud, and then sequestered his estate at La Durantie. By 1791 he and his wife and their youngest daughter were in prison, there to remain until the fall of Robespierre in 1794. Their oldest sons had emigrated, and only the Bugeauds' three other daughters remained with their brother Thomas-Robert in the family home in Limoges. Survival was difficult for both children and parents. Financially, the sisters made ends meet by manufacturing shirts which the little Thomas-Robert delivered to customers in the city. Sixteen-year-old Phyllis was able to succeed, by frequent testimony before the local revolutionary tribunal, in postponing execution of her parents. During her testimony, she

usually had Thomas-Robert at her side. The two conducted themselves with a sophistication beyond their years, helping to assure
that all members of the family were still alive at Thermidor. Thomas-
Robert's early encounter with political extremism constituted an
experience which he probably never entirely forgot. For their parents, liberation brought little relief, however: Françoise Bugeaud
died of general debilitation in late 1794, and Jean-Ambroise, impoverished and embittered, became increasingly erratic and violent
in behavior. For all the Bugeauds, five years were apparently enough
to destroy totally the promise of pre-Revolutionary France.

However, their plight markedly improved after Thermidor.
Control of La Durantie was returned to them by the Directory, and
after 1795 the old country house became home to Jean-Ambroise's
daughters as well as a constantly changing collection of relatives.
He kept his son Thomas-Robert with him in Limoges, but gave the
boy little but abuse. Ill-clothed, hungry, and increasingly frightened
by the unpredictable rages of his father, Thomas-Robert finally fled
the city in 1797 and walked more than fifty kilometers to rejoin his
sisters at La Durantie. There, in the fields and woods that fell away
in all directions, he first developed the agrarianism and interest in
the region's inhabitants that characterized his subsequent career.

The years of his adolescence were happy ones. Bugeaud roamed
the area between Lanouaille and Nontron with his friends, learned
to speak the local patois fluently, and provided La Durantie with a
regular supply of rabbit and fish. He became adept at snaring hares
with a noose, and in identifying the places where trout were most
likely to be found. For most of six years, Bugeaud spent much of his
time with impoverished young sharecroppers, and he developed an
understanding of land and people which years and distance never
erased. Meanwhile, his sisters attempted to provide him with an
education. They insisted that he learn to read and write, and that he
commit to memory lengthy passages from Molière and Racine. So
well, indeed, did Bugeaud memorize them that he was able to recite
them without error forty years later. On several occasions he was
sent back to Limoges to attend school, and in 1799 he even won a
prize for excellence in French grammar. Still, most of his learning
occurred in the primitive Perigordin countryside. Even as he became far more literate than any of his boyhood companions, he
remained firmly one of them by preference and sentiment.

In 1802, as war broke out again in Europe, the eighteen-year-old Bugeaud confronted the problem of selecting a career. Prospects for farming at La Durantie appeared dismal: Much of the estate had reverted to wasteland, ownership was held by speculators and various family members, and there was no capital available either to improve the property or to consolidate ownership. Not wishing to leave Perigord, Bugeaud decided to seek employment locally. He investigated a variety of possibilities and made a particular effort to obtain a position as assistant to an area blacksmith. All his inquiries, however, proved fruitless. The military alone seemed to offer both immediate openings and some promise of advancement. With great reluctance, Bugeaud finally left La Durantie and, on June 29, 1804, enrolled at Fontainebleau in the foot grenadiers of the French Imperial Guard.

Army life, and the general military environment, proved even more uncongenial than he had anticipated. Throughout 1804 Bugeaud complained to his sister Phyllis about the womanizing of his fellow soldiers, and lamented that barracks life outside Fontainebleau gave him little opportunity to become acquainted with respectable individuals in the town. Isolated and lonely, the new recruit took refuge in books and private study. By year's end, his antipathy to the military had become profound: "One is such a slave," he wrote, "and subject to mistreatment by so many persons. To be a soldier one must be absolutely unfeeling—like marble."[1] The opening of the campaign of 1805 put Bugeaud's capacity for insensitivity to its first serious test.

That test the young soldier failed miserably. From Bologne, where the Third Company of the Fourth Batallion of the Imperial Guard had been stationed in early 1805 as part of Napoleon's cross-channel invasion force, Bugeaud's unit moved rapidly toward the upper Rhine and the approaches to Vienna, where it took part in the battle of Austerlitz in early December. The march south was replete with excesses, which left Bugeaud deeply troubled. "What particularly bothers me," he observed, "is the amount of molestation and the thefts to which the peasants are subject: their fowl, their wood, their bacon are all appropriated whether they like it or not."[2] When a sergeant urged the rape of a young woman in a home which had offered the grenadiers hospitality, Bugeaud promptly challenged him to a duel. The unlucky sergeant accepted the challenge but lost his wager: his wound proved fatal. Battle and pillage left Bugeaud shocked and saddened. "I will not describe...the horrors of war, the villages sacked, the wrongs and barbarities which it entails," he wrote. "I will only [say] that the profession of a hero is so much like that of a brigand that I hate it with all my soul. A man must have a heart of stone, destitute of all humanity, to love war."[3]

As a result of Austerlitz, where his batallion was in the thick of the fighting, Bugeaud's dislike of war intensified: "I have no desire to describe the horror of the battlefield—the wounded, the dying beseeching the compassion of their comrades....I would like the emperors and kings who go to war without legitimate cause to be condemned, throughout their life, to hear the screams of those unfortunate wounded soldiers who remained on the battlefield for three days without any assistance being provided them."[4] By 1806, he had concluded that combat led only to "calamities, inhumanity and ruin,"[5] and, in consequence, he decided to resign from the military.

Before that decision could be carried out, Bugeaud was wounded in the thigh at the battle of Pultusk. Prolonged rest and recuperation in Warsaw, and exposure to that city's cultural offerings, delayed execution of his decision. Finally, Bugeaud wrote a letter of resignation to the minister of war in early 1808, while on leave at La Durantie. That letter, entrusted to his sister for posting, was never mailed, however. When he received orders to join the 116th Regiment of the Line as a lieutenant and report to Spain, Bugeaud did so without complaint. By midsummer of that year, he was deeply involved in Napoleon's ill-fated Peninsular Campaign.

Participating in Napoleon's conquest of Central Europe had enabled Bugeaud to develop significant leadership capabilities which bore immediate fruit in Spain. In late July, 1808, Bugeaud's unit received news that the French garrison at Baylen, a half-day's march away, had capitulated. Rather than also surrender, Bugeaud urged that the unit attempt to escape to Madrid by a forced march through the mountains. This advice was accepted, and the march made successfully with Bugeaud commanding the rear guard. Thereafter, his rapid promotion seemed guaranteed. Nevertheless, the young officer's attitude toward militarism and the usages of war did not decisively change until 1809, and then as the result of bitter street fighting in the city of Saragossa. Saragossa, indeed, acted as a catalyst in Bugeaud's career, convincing him that any and all measures were legitimate in that total war which was necessary for repression of a people in arms. The lessons Bugeaud learned in Saragossa were to work themselves out in Algeria and France during and after the 1840s.

The French siege of Saragossa in January and February of 1809 exposed Bugeaud to an all-encompassing violence which he had never before experienced. The Spanish Catholics detested the "Godless" invaders, and they totally rejected the principles of the Revolution. Thus, the Saragossans engaged their attackers with an uncompromising and even suicidal fury. To Bugeaud, they seemed to desire to bury themselves beneath the ruins of their city. "Every convent, every house offers the same resistance as a citadel," he reported, "and each has to be individually besieged." Fanaticism, fury, and mass popular involvement meant that "everything is disputed foot by foot, from cellar to attic," and not until everyone had been "bayoneted to death or thrown out the windows" did resistance end.[6] In Bugeaud's opinion, the guidelines of traditional military doctrine were insufficient to meet the challenges newly posed by a fusion of ideology with generalized partisan resistance.

For the French command, the only apparent solution was to destroy much of the city and liquidate its inhabitants. Consequently, sappers were ordered in February to deposit explosives near strongpoints occupied by the Saragossans and, on signal, to blow buildings and defenders to bits. Bugeaud offered no objection: Saragossa and its inhabitants by then seemed "cursed" and "infernal" to him.[7] After Saragossa, Bugeaud never again protested military severity, particularly when brought to bear against a population in arms. Indeed, only a year later he proudly related his role in the bloody French conquest of Lerida and his success in sabering or bayoneting to death several defenders. He described, with evident amusement, what transpired after the city fell: "The soldiers, eager for loot, fanned out through all the houses; carnage ceased and gave way to scenes of quite another sort: everywhere one saw the conquerors in the arms of the conquered. Carmelites, old grizzled nuns, young sisters, all experienced the ecstasy of our grenadiers, and several cried out to the effect that 'If we had known that this was all that would happen, we would not have been so afraid!'"[8] Surely, his Rhenish campaign must have seemed a very long time ago.

Bugeaud's experiences in Saragossa convinced him that French tactical inflexibilities accounted for much of the bitterness and duration of that siege. In 1809, he began to insist that if troops were to respond effectively to irregular warfare, more was required of them than the ability to "execute on a parade ground the various lessons taught in the military handbook."[9] Campaigns in the Catalonian countryside during 1810 persuaded him that it was not always superior numbers which led to victory. "Forces inferior to an enemy in size but made up of brave men and commanded by a clever individual have nothing to fear," he observed. "They may sustain a momentary setback, but their steadfastness and determination will provide their commander the wherewithal to take advantage of a favorable turn of events and recoup everything in an instant."[10] During the next two years, Bugeaud lectured his subordinates regularly concerning tactics which he had personally found effective in curbing guerrilla resistance.[11] In 1811, he was promoted to *chef de bataillon* and inducted into the Legion of Honor. Thus, within only a few years he had evolved from an embittered critic of soldierly values to an acknowledged authority on some of the more uncompromising of military usages. In December 1813, Marshal Suchet recommended that Bugeaud be promoted to lieutenant colonel of the 14th Regiment of the Line. On the eve of the Hundred Days, he was recognized as one of the most promising junior officers in the French army.

Bugeaud's developing commitment to the French military, however, was unassociated with any loyalty to Napoleon or the principles of Bonapartism. Withdrawn from Spain early in 1814 with the remnant of the French Peninsular forces and assigned to garrison duty in the strongly Royalist town of Orleans, he received the news of the emperor's abdication with equanimity. In fact, during the early summer of 1814 Bugeaud participated in Orleans's official welcome for the Duchesse of Angoulème, and composed a military ballad which was set to music to grace the occasion:

> Far from our Fatherland
> Have we recently traveled
> And the springtime of our lives
> Has been sown by battles alone;
> Destiny today, less harsh,   ~

Has blessed us doubly:
In *Louis* has it given us a father
And to Orléans has it brought us.
"Go," this good king tells us,
"Be happy, it is high time;
I desire a merry issue
For my children's every day.
Entertainment, games and warm communion
Will here fill your leisure time.
But amid all your pleasures sweet
Do not forget the God of War."[12]

When Louis XVIII promoted him to colonel on June 11, 1814, Bugeaud's satisfaction was marked[13] and his support of the Bourbon Monarchy and the principles of the Settlement of 1814 born.

Rumors of impending difficulties along the lower Rhône were sufficient early in March 1815, for the monarchy to order Bugeaud to move the Orleans garrison toward Lyons to bolster a corps being concentrated there under the command of the Count of Artois. At Montargnis, some twenty-five miles east of Orleans, Bugeaud received news of Napoleon's landing on the Mediterranean coast. Unable to join with the forces north of Lyons as he had been ordered in order to prevent a breakthrough by the emperor into the Loire valley, Bugeaud led a determined struggle from March 6 through March 16 to maintain the loyalty of his troops to the restored Monarchy. To the best of his ability, he attempted to prevent collapse of the Burgundian defenses on the road to Paris.

That effort, of course, was doomed to failure. Already at Montargnis the people were drinking to Bonaparte's health in the local taverns, and disaffection was evident among the soldiery. Bugeaud's response was to remind his officers of the "loyalty we have sworn to the king," and to issue a proclamation to his troops informing them that Napoleon's landing "would be disastrous for France if the country did not have soldiers loyal to their oaths and their duties. You will not listen, I am sure, to the urgings to which certain malevolent individuals may subject you. You have too strong a sense of honor to abandon the flag which you have sworn to defend. I count on you as I count on myself; we will do our duty whatever the circumstances. Long live the king!"[14]

As Bugeaud advanced through Joigny toward Avallon during the second week of March, he found the countryside increasingly excited and became convinced that 90 percent of the population of Burgundy had rallied to Napoleon. At Avallon, where the tricolor was publicly displayed, he learned that the emperor had taken Lyons on March 12 and intended to march on Paris immediately. He consequently determined to fall back toward Auxerre since his troops were "too disaffected to bring them any nearer to the source of the problem."[15] The troops' opposition to this reversal of direction, and the sudden arrival of news that Napoleon was approaching the outskirts of Avallon, led them to send a deputation representing the rank and file to Bugeaud to inform him that his soldiers would no longer acknowledge his command unless he rallied to the emperor. Bugeaud thereupon informed the Ministry of War that the collapse of discipline and mass popular disaffection made further resistance impossible. "It was," he reported, "no longer possible to hold the 14th in check," and he confessed that he himself had been temporarily carried away by the "unanimous support [for Napoleon] of the troops and the people who came swarming in from the countryside, rending the air with their cries."[16] At Auxerre, on March 17, Bugeaud quietly drew up his troops for review by Bonaparte and ended his effort to defend the monarchy by denying the emperor access northward. Three days later Napoleon was in Paris.

With the dynastic question apparently settled by popular acclamation, Bugeaud turned his attention to how to counter an invasion by the Allied forces now poised on the frontiers. Planning was interrupted, however, when he was denounced in April as a Royalist and ordered furloughed by Marshal Davout, Napoleon's new minister of war. Intercession by generals Grouchy, Gérard, and Bertrand and direct intervention by the emperor himself were necessary to bring about Bugeaud's reinstatement. Demonstrating his continuing political adroitness, and an ability to separate talent from ideology, Napoleon informed Bugeaud on May 8 that he had been "satisfied" with his behavior. "You were unjustly removed from command of the 14th Regiment of the Line with which you joined me at Auxerre," the emperor wrote. "I have ordered that it be returned to you, and, as proof of my satisfaction, I have named you commander of the Legion of Honor."[17] Nevertheless, Bugeaud's adherence to the principles of the Restoration of 1814, and his commitment to defend the territorial integrity of France rather than the particularities of any reconstituted Napoleonic regime, had almost cost the country the services of an outstanding young officer. Always, Bugeaud emphasized that the only reason that he departed under the Napoleonic banner to check the Austro-Sardinian advance into Savoy was from a "desire to keep my country from foreign invasion... and a passion to defend the Fatherland."[18] However forgotten under the Second Restoration, the sincerity of Bugeaud's Royalism was certainly recognized by the Napoleonic general staff in the last few weeks before Waterloo.

During the last half of June 1815, the 14th Regiment of the Line constituted the avant-garde of the Army of the Alps and performed brilliantly under Suchet and Bugeaud. Despite being outnumbered by four or five to one, the regiment helped to halt the Austro-Sardinian advance and won a signal victory at L'Hopital-les-Conflans. There, it killed two thousand of ten thousand attacking Austrians and took eight hundred prisoners. Bugeaud put to good use the lessons he had learned in Spain concerning mobility and military outposts and forward patrols. However, following news of the occupation of Paris morale rapidly collapsed, and proscription on July 24 of leading Napoleonic commanders by the restored Monarchy brought effective resistance to an end. Furthermore, beginnings of the White Terror in the Midi stimulated widespread rank-and-file desertions. For Bugeaud, final dissolution of the Napoleonic imperium offered a chance to rally support for that Monarchy which he had recently so unwillingly abandoned. At month's end, he composed and distributed a broadside appealing to all deserters to return to their posts. Promising amnesty to returnees and reprisals against those who failed to do so, he concluded by imploring everyone to "*Return, return, it is your Colonel who calls upon you to do so; the entire army is rallying to the king for the welfare of France.*"[19] Probably, Bugeaud felt considerable relief at finally being free to give unqualified public expression to his Royalist convictions.

Any such relief was short-lived. Despite all his efforts on behalf of the Monarchy, Bugeaud was denounced as a "brigand of the Loire" during the autumn, placed on half-salary, and furloughed from the army on November 11, 1815. Surprisingly, even this compensation for his efforts failed to shake his support for the Restoration and the principles of the Charter of 1815.

Early in the new year, Bugeaud observed that his devotion to Louis XVIII was increasing daily, and that the king was "as essential for the survival of France as air is for that of an animal."[20] Such Royalist enthusiasm, however, did not extend either to the Monarchist extremism of terrorists who rampaged through the Midi in the late summer of 1815, or to the Ultra Royalist faction which soon coalesced to the right of the king. Support of the revised Settlement of 1814 soon led Bugeaud to champion the king against extremists of the Right as vigorously as he had previously attempted to protect him from attacks from the Left. From his country house in Perigord, Bugeaud increasingly came to advocate the juste milieu as vital to the equilibrium of France.

As frenzied mobs murdered Napoleonic commanders and reputed Bonapartist sympathizers in such cities as Avignon and Nimes, Bugeaud condemned the way in which "the inhabitants of the Midi, or at least the Royalists, are covering themselves with infamy through their numerous assassinations." He deplored the killing of General Ramel in Toulouse, and expressed hope that "as soon as his Majesty is able to do so" he would "punish these brigands who sport the white and green cockade." In any event, such "false Royalists" had no claim on the loyalty of true supporters of Legitimacy, since they preferred the Duke of Angoulême to the king.[21] Basically, the anarchy for which Bugeaud held them responsible seemed to him to threaten the integrity of France at least as much as had the passions evoked by the emperor's return five months earlier. This conviction was strengthened by his knowledge that his name had been placed on a list of those marked for assassination in the Dordogne. "One of my relatives," Bugeaud wrote later, "who participated in a meeting with the assassins told me to be on my guard, and from then on I only went out armed. I barricaded myself in each evening.... You can imagine how pleasant my life was."[22] Clearly, the postwar Right offered no home for a supporter of political moderation.

If Ultra-fomented anarchy and civil war were anathema to Bugeaud, he made no attempt to respond by alliance with the Ultra's ideological opposites. However, he had every reason to do so. During the first several months of 1816 he was subjected to close surveillance by Louis de Montureux, a former émigré who had become prefect of the Dordogne. Of Ultra persuasion, Montureux judged Bugeaud dangerous and "capable of undertaking anything against the government of the king." He ordered Bugeaud's hunting rifle confiscated, and established close contact with the Ministry of Police in Paris. In February, Montureux informed the ministry that Bugeaud planned to visit the nearby town of Bergerac, where it was likely that he intended to make seditious contact with General Mesclop.[23] In fact, Bugeaud desired nothing more than to reminisce about the war in Spain with an old friend. The minister of police reported the matter to the Ministry of War, and charged Montureux to pass on any information that he had uncovered concerning results of Bugeaud's trip to Bergerac.[24] Bugeaud protested all of this attention, and inquired of one friend whether he believed such surveillance was "the way to serve the king well."[25] Nevertheless, alliance with the Left was unattractive to one who "despised extremism," and Bugeaud determined to keep company "neither with one side or the other."[26] He simply was "too much of a Frenchman," he insisted, ever to consider shedding the blood of his fellow citizens if they did not threaten his life.[27] By late 1816, Bugeaud was articulating the Centrist doctrine which was the basis of his political posture until the early 1840s. Opposed to all political enthusiasms, he had already become convinced that the juste milieu required maintenance of a position of moderation and an avoidance of all doctrinaire ideologies.

Political debate and parliamentary maneuvering during the early Restoration years revolved around the Monarchy's relationship to the Charter of 1815. Maintenance of the charter, Bugeaud believed, was vital in order for the politics of Centrism to survive and prosper. When in 1816 an emergent faction of Ultra Royalists challenged the Monarchy's interpretation of the charter, Bugeaud rallied to the king's defense. Describing himself as a "true constitutionalist," he emphasized the "absolute necessity" of upholding the Settlement of 1814. He spoke disparagingly of "dissemblers" among those who described themselves as great friends of the king and who pretended to be more committed to the charter than was Louis XVIII.[28] For Bugeaud, maintenance of the Restoration required that the Bourbon dynasty be strengthened, and that it retain that principle of hereditary succession, which was "very propitious" for liberty.[29] In Bugeaud's opinion, liberty was both a product and a constituent part of Legitimacy. The juste milieu would be shattered, he clearly believed, were revolution to issue from any quarter of the political spectrum and threaten a Monarchy which "alone [could] guarantee the welfare of France."[30]

Before 1820, however, Bugeaud was convinced that the source of possible revolution lay entirely on the Right. Throughout the five years after 1815, he continued to fear Ultra extremism deeply and to work to neutralize it. For their part, Royalists had little use for Bugeaud. His criticisms of their more strident spokesmen alienated them, and they misunderstood the motives which had led him to campaign under Napoleon during the Hundred Days. Pierre Magne, later to serve with Bugeaud in the Chamber of Deputies, described Royalist sentiment well in recalling Bugeaud's visit to the Magne family home early in 1818. "For my fervently Royalist parents," he observed, "this visit was a matter of great unpleasantness. They had an instinctive distaste for the Empire and everything connected with it....Colonel Bugeaud was highly suspect in the eyes of the Royalist party....For us, he was an ogre."[31] Such antipathy probably was not diminished when, a year later, Bugeaud reprimanded his friend d'Esclaibes d'Hust for joining a group made up mainly of Ultras. He was confident, Bugeaud noted in 1819, that d'Esclaibes possessed "too much good judgment to subscribe to the extremism of their views." He added that "those individuals do us serious harm by continually impeding the gradual and natural evolution of our institutions. We have an electoral law which, without being perfect, provides us with guarantees; they want to take it away from us...." In his response to what were apparently suggestions by d'Esclaibes that he modify his opposition to the Ultras, Bugeaud manifested an already well-developed denunciatory rhetoric. "If you mean the group which includes the fanatics of 1815," he stated, "the writers of the staffs of the *Conservateur*, the *Drapeau blanc*, the *Quotidienne* and those who read these papers with enthusiasm, the persecutors of the army, the detractors of France, the enemies of our glory and our liberty, the authors of the crimes of the Midi, the apologists who continually excuse them by citing in response the horrors of '93, never, never, never will I be a part of this infamous faction...."[32] Although he considered Jacobins "odious" and "irreconcilable monsters," they did not in 1819 provide a comparable threat to the Settlement of 1814 because they were more discredited.[33] The Ultra, however, was dangerous because of his ubiquity around the throne. The dogmatism of those Ultras who had shown themselves ready to have "all who were not *pure* removed from office and replaced by the most inept and frequently the most immoral individuals"[34] was for Bugeaud as much an obstacle to preservation of the juste milieu as it apparently had proven to advancement of his own military career.

Despite the surfacing of Carbonarist conspiracies in the early 1820s, Bugeaud continued to worry over possible implications of Ultra charges that the king's councilors (and even the king himself) were in fact Jacobins. Throughout the decade his most fundamental concern was that the Monarchy remain strong in order to protect the constitution. Increasingly, Bugeaud came to perceive the restored Bourbons as the very embodiment and exemplar of France. For example, in 1826 he led the assembled peasantry of the canton of Lanouaille in the following toast: "To his Majestry Charles X! May his reign, as he so devoutly wishes, grant to our dear France all the prosperity which its prominence and the genius of its inhabitants demand."[35] Obviously, Bugeaud believed that the king should rule as well as reign. Nevertheless, shortly before the Revolution of 1830 he had begun to emphasize how important it was that the "Chambers [be left] all their rights," and that political concessions not be too long delayed.[36] If by 1830 preservation of the Settlement of 1814 seemed to require compromise with the Left rather than repression of the Right, Bugeaud was sufficiently sophisticated to counsel the course of political prudence. The juste milieu, soon to be threatened by the fall of the Monarchy and the unrest of the 1830s, obviously constituted the axis around which his political views revolved during his fifteen-year provincial exile.

During those years in Perigord, however, Bugeaud devoted more attention to agricultural than to political problems. Improvement of farmland at La Durantie through a variety of innovations, and a growing conviction that he was destined to effect an agricultural revolution in the region led him after 1820 to proselytize the landowners and impoverished sharecroppers of the area. In 1816, however, all that was in the future. Indeed, there then seemed little likelihood that the Bugeaud family home would ever lodge a master sufficiently prosperous to launch a major effort to improve it. Everything changed, however, with Bugeaud's marriage early in 1818 to Elisabeth Jouffre de Lafaye, an attractive eighteen-year-old who belonged to one of the Dordogne's oldest, wealthiest, and most influential families. The bride brought her thirty-four-year-old husband the magnificent dowry of 240,000 francs. In addition, she granted him title to family property in the Vendée which Bugeaud promptly sold for an additional 250,000 francs. Of this new wealth,[37] 180,000 francs were spent to purchase control of all of La Durantie. By late 1819, Bugeaud was sole owner of most of his family's eighteenth-century holdings. Apart from forest lands, these consisted of approximately seven hundred hectares (some seventeen hundred acres) of potentially arable soil. The following year, he initiated those agricultural innovations which soon attracted imitators in all strata of society, and later were to inspire an important part of his campaign for effective French control in Algeria.

The challenge which Bugeaud faced was clear. After three decades of neglect, large sections of his property had reverted to wilderness. On it, some dozen *métayers*, or sharecroppers, grew only a little buckwheat, rye, and turnips. Like their kind everywhere south of the Loire, they lived in wretched hovels and often were close to starvation. From time immemorial, farming routine at La Durantie and elsewhere consisted of the *assolement biennal*, or the annual alternation between the planting of wheat and the leaving of land fallow. During fallow years, animal dung was typically plowed into the land in hopes of fertilizing it. However, this *jachère labourée*, involving the turning over and exposure of several inches of topsoil to the summer sun, tended to deprive the land of most of the benefits which fallow years might otherwise have provided. Thus, at the end of fallow periods the earth was often little richer than it had been at the start. This fallow-farming sequence offered little possibility of significant improvement to either the soil or the livestock: "Wheat and fallow land, always the same amount of fodder for the animals—hay, perhaps a little alfalfa," a local expert observed years later. "Absolutely no progress, no improvement."[38] First on his own estate, and later in the Canton of Lanouaille and elsewhere, Bugeaud launched a three-pronged campaign to change these ancient customs. That campaign emphasized (1) suppression of the established fallow field system; (2) enrichment and increase of farmland; and (3) modest improvement in the condition of the métayer.

Of course, an end to the assolement biennal was dependent on enriching or augmenting farmland to the point that the fallow field system was rendered unnecessary. In Bugeaud's opinion, cultivation of such forage as clover (for which the region's soil was particularly well suited), alfalfa, and sainfoin would add significantly to the land's fertility, support a larger number of animals, and provide métayer and proprietor alike more income and a brighter future. His laboratory was La Durantie, and the initial results there were little less than spectacular. During 1820 Bugeaud terminated the jachère labourée, and planted much of the property with clover. Not only was the soil enriched, but the clover grown in 1821 enabled him to project the doubling of his herds.[39] Additional animals fattened on this crop meant more manure, which could be used to fertilize lands that now were planted with wheat or potatoes rather than reserved for use during the jachère labourée. Suppression of the fallow field system through application of herbaceous and animal fertilizer enabled the amount of land under cultivation to be doubled. In addition, it persuaded Bugeaud to begin to publicize his innovations. From 1821 on, he made regular presentations on farming techniques to the Dordogne's infant Agricultural Society, an organization which he had helped to found in 1820.

Constantly, Bugeaud maintained that all agriculturalists should "devote themselves to the *cultivation of forage, the basis of all enlightened farming.*" He observed that he could "not repeat this too often, until everyone has got it through his head." To accelerate soil enrichment, he recommended the removal of topsoil from areas where there was an excess and redistribution of it to places where it was in short supply.[40] Typically, such topsoil-hungry locations were on the upper reaches of hillsides and in areas whose soil was characterized by a significant admixture of clay. For the same purpose, Bugeaud underlined the importance of sheep, and urged that they be stabled in movable enclosures in the fields themselves. Such "parking" of animals would make it unnecessary to transport manure to fields from a distance, and guarantee that dung would lose none of its ingredients while awaiting application. Indeed, so important did Bugeaud consider an increase in the number and size of four-legged "manure machines" that he persuaded seven other landowners to join with him in 1821 to found the Canton of Lanouaille's first livestock improvement society.[41] Such efforts won him the favor of Huchet de Cintré, who had replaced Montureux as prefect in 1819, and the backing of other large farmers. Cintré was particularly admiring: "Colonel Bugeaud has helped me greatly by his sacrifices and the splendid experiments he has undertaken," he observed several years later. "His ability and experience have significantly improved the backward agriculture of Perigord."[42] The Dordogne's Agricultural Society officially endorsed Bugeaud's activities as early as 1821: "Colonel Bugeaud speaks on the basis of his own experience," the minutes of a meeting on April 24 note. "What he advises, he has done; in imitating him, others will succeed as he has."[43] Thereafter, agricultural improvements inside and outside La Durantie maintained something of a symbiotic relationship.

Always, however, the central exhibit was La Durantie itself. In late 1822, Bugeaud described in detail what had been accomplished here. "My first concern was to suppress the pernicious fallow field system,"[44] he wrote. By May of 1822, clover stood "three and a half feet high" in his fields. With the help of clover, Bugeaud reported, he had "got rid of several acres of wasteland, and been able to cut down a large stand of chestnut trees which wasn't producing anything. Without the clover," he added, "I would never have thought to do so, for I would already have had more land than I could have worked."[45] Thus, ending the jachère labourée freed human resources to open new lands to planting and improvement. Bugeaud's sharecroppers were quick to recognize that his innovations promised more food—and probably made survival more certain. By the end of 1822, all of them had adopted his system, and they themselves had begun to reclaim wasteland and remove chestnut trees in order to plant clover.[46] Only three years after its consolidation under his ownership, La Durantie had clearly become the lodestar for the transformation of a portion of rural Perigord.

During the next ten years, that transformation was stimulated by Bugeaud's leadership in the Dordogne's Agricultural Society. Objections or inattention to the importance of forage and livestock elicited his formal criticism. For example, he dismissed arguments that an increase in land planted with forage would be at the expense of land planted with wheat. Forage, Bugeaud maintained, meant that harvests of wheat would become more bountiful, since more wheat would be able to be grown on land so enriched. Forage was essential if more manure were to be available for use as fertilizer, and he continued to insist on cultivation of clover and other crops for consumption as fodder by larger numbers of livestock.[47] In 1823, Bugeaud even suggested a way of crossbreeding the Dordogne's cattle to enlarge and improve the race. Several years later he described a new type of wheat thresher employed at La Durantie and offered to demonstrate it publicly in Perigueux. He also displayed to Agricultural Society members an improved plow which he had recently imported from Grenoble. In 1830, Bugeaud persuaded twelve other notables to join with him and contribute funds to establish a model farm near Lanouaille. He agreed to serve as director, which, as one observer remarked, "itself guaranteed success." Among the original subscribers to this model farm were another landowner and the mayor, curé, and principal of the *collège* of Excideuil, two doctors, a lawyer, a notary, and a retired officer.[48] At decade's end, Bugeaud's "zeal and insight into agriculture"[49] were well recognized by the elite in the Department's northern sections.

However, the greatest appreciation of his accomplishments may have come from Bugeaud's own métayers and domestic servants. In 1823, there were at La Durantie twelve domestics plus thirteen sharecropper families, totaling 106 persons.[50] By the mid-1820s, métayers and domestics alike had begun to benefit from the use of Bugeaud's methods everywhere on his estate. Indeed, improvements in their status may have contributed to their initial support for establishment of an elementary school in Bugeaud's home for the commune's children. At the time, 80 percent of the Dordogne's population was illiterate. Founding of a school by a Perigordin landowner was unprecedented, few then believing that the generally impoverished country folk were even minimally educable. Unfortunately, results were limited. The number of pupils in attendance at Bugeaud's school never exceeded thirty, and the total was usually far less. None ever remained for an entire school year. By the early 1830s, Bugeaud had concluded that much greater agricultural progress was required before parents would be willing to release children from fieldwork for schooling. In his opinion, improvement in the conditions of rural life had to precede efforts to reduce illiteracy.[51] His educational experiment found no imitators elsewhere in the Department.

Institutionalization of Bugeaud's agrarian reforms was most effectively accomplished by the *comice agricole* (agricultural committee) of the Canton of Lanouaille, founded at La Durantie in the late summer of 1824 with the declared purpose of "accelerating as much as possible agricultural progress in the surrounding country-

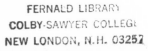

side."[52] Bugeaud was chosen president, a title he retained without interruption until 1841. This was the first of the comices which were established throughout France during the next thirty years, and which functioned (unlike the more academic agricultural societies) as combined country fairs and rural supply depots. Bolstered by prefectural support and donations from both landowners and the local bourgeoisie, Lanouaille's comice declared itself open to all cultivators in the canton, established annual dues, and endorsed the periodic distribution of prizes for the best forage and fattest livestock produced by the area's sharecroppers. Suppression of the jachère labourée was specified as a primary objective. Bugeaud expressed his willingness to provide counsel and assistance to all attempts at innovation which the new organization might stimulate.[53] It was a commitment which he fulfilled with enthusiasm for almost twenty years.

For Bugeaud and the other founders of the Lanouaille comice, direct involvement of the rural masses in agricultural reform was essential. This the Departmental Agricultural Society had never sought to accomplish. From its inception, the comice at Lanouaille attempted to forge links between landowner and sharecropper throughout the canton similar to those Bugeaud had already created on his own property. Fundamentally, its purpose was to enlist other large proprietors in a campaign to convert the region's métayers to Bugeaud's farming methods. The Agricultural Society, a number of whose members were also members of the comice, endorsed this effort, and beginning in 1826 granted the comice biannual contributions of 200 francs. The society expressed a desire that as many new comices be established as possible.[54] By late 1826, the recognition and festivities connected with the Lanouaille comice's distribution of prizes had evoked a positive response from both proprietors and sharecroppers. Soon, this annual fair became a major event in the local rural year.

In 1826, the comice began the tradition of sponsoring the fair in the late spring. On June 4 of that year, festivities took place under an enormous tent pitched to shelter participants from the weather. Officers of the comice sat at a high table in the center, and spectators placed themselves wherever space could be found. Attendance totaled approximately sixty persons. Flowers decorated every corner. On one side plows, pitchforks, hoes, wheelbarrows, and oxen yokes were displayed, and on the other were tethered the canton's heaviest bulls, heifers, and oxen. Monetary prizes were distributed to the animals' owners and wreaths placed around the beasts' necks, and awards were given to those judged to have grown the best clover. Bugeaud concluded the business session with a rousing speech reiterating his principal agricultural proposals. Everyone then repaired to enjoy a banquet followed by dancing to music played by performers Bugeaud had imported from Excideuil.[55] Subsequent fairs followed the same pattern, and Bugeaud was usually the principal speaker. Establishment of additional comices in 1827 and 1828 at Montagrier, Fayolle, and Jumilhac-le-Grand demonstrated the popularity of the activities at Lanouaille. Covered as it was by lush fields of clover, wheat, potatoes, and sugar beets, La Durantie increasingly became a catalyst for agricultural innovation.[56] On the eve of the July Revolution, Bugeaud doubtlessly considered his future to lie entirely in the area of provincial agrarian reform.

By 1830 Bugeaud had already come to identify agricultural with military values, and to see congruencies between bucolic and martial enterprises. His estate's dependents, whose "maneuvers" he directed, constituted for him the "effective force of a company." If one "included animals with dependents" (evidently an easy association for Bugeaud), he commanded, as he proudly stated, a "good-sized battalion."[57] Despite the passage of time and his deepening involvement in rural affairs he never completely adopted civilian mores or shed military values. Throughout the 1820s, he maintained contact with Marshal Suchet and generals Valée and Saint-Cyr. His observation that "several Roman dictators"[58] lacked a retreat as pleasant as La Durantie had overtones of attitudes sown by the Peninsular Campaign, and constituted an augury of his ultimate political and moral evolution. Bugeaud's enthusiasm for the plow and the sword, nurtured in Perigord and Spain, would ultimately blossom in Algeria.

2

The 1830s
Domestic Policy
and French Society

In the year following the Revolution of 1830 Bugeaud was elected to represent Excideuil in the Chamber of Deputies by that district's electoral college. Excideuil reelected him without interruption until 1847,[1] and the chamber became, along with Lanouaille's comice agricole and the army, a principal stage upon which his public career was enacted. Throughout the 1830s, Bugeaud emphasized his conviction that the values and practice of agriculture constituted the basis of a good society and offered the major avenue to national and individual betterment. His holistic agrarianism, strengthened by more than a decade of struggle for rural reforms in Perigord, led him to denounce the increasing ascendancy he perceived of city over countryside, to advocate establishment of comices agricoles throughout France, and to insist that broad political participation was irrelevant and even inimical to agricultural progress, moral improvement, and "responsible," representative government.

Bugeaud won his first political victory in 1831 only by the narrowest of margins. Following the overthrow of Charles X, the Dordogne had been divided into seven electoral districts, the number of electors varying between 219 in Excideuil and 413 in Bergerac. Bugeaud, convinced that the time had come to carry his beliefs to Paris, campaigned in Excideuil on the basis of his long-standing support for the juste milieu. His opponent, a Doctor Montagut from Perigueux, campaigned as spokesman for the liberal and republican Left. The election was hotly contested, and neither candidate received the absolute majority required for victory on the first round of balloting. When second-round votes were tallied on July

7, Bugeaud emerged as the winner, garnering 93 of 181 votes cast. However, his margin of victory was only five votes. Shortly thereafter, he launched a campaign to solidify his political base by advocacy of locally popular economic and agricultural policies, and encouragement of stronger regional support for the juste milieu. That effort soon bore fruit, and more than a decade passed before Bugeaud again encountered serious political opposition in Excideuil.

Meanwhile, he was reactivated by the military. In September 1830, Bugeaud was named colonel of the 56th Regiment of the Line stationed in Grenoble. On April 2, 1831, he was promoted to *maréchal de camp*, a rank approximating that of brigadier general. This recognition delighted him, although he did consider it substantially overdue.[2] When he assumed his responsibilities in the Chamber of Deputies late that summer, it was as both a prominent local notable and a soldier of high rank.

During the 1830s, Bugeaud emerged as France's principal exponent of social holism, paternalism, and antimodernism. Repeatedly, he emphasized that agricultural reform was the prerequisite for all economic and educational improvement. "Each social class is directly or indirectly involved with farming," he observed in 1832, "and each has need of stability and prosperity."[3] He condemned theories that "placed the worker at odds with the manufacturer or foreman, or the merchant with the producer." He denounced the belief that employers always "exploited" workers, and lived as "bloodsuckers" on the fruits of their labor. For Bugeaud, intrinsic to societal holism was the ineluctable service performed for workers by possessors of capital as bankers, job creators, and (perhaps most importantly) "fathers."[4] Indeed, paternalism pervaded his thought. He was convinced that the best regime was a "wise and paternalistic" one which all would have an interest in defending.[5] To such paternalism he soon added a profound antimodernism. Thus, to the assembled comices agricoles in Excideuil in 1839 he went so far as to compare the head or "soul" of a rural family to the "patriarch of antiquity." Characteristically, he struck a moralistic note: "If you have money to spend," he advised his listeners, "let it not be in a tavern. Buy some wine and some meat; the money you might have wasted alone in an alehouse will suffice to feed the whole family this evening."[6] Better farming methods, rather than more widespread education, were the first requirement for improvement in the human condition. "Only when basic needs have been satisfied," he maintained in 1834, "can education be expected to take hold and spread." In the future, primary instruction might possibly be desirable, Bugeaud argued in reference to the Guizot Law of 1833, but only if significant reforms were first achieved in agriculture. Requiring that every commune maintain an elementary school for boys, and each department a teacher's college, was well and good but it would be fruitless unless progress in farming was realized. Probably, the failure of his own educational experiment at La Durantie contributed to these views. In any case, for Bugeaud the purpose of classroom instruction was to inculcate morality rather than to achieve societal melioration.[7] This traditionalist world view underlay the policy positions which he adopted during his first ten years in parliament.

From his earliest months in the Chamber, Bugeaud's commitment to a less onerous, more cohesive and demographically stable agrarianism motivated his opposition to the urban and political thrusts of modernity. In particular, the rural depopulation which had occurred in much of southern and southwestern France during the 1820s troubled him. Rural emigration had been mainly responsible for the growth of the country's twelve largest cities by 9.5 percent between 1821 and 1831, while France as a whole increased in population by only 6.4 percent. This situation had been exacerbated by relocation in Lyons and various northern cities of the thriving cottage textile industry that had characterized rural France during the immediate post-Napoleonic years. Despite his status as a political neophyte, Bugeaud took the lead in condemning this relocation as a principal contributor to flight from the countryside. In his opinion, opportunities in the new manufacturing cities threatened a general "desertion of agriculture for the factory," and an erosion of the rural family unit.[8] For Bugeaud, the industrial revolution underway in France since 1825 constituted a menace to preservation of a bucolically communitarian order. Politically, he concentrated his efforts after 1831 on fighting legislative initiatives which he believed reflected the antiagrarian biases of urban society.

During the early 1830s, he directed these efforts against proposals from economic liberals and maritime interests to lower the wall of protective tariffs erected between 1814 and 1826. As early as 1819, substantial duties had been imposed on all imported livestock, meats, eggs, and grain. In 1822, tariffs on foreign oxen, bulls, cows, calves, and sheep were raised significantly. Four years later, the Restoration's protective system was completed by new hikes in tariffs on oxen, horses, and wool. However, after the July Revolution attempts were begun to solve problems of domestic supply created by such duties, and a modest lowering of tariffs in selected categories was proposed. This campaign was led by Charles Tanneguy Duchatel, deputy from the Charente, and by spokesmen for the shipping interests of Bordeaux and Le Havre. To Bugeaud, such efforts represented an unholy alliance between commercial and urban interests and constituted a serious threat to the viability of rural society.[9] Of course, Bugeaud himself owned a sizable herd, and the position he articulated was highly popular among Excideuil's landed electors. The same mixture of self-interest and political shrewdness characterized his opposition to attempts to so reform the salt tax that large landowners would pay a higher percentage of the total levy.[10] By defending the economic interests of politically significant proprietors in the Dordogne, Bugeaud certainly increased his popularity there. Nevertheless, he truly believed that urban contributions to rural problems were of major proportions, and he demanded immediate remedial action.

To obviate effects of the new industrialism and diminish the cities' apparent ascendancy over the countryside, Bugeaud suggested that the large urban population be reduced by transfer of a portion of the city population to the countryside where it could easily be absorbed and put to work. "I will take the responsibility for employing in Limousin," he informed his colleagues in 1832, "all of the excess population of Lyons, Bordeaux, Rouen, Marseilles and Paris."[11] The orientation of urban immigrants to their new tasks would be helped by a substantial increase in the number of comices agricoles. The resultant increase in agricultural production would ultimately reduce food prices for city dwellers, Bugeaud argued, and earn rural inhabitants an unprecedented financial return. Increased rural purchasing power would create a new national market for manufactured goods and remove the need to seek outlets abroad. Above all, a return to the land mediated by the comices would help to recreate an organically integrated community free from class conflict. Bugeaud proposed, therefore, that a comice composed of at least twenty-five members be established in every canton in the country, that each comice create its own development fund from membership dues, and that every such organization be granted a governmental subsidy for a five-year period.[12] For 1832, he requested state support of 200,000 francs, and suggested that this subsidy be increased to a maximum of two million francs as the number of comices increased. Governmental assistance for the comices agricoles was essential, Bugeaud was convinced, in order to provide a solution to urban population problems, restore a balanced economy, and shore up the agrarian foundations of a holistic society.

As events turned out, he was able to obtain approval only of a 100,000-franc subsidy. Nevertheless, that was a significant accomplishment. Throughout the parliamentary debate preceding the vote nobody challenged Bugeaud's contention that a flourishing agriculture was fundamental to general societal viability, and that French agriculture had not received the attention from which farming in other countries had benefited. Indeed, his colleagues in the chamber endorsed Bugeaud's bucolic preferences. For example, Raimbert-Sevin emphasized that no material progress or enlightenment was possible without "encouragement by every possible means" of farming, that "most noble and useful" of enterprises. "If we can point with pride to Flanders, Alsace, and a few isolated farms," Saubat commented, "the rest of France is far behind England, Switzerland, Hanover, Meklenbourg, Wurtemberg and several other German states." The minister of commerce and public works and spokesman for the government, Comte d'Argout, remarked that it was "impossible not to give serious attention to the questions raised" by Bugeaud, and that his arguments were "eminently patriotic and express the desires of all Frenchmen."[13]

Despite this parliamentary endorsement, most comices founded in the Dordogne during the next two years did not utilize governmental funds. By 1834, notables in Excideuil, Vern, and Champagnac had established comices with their own resources, and similar efforts were underway in Terrason, Monpazier, and Saint-Pierre de Chignac. Nevertheless, in May of 1834 Bugeaud urged the Chamber to vote an additional 200,000-franc subsidy on the grounds that it would constitute a "moral endorsement" of farming.[14] In fact, it was to the "excellent effect" of the 1832 vote on rural psychology that he attributed the recent increase in comices. To this observation, Martin replied drily that he did not believe that the national budget ordinarily included "moral votes."[15] Martin's scruples were shared by a majority of other deputies, and proposed subsidies of 200,000 and 80,000 francs were deferred until all funds voted in 1832 had been expended. General support for agriculture was again expressed, and there was no opposition to additional support for the comices once the money already appropriated had been used.

During the middle and late 1830s the number of comices increased rapidly in southern and western France. In mid-1835, Bugeaud reemphasized his desire to "cover France" with them to assure that every canton had its own "truly progressive" agricultural catalyst.[16] He spoke at length in the Chamber about the mechanics of founding comices, about differences between the comices and the agricultural societies, and about the importance of governmental endorsement and financial assistance for the comices. State subsidies, Bugeaud maintained, were so important that they should be provided even if it were necessary to reduce governmental support for such maritime enterprises as whaling. To guarantee that the political dividends of his efforts were maximized, he had his arguments inserted in the Dordogne's *Annales agricoles*. By 1840, the villages of Belvis, Issegeac, Lalinde, Saint-Astier, Saint-Alvère, Savignac, Sigoulès, Vergt, and Villefranche-de-Longchapt had all established comices agricoles. Many comices had by then also been founded in Charente, Haute Vienne, and even north of the Loire. As early as 1836, for example, a comice was functioning in Chartres and sponsoring an annual fair. Almost all were patterned on the Lanouaille model, and many received state subsidies. By decade's end, the total agricultural subvention voted by the chamber was more than four times what it had been in 1832. Although no resettlement of urbanites in the countryside had taken place and demographic trends showed no signs of reversal, Bugeaud nevertheless had secured official sanction, substantial financial support, and widespread exposure for agricultural principles which he had first formalized in Perigord sixteen years before.

Meanwhile, Bugeaud continued to cultivate a network of relationships in Excideuil. Agricultural reform stimulated by Lanouaille's comice proceeded apace, and the annual spring fair increasingly assumed the character of a political rally. In at least eight of the ten years between 1831 and 1841, Bugeaud left Paris to return to the Dordogne for Lanouaille's spring exposition. He was also present at many of the business meetings of the comice during that period.

At the annual fair, Bugeaud ordinarily addressed the assembled métayers in patois and the proprietors in French, and he personally distributed prizes for the best livestock and forage. Paternalism mixed with politics, and both reflected Bugeaud's commitment to a more prosperously organic and traditional society. By 1835, almost all local opposition to his parliamentary mandate had disappeared.

In April 1832, Bugeaud returned to Excideuil to dramatize his recent success in securing a governmental subsidy for the comices. To his colleagues in the Lanouaille organization he read a letter from the ministry announcing a grant of 700 francs and promising future support on an annual basis. Bugeaud proudly stated that the additional funds would enable new or larger awards to be offered for livestock and a variety of forage crops.[17] The comments of the Lanouaille comice's secretary probably accurately reflected the sentiment of the membership: "The general subsidy [Bugeaud] obtained," he observed, "although considerably reduced, certainly resulted in capturing the attention of France and making it aware of the absurd parsimony with which agriculture, which pays all the expenses of the state and supplies the largest part of its requirements, has been treated. A sum of 100,000 francs has been voted by the Chamber, and [Bugeaud] has obtained 700 francs for our comice." Apparently Excideuil now had ready access to Parisian funds, and the future seemed promising. "Through this allocation and our own private resources," the secretary continued, "we will be able to expand our awards in all sorts of areas. Thus, we will offer this year fifteen different prizes for forage, and two for bulls."[18] New awards for the heaviest oxen also were announced. On June 3, this new optimism found expression in the most ambitious fair yet sponsored by the Lanouaille comice.

Bugeaud presided over the festivities from beginning to end. The day began with him leading the participants to mass in the village church. Then, to music played by a military band which he had invited, everyone repaired to the usual large tent for speeches and the distribution of prizes. A number of local women and visitors interested in learning about the comice attended this session for the first time. In the local patois, Bugeaud reminded the assembled métayers that clover was the most valuable crop that they could cultivate. "After God, your wife, and your children," he declaimed, "it is clover which you must adore. Clover will provide you an abundance of wheat and a variety of other crops. With clover, one can feed those large numbers of livestock which produce vast amounts of dung—and with manure, one has everything." He then repeated his remarks in French. When he distributed the prizes, it was certainly with satisfaction that he noted that three of his own métayers had won awards for clover.[19] Bugeaud's image as father and protector—the *père Bugeaud* of later song and legend—obviously was already in the process of formation. When the mayor of Excideuil announced in 1833 that the Chamber of Deputies had released 2,000 francs to be shared by the Dordogne's comices, Bugeaud's status as patron and political provider was further enhanced. The fact that he had been planting mulberry trees at La Durantie since 1830, and had thereby introduced the silkworm industry into the Department, added to his popularity.[20] By the middle 1830s, it may well have seemed to Excideuil's electors that Bugeaud had become as adept at reorienting Paris toward the countryside as he had been at reforming farming. Elections in 1834 and 1836 returned Bugeaud to parliament with large majorities.

The idea of agrarian holism was at the heart of Bugeaud's critique of modernity and his opposition to those who perceived in political liberalization the key to societal improvement. "Of what use are political rights," he inquired rhetorically in the Chamber in 1834, "if one has no bread, no furniture, nothing which is necessary for a decent life? Farming alone can provide material improvement—not that which demagogues dream about, which would lead to a lowering of the upper classes to the level of the lowest groups in society—but that general improvement which enables all social classes to rise one or two degrees on the social scale at the same time."[21] He rarely missed an opportunity to repeat such sentiments in the Dordogne. "Political liberty will not provide you with bread, clothes, shoes, a decent house, furniture, and all the rest," he reminded sharecroppers at one of Lanouaille's spring galas. "Poverty is the cause of your ignorance, and the only oppression from which you suffer."[22] These convictions were certainly well received by Excideuil's electors. Still, Bugeaud honestly believed that the requirements for a good society were a limited franchise and the freedom from all experiments in political utilitarianism.

In fact, opposition to liberalization of the franchise constituted the essence of the juste milieu whose political parameters he had sketched before 1831. To Bugeaud, agricultural reform was a prerequisite to the spread of education, and both were necessary for the responsible exercise of the right to vote. Realistically, Bugeaud expected no great improvement in either agriculture or education in the foreseeable future, and certainly none of such significance as to justify extension of the franchise. Thus, when he expatiated on his commitment to Centrism, it was to the juste milieu as a political ideal within the contemporary *pays légal*, or within that still-minute proportion of the French people who were permitted to participate in the political process. Basically, in politics what mattered to Bugeaud was the balanced functioning of the system that had been established in 1830. However traditionalist his agrarian sentiments, they did not skew his Centrist political convictions.

Throughout the 1830s, Bugeaud proclaimed his moderation in declarations of support for the July Monarchy and professions of his "democratic" inclinations and commitment to reasonable increases in living standards. To some degree, this Centrism was the result of his being repudiated by both Legitimists and Leftists. To the Legitimists, he was anathema, for he was the "jailor" of the Duchesse de Berry at Blaye. The Leftists considered him an enemy because of the death at his hands of deputy Charles Dulong, who had charged Bugeaud with improper conduct at Blaye, provoking a duel between the two men.[23] So determined was Bugeaud's opposition to both revolutionary Carlism and Republicanism that, along with his parliamentary efforts to secure funds for the comices, he attempted to establish in the Dordogne a political mechanism protective of the modestly reformed electoral system established in 1830.

On the occasion of his election to the Chamber in 1831, Bugeaud summed up for Excideuil's electors both his conception of himself as a Centrist politician and the meaning to him of the juste milieu as a political posture. "It has been said that I am a man of the juste milieu," he observed. "Gentlemen, I am in favor of change, but change which can always be kept from getting out of control. I am not reactionary in any way. I will always favor progress which is gradual, and which does not compromise the constitutional monarchy of Louis Philippe. With calmness and constancy I shall support all sensible consequences of the July Revolution."[24] Here as later, Bugeaud showed a tendency to identify the juste milieu with what was or had come to be, and to make the best of the political storms which racked France. Always the realist, he did not hesitate to adopt the pragmatism necessary for success as a public figure. Nevertheless, throughout the 1830s his contemporaries in Perigord recognized him as both as man of principle and an adherent of the ideological Center. At the same time, Bugeaud already was manifesting another, darker side, a proclivity to violence. In the Dulong affair, his excessive anger and cold determination in shooting to kill a man who lacked comparable military skills foreshadowed his later moral evolution and the extremism to which he succumbed in Algeria. In 1831, however, all that was in the future. Whatever violence Bugeaud's instincts tempted and occasionally persuaded him to commit, his political allegiance throughout the decade remained to the new juste milieu, symbolized by Louis Philippe and the July Monarchy.

For Bugeaud and other supporters of Centrism, the political structure of all Europe seemed frighteningly fragile. In 1830-31, political systems had been overthrown or apparently seriously compromised across much of the Continent. Although the results of uprisings in France, the Netherlands, Poland, and the Italian states were dissimilar, the series of upheavals seemed to augur a dangerous and most uncertain future. In 1831, England seemed on the verge of revolution, as thousands of protesters demanding political reform massed in Birmingham and plundered shops and burned buildings in Bristol. These threats, of course, were known to have issued mostly from the Left. Bugeaud, however, still considered the principal danger to France at the time to stem primarily from the domestic Right. The occasional agitation from Republicans and Saint-Simonians was seen as inconsequential when compared with perceived clerical conspiracies, widespread Carlist sentiment, and the outbreak in 1832 of counterrevolution in the Vendée.

Rumors of plots by clerics and foreigners with the Vendéan West especially concerned Bugeaud. Such intrigue was apparently confirmed by the arrival of the Duchesse de Berry, mother of Henry V, Legitimist heir to the throne, in the Vendée in May 1832, to direct Carlist forces. In fact, the Legitimist danger was considerably overblown. No foreign powers extended assistance to the Legitimists, and the duchesse was soon hunted down and her partisans crushed after sporadic, if occasionally fierce, combat with government forces. In France as elsewhere, in the long run the Left constituted the major threat to maintenance of political Centrism. Perhaps because he had so long been obsessed with the Right, Bugeaud did not recognize the revived Leftist challenge until midway through the 1830s.

Nevertheless, his new career as a representative from the Dordogne made him aware of Leftist agitation in Paris and elsewhere. Indeed, being exposed in the nation's capital to competing extremisms on the Right and Left led him to the conclusion that the forces of moderation were in need of conscious cultivation by the government. Therefore, in mid-1833 he urged that each of the Dordogne's *arrondissements* form its own "election committee" for the juste milieu. "It is particularly vital that such a committee be established in Perigueux," Bugeaud advised the Department's new prefect. "You will know best how to suggest this to those most capable of managing it."[25] Organization of electors into such committees, he thought, might neutralize the influence of extremist newspapers and help to diminish the "moral disorder" troubling the country. All in all, Bugeaud was optimistic about the possibility of broadening support for Centrism: "There is progress," he observed in early 1834, "and each day the system of order and of prudent liberty which we have supported further consolidates itself. We will see a large proportion of the Republicans and unfanatical Carlists rally to our side. Good elections and we are saved."[26] Good elections of course were those in which only a limited number of significant notables participated. Obviously, Bugeaud believed that the leading local citizens had the responsibility to assure that such elections were properly conducted.

In his own case, results of the 1834 contest were satisfying indeed. On June 21, he was reelected to the chamber, winning 124 of 200 votes cast. Two years later his dominance was even more marked: On September 24, 1836, he was returned with the support of 127 of 131 voters in Excideuil. The political system which had proven of such personal advantage was also essential, Bugeaud was convinced, for societal order and national security.

To expect better government to result from granting of the franchise to the masses, he maintained, was a major error. Such "simple souls" knew nothing about representative institutions and could not be expected responsibly to exercise a right to vote.[27] Exercise of the franchise was not a "right" which belonged to everyone, but a "responsibility" (*mandat*) possessed uniquely by the nation itself. The country's responsibility for its own defense and for the security of its citizens required that it select representatives from among those propertied individuals most likely to prove "capable" and "really patriotic."[28] Ownership of property was crucial. "For one to put his torch to my barn," Bugeaud observed, "I want him to have his wheat in it along with mine. In the same way, it is necessary that one have a stake in society to be permitted to contribute to the process of government."[29] To advocate a major extension of the franchise was an "excellent means of acquiring popularity," but would not help to preserve a juste milieu in which the interests of all classes inhered.[30]

Thus, proper exercise of their responsibility to Centrism required that the country's leading property owners elect representatives who could be relied upon to make "good laws" and establish a "good administration." Bugeaud hoped that such laws and administration, issuing from the pays légal, would prevent political change from ever getting out of control, regardless of who the monarch or the legislators who formulated legislation and managed the system happened to be. Law, in Bugeaud's opinion, affected deputy, elector, and citizen equally, and the right to sit in parliament or to exercise the franchise did not endow its possessors with any greater liberty than that retained by their fellow citizens. Liberty was the offspring of good laws and a good administration, and Bugeaud insisted that both the legal and administrative bases of the juste milieu would be eroded by extension of the right to vote. Fundamentally, Bugeaud's loyalty was not finally or exclusively to Louis Phillippe and the regime in power, but to the evolution of politics and the political system within a perceived framework of ideological moderation. Universal suffrage would invest a government with ignorance, which, in the interests of the "people itself" whom Bugeaud stated he "loved and cherished more than those who want to give it theories with which to assassinate itself," was at all costs to be avoided.[31] Only to the extent that active political participation was restricted to an electorate no larger than that established by the July Revolution, Bugeaud believed, could a governmental system supportive of moderation be considered either efficient or responsible.

Corollary to Bugeaud's insistence that maintenance of the juste milieu required a limited franchise was his conviction that policymaking should not be broadened, and that the challenges of the press had to be met. The general population should not be encouraged to be interested in debates of deliberative assemblies, or to participate in discussions of political or policy questions. "What it is important for the public to know," he maintained, "are final votes and not the reasons which led to them. If [the votes] are good, the rest is of little importance; if they are bad, familiarity with the debates will not improve them."[32] In particular, Bugeaud opposed publicizing the proceedings of the departmental Conseils generaux. However, the "horrible despotism" increasingly exercised by an "odious press" made privacy in political or governmental deliberations difficult.[33] By late 1833, Bugeaud was arguing that extremist newspapers had become one of the most serious threats to preservation of the juste milieu. Parliamentary debates were "completely transformed" by publications such as the *Courrier Français* and the *Messager*. "They are no longer those which we have experienced and heard," he complained. "They are something completely different."[34] Politicization of France by a "poisonous elite" seemed to him likely to stimulate an activism which the juste milieu could not long endure.[35] During the middle 1830s, Bugeaud excoriated the press as the primary obstacle to preservation of that holistic society without which Centrism could hardly be expected to survive. In so doing, he demonstrated an irascibility and rhetorical violence which foreshadowed the great transformation that would ultimately be brought on by his experiences in Algeria.

Bugeaud considered journalists responsible for most of the evils in society. It was the press, he insisted, which enabled ideology to make inroads, stirred up conflict, and waged war against the monarchy. In 1834, Bugeaud challenged the government to demonstrate its "courage" by muzzling newspapers in Paris.[36] One ideological extreme, he stressed the following year, was as dangerous as another. "There is nothing more abominable than the Republican press," he wrote to the Dordogne's prefect, "unless it is the Third Party and Legitimist Press. I do not have words adequate to express how these [illegible] of hell make me feel."[37] Although he professed belief in a freedom of the press which would "sustain public officials in their duties, uphold legality, and proclaim all useful verities," Bugeaud saw little reason to tolerate publications that spread "sophistries, lies, and slander throughout the citizenry and on the laws and acts of the government, whether good or bad." Rather than fulfilling their responsibility to uphold the juste milieu through the promotion of temperance, newspapers now so violated their commission that every new public official seemed intimidated by unrelenting journalistic attack.[38] In the summer of 1835, Bugeaud advanced his own proposals aimed at bringing to heel publications whose restriction he considered essential for the survival of political moderation.

From Perigord in early July he wrote to François Guizot to recommend halting of the "ravages" of the press through imposition of appropriate sanctions. Then minister of public instruction, Guizot had developed a warm friendship with Bugeaud. The urban, bourgeois values Guizot professed did not prevent him from collaborating with the nation's leading advocate of agrarian antimodernism.[39] Since "toleration" had proven ineffective, Bugeaud recommended that his friend support "severity" so that journalists might learn to fear the government.[40] Yet repression alone, he predicted, would not be enough to halt a process of politicization which had developed its own momentum. An effort to establish publications that supported the regime was necessary, Bugeaud suggested, in order to contain the ideological threat to the juste milieu. Therefore, he urged that the ministry's special contingency funds be used to subsidize journalistic defenders of the established political system. Preservation of moderation, Bugeaud argued, now required representatives of the nation seriously to compete in the arena of ideas.[41]

His own recent efforts to establish a pro-government press suggest what Bugeaud may have had in mind. In 1833, he attempted to create a "press to fight the press" in Paris using private funds. From the nation's capital, he hoped, newspapers supportive of the juste milieu would "spread throughout the rest of France." Bugeaud anticipated formation of some ten associations in the capital, each composed of between fifty and sixty men of means, to found and subsidize journals whose financial resources would enable them to undersell the competition and "buy up the best writers of the opposition." Purchase of adversary talent would constitute a "double victory," since it would enable the forces of Centrism to "wage war with the soldiers of the enemy."[42] Although nothing came of these plans, Bugeaud continued his personal campaign against what he considered extremist newspapers. In 1834, he urged prefectural action against the *Écho de Vésone*, a Republican newspaper published in the Dordogne which had opposed him in the elections of 1831 and 1834. Unless the *Écho* were to begin to "support the only reasonable system, the only system which inheres in the nature of things and in our civilization, the only one which is capable of consolidating true liberty," Bugeaud recommended imposing punitive sanctions on it.[43] However, Prefect Romieu had no more interest in challenging the press openly than Guizot did in 1835. Neither in Perigord nor in Paris were people inclined to act on Bugeaud's advice. Neither private nor public funds were available through 1835 to wage the struggle which Bugeaud advocated. Soon, events dramatically altered this situation.

During the summer of 1835, Bugeaud insisted for the first time that the juste milieu's most dangerous ideological opposition issued from the Jacobin Left rather than the Legitimist Right. Carlism's romanticism and political misjudgments had destroyed it as a credible threat to the regime, and Bugeaud had experienced Leftist rioting at first hand while commanding troops in Paris only a year before. Reports already were circulating about the establishment of a new network of Leftist revolutionary secret societies. Conditions had clearly changed from those of earlier years, and Bugeaud's political target changed accordingly. It was now Republican, rather than Legitimist publications, he informed Guizot, that would inflict grave damage if permitted to continue to attack the governmental system. That "liberty" which the government had been "silly enough to permit," he now emphasized, had created a resurgent Jacobinism which would, if no countermeasures were taken, topple the regime at the first moment of crisis.[44] Indeed, 1835 marked the date that Bugeaud's campaign against both Ultra and Jacobin ideologies was transformed into a single-minded assault against the revolutionary Left. Throughout the remainder of the decade he clearly identified the principal challenge to Centrism with the radical Left, as between 1815 and 1820 he had identified it with the Ultra Right. In Bugeaud's opinion, the survival of political moderation after 1835 required elimination of what he now considered an uncompromising Jacobin assault against the juste milieu.

By mid-1835, in the words of one commentator, radical newspapers had come to "abound with more appalling insults than usual, including some tasteless expressions of surprise that the king had so far not been assassinated."[45] Several of these newspapers had close relations with the new underground network of revolutionary cells which had dedicated itself to warfare against the established order. This new Carbonarism, which had been stimulated by the regime's use of the penal code of 1834 to dissolve such public advocates of Republicanism as the Friends of the People and the Society of the Rights of Man, was exemplified in Paris by the rapid growth of the Society of Families. By 1835 this clandestine organization enrolled some one thousand potential insurgents, and had penetrated two regiments stationed in the capital. Coordination between the ideological and military challenges to the juste milieu, Bugeaud informed the minister of justice, was undermining both popular and official support for the politics of moderation. There was, he observed, a growing reluctance on the part of those favorably disposed to the regime to support it publicly, and leading citizens increasingly were "echoing the line of the revolutionaries." The government now was "never defended in conversation and rarely by the actions of the authorities." Bugeaud concluded by caustically noting that if "occasionally, pushed by the force of things, our timid officialdom manifests a semblance of resolution, the very next moment it pulls back and hastens to apologize to the mighty lords of the country, the journalists."[46] Since Leftist journals had become so violent, it was urgent that the ministry end its policy of toleration and bend every effort to apprehend Jacobin conspirators. Employment of harsher methods was essential, Bugeaud insisted, if the regime's determination to defend the juste milieu were to remain credible.

To that end, he proposed that army units be concentrated at strategic points within the city of Paris. Display of military force might intimidate radical journalists and abort any outbreak of revolution. In the event of an uprising, the government should employ the "very greatest severity" to end the revolutionary danger permanently. Adoption of such policies, Bugeaud maintained, would be excused by a citizenry which would understand that the policies had been employed in defense of the only political system capable of maximizing both the citizens' economic welfare and their personal security.[47] As in the Dulong affair, here again is a hint of the incipient ethical deformation which Bugeaud's North African experience was greatly to worsen. Perhaps Bugeaud's very ardor and consistency in defending the juste milieu was what nourished the moral confusion that later events were dramatically to exacerbate. A semblance of both the explosion which Bugeaud feared and the energetic governmental reaction which he urged were close at hand in early July of 1835. As celebrations to commemorate the great revolutionary *journées* of 1789 approached, rumors multiplied that one of the observances would be marked by an attempt to assassinate the king. On July 28, as the royal family, several marshals of France, and other leading personalities paraded through Paris, the Corsican revolutionary Fieschi fired a primitive machine gun, killing or wounding forty-one dignitaries and onlookers around the king.[48] Although the royal family escaped unscathed, the chambers responded in early September by passing a series of laws whose purpose was to withdraw the rights of the Charter from political groups that did not accept the form of government established in 1830, and to silence Legitimist and Republican newspapers. The new laws made it a criminal offense to mention the king's name when discussing any action of the government or to suggest or propose the monarchy's overthrow or the restoration of the former dynasty. Fines on the press were doubled, the required financial deposits ("caution money") were quadrupled, popular subscriptions to pay either were forbidden, and conviction of offending publications was made more easily obtainable. All newspaper cartoons were henceforth subject to censorship by either the minister of the interior in Paris or the appropriate provincial prefect. That September, for the first time since 1830, the representatives of the nation doubtless seemed to Bugeaud to be seriously defending a governmental structure supportive of political moderation.

During the period of well over a decade that ensued, this restrictive September legislation buttressed the juste milieu, which in Bugeaud's opinion the ministry had long left vulnerable to opposing extremisms. If no broad network of publications favorable to the regime was established, the journalistic "advocates of violence" were after 1835 generally silenced, and the opposition press as a whole ceased to advocate the king's assassination or the overthrow of the monarchy. The same was not true, however, of the secret societies whose spokesmen some of the Jacobin newspapers had

been, and Bugeaud's fears of both the journalistic and insurrectionary threats to the politics of Centrism were not permanently abated
even by this important legislative victory of September 1835.

Late October, in fact, found him attempting to impress upon
the government the necessity of energetically enforcing the restrictive legislation of the month before. "It is essential to suppress the
liberty of the press," Bugeaud insisted, "if you do not wish to perish
by the press." Tolerance of incendiary journalism only made civil
war inevitable. Jacobin conspirators could not be foiled by "concessions or kindness." Rather, it was necessary "either to dominate
or to crush them."[49] Still, the relationship between such severity and
maintenance of the politics of the juste milieu remained clear to
him. "We have a representative government and we cannot have
any other without frightful upheavals," Bugeaud reminded an old
friend several months later. "We must therefore make do as well as
possible—or the least badly as possible—with the one we have." He
admonished his correspondent for his Legitimist enthusiasm: "I
recommend that you silence your dislike of the upcoming elections,"
he observed, "and if you are unable to secure the victory of the
candidate of your choice, vote for the man of the juste milieu. That
is the most sensible and ethical course."[50] There were no direct challenges to either the regime or political moderation until the uprising
of Society of the Seasons on May 12, 1839.

Successor to the Society of Families, which had finally been
destroyed in 1836, the Society of the Seasons was uncompromis-
ingly Jacobin and was directed by Armand Barbès, Auguste Blanqui,
and Martin Bernard. Although by 1839 it had approximately a
thousand members capable of bearing arms, only some three hundred participated in its poorly coordinated uprising in May. The
national guard and troops stationed in Paris easily aborted the
attempted coup. Shortly thereafter, the ringleaders were put on trial
before the Chamber of Peers, and Bugeaud found the proceedings
not at all to his liking.

What upset him about the trial were both the verdict and the
defense's justification of their clients' actions on ideological grounds.
A confounding of crime with politics had been encouraged by a
king and ministry which had "lost their heads," Bugeaud insisted in
late July, and politicization of society had been advanced by the
failure of the authorities properly to punish revolutionaries whose

sole defense consisted of protestations concerning the purity of their Jacobinism and their effort to effect radical change.[51] The impact of ideology on the juste milieu was clearly revealed, Bugeaud argued, in the conduct of the trial and in the sentences handed down. He was "outraged but not surprised" by the "extraordinary doctrines" with which the country's "pretentious lawyers" defended their Jacobin clients. They had argued, Bugeaud insisted, that Barbès was "not in the least a criminal subject to trial in the courts, no matter how high they might be." Rather, he was portrayed as a political reformer who had merely wished to rectify problems which contributed to the sufferings of the people. Barbès and his associates had "perhaps erred," but their cause, so Bugeaud insisted that their lawyers had argued, was an "expression of rationalism" more likely to improve the condition of the masses than was gradual institutional evolution. This kind of justification of criminal acts could only encourage the "killing of citizens and soldiers by the hundreds" by "every diseased ideologue" who desired to create an alternative society. Acceptance of the politicization of crime would allow the state no recourse against the insurrectionary who variously defended his actions by arguing that he only wished to "solve a great social problem," that he was "defeated but not a criminal," and that had he prevailed he would have had a moral right to judge those presently judging him.[52] Centrism could hardly remain viable, Bugeaud maintained, in the face of such excitation to extremism.

The worst of the situation was that the king and ministry, by agreeing to commute Barbès's death sentence, had not only accepted the politicization of crime but had granted it a kind of royal imprimatur. Sentences meted out to the eighteen other leaders on trial were in Bugeaud's opinion far too light. Such "cowardice" and evident scorn for those defending the social order would only strengthen the "horrible sophistry" that "political crime is not punishable as are other crimes." Commutation of Barbès's death sentence, Bugeaud noted, had won the regime few political dividends. Even the pro-government *National*, for example, had declared that Barbès had been treated like a common criminal in being condemned to the galleys. All "wild and arrogant spirits" could be expected to take heart at the government's failure to maintain its defense of the juste milieu. Insurrectionary Jacobinism could be expected again to increase. Bugeaud pronounced himself shocked that the regime seemed

incapable of comprehending that clemency would prove totally ineffective in silencing revolutionary enemies of society. Such irre-
sponsibility, he forecast, would make the ultimate day of reckoning
bloody indeed.[53] So stated, his argument anticipated that which he
was to make from North Africa in far grosser form in 1845, when
he insisted that solicitude for the indigenous population itself required widespread liquidation of Muslim Algerians.

By the subsequent summer, Bugeaud had come to view the
erosion of royal authority as one of the most worrisome results of
the monarchy's apparent acceptance of the justification of crime on
ideological grounds. The king's magnanimity had encouraged many
in the chamber to join with the enemies of Centrism, Bugeaud
suggested in August of 1840, to undermine further a monarchy
already weakened by its handling of the May uprising. The instabil-
ity of the ministry could hardly be expected to contribute to the
monarchy's maintenance of the juste milieu against challenges from
"communists, equalizers and other such types begotten by the un-
ruly imagination of that swarm of intellectuals [lettrés] which battles over the body of France to determine who shall devour its
corpse."[54] For Bugeaud in 1840, the Left, in its ideological and insurrectionary forms, still represented what it had first clearly become
for him in 1835: the primary threat to the continued viability of a
workable Centrist system.

Near the end of his first decade in parliament, therefore, Bugeaud
continued to support the political moderation he had advocated
since 1815. Despite increasingly shrill rhetoric and evidence of moral
disorientation, he still believed in 1840 that a juste milieu yet survived the ravages of ideology, and continued to protect the stability
and spiritual cohesiveness of rural society against inroads of modernity. Rightist opposition to the Settlement of 1830 had largely
disappeared, and journalistic and revolutionary challenges from the
Left to the political expression of agrarian values had not yet resulted in incorporation of the masses into the electoral and legislative processes. On the eve of his appointment as governor-general
of Algeria, Bugeaud's convictions concerning the agricultural bases
of societal improvement, the advantages of a limited franchise, and
the representational inclusiveness of the juste milieu remained
unshaken.

3

The 1830s
Foreign Policy,
France and Algeria

During the 1830s Bugeaud's views on foreign and military policies demonstrated his continuing concern with the preservation of a cohesive community. Throughout that turbulent decade he insisted that maintenance of a juste milieu necessitated avoiding adventures abroad, and most especially avoiding direct armed intervention in Eastern Europe, Belgium, or the Ottoman Empire. Bugeaud was convinced that a pacific orientation toward international affairs, based on a defensive deployment of military forces, was the only way to minimize internal challenges to Centrism and societal cohesion. Attempts to embroil France in revolts or domestic strife in Poland in late 1830 and 1831, and in the Low Countries and Syria at the end of the decade, evoked his outspoken opposition. By the late 1830s, he was among the most prominent parliamentary supporters of a policy of noninvolvement in European disputes and a defensive and continentalist military posture. Only where Algeria was concerned did Bugeaud, by 1840, manifest any willingness, despite extensive rhetoric to the contrary, to commit substantial French forces to offensive and distant campaigns.

In the fall of 1831, Bugeaud stated in the Chamber of Deputies that France's refusal to support the war for Polish independence, which had broken out a year earlier, had enabled the country to maintain sufficient armed strength to "hold the factions in line."[1] Such factions, of course, ranged from Carlist to Jacobin. However, the Left alone had advocated immediate military intervention, and it found Bugeaud's views particularly objectionable. To neutralize "malcontents" within the country, and thereby to preserve the juste milieu, Bugeaud argued that it had been essential that France avoid the military quicksand of Eastern Europe. The wisdom displayed by a monarchy supported by a rural majority opposed to war had fortunately spared society the strains of armed intervention in Poland.[2] In fact, the monarchy's success in resisting Leftist calls for war was what finally persuaded Bugeaud to grant it his support.[3] Preservation of political and ideological moderation, he clearly believed, required prudence in foreign, and particularly military, policy.

Furthermore, Bugeaud argued that there were immense difficulties in any campaign in a distant theater. An army, he informed the chamber in late 1831, could not operate without secure communications with its homeland. In the case of Poland, significant French military support would have necessitated supply lines some 750 miles long. Military involvement there would have required that one army be stationed on the Rhine to support operations farther east, and that another be assigned to the Pyrenees to maintain French security on the nation's southern frontier. Therefore, a war machine sufficient to guarantee domestic order while simultaneously fighting in Poland would have totaled some 800,000 men, or approximately four times the size of the French army in 1831.[4] Despite his "admiration and sympathy" for the "heroic Polish nation,"[5] Bugeaud was sure that France had done well in refusing major military assistance.

Two years later he was even more confident that his 1831 analysis had been valid. Would not the commitment of a major army to Poland, he inquired in early 1834, inevitably have precipitated a general European war? "Would it not have been essential to form a huge army to secure our line of operations and to defend against the German Confederation? And what about the Austrian armies? Would it not have been necessary to send one army to the foot of the Alps to defend our Swiss and Italian frontiers and another to the base of the Pyrenees?"[6] Expeditionary forces dispatched by ship to help Poland from the Black and Baltic seas, he insisted, would have been useless, since the presence of English sea power in those areas precluded obtaining secure bases there.[7] Apparently, Bugeaud believed those imprudent Frenchmen who insisted that with enthusiasm alone one could take on all Europe, to be as much of a menace to the international order as they were to domestic tranquillity.[8]

In addition, Bugeaud observed that it was not French restraint by itself that had caused the uprising in Poland to fail. In his opinion, the threat of France's uncommitted army had prevented the struggle in Poland from ending within a week or two. "There is no reason to keep insisting that we let Poland perish," Bugeaud stated in 1834. "By keeping the peace we did more for Poland than we could have done by war, for by maintaining peace we kept all of Europe at bay and prevented the entire continent from marching against Poland. If we had fired a single cannot shot on the Rhine, Europe would no longer have had to treat us with caution and would have crushed Poland in eight days."[9] No conceivable French assistance could have prevented the destruction of the Polish forces, he believed, and any military aid would only have invited formation of a coalition against France. Here as elsewhere, when Bugeaud spoke of war he had the Revolutionary or Napoleonic "worst case" model in mind: France confronted by a coalition of Austria, Prussia, and Russia which was abetted by the British navy. In the late 1830s, the key military experience of his career remained that obtained in the emperor's *grande armée*, with all that force's triumph and tragedy. Generally, the potential domestic impact of a hostile foreign coalition needed little explanation in a forum where recollections of the Napoleonic era remained vivid.

In 1839, when it briefly appeared that the Belgian Settlement of 1831 might be overturned and France might again march into Flanders, Bugeaud repeated his concern about the probable effect of such action on the juste milieu, and resumed his campaign against the Left. In February, under the erroneous impression that the Belgian king had abdicated and that war was likely to result, he confessed himself "thunderstruck" by the fervor with which "manufacturers and merchants express their hope that war will break out," and the extent to which they had "adopted the ideas of disorder" articulated by some newspapers.[10] The consequences of this journalistic agitation, he averred, would likely be visited not upon merchants or journalists but upon the rural majority from which infantrymen would be recruited. "How happy our publicists and our bellicose orators would be [should war break out]," Bugeaud observed. "What a stroke of good luck it would be for them! Imagine how much ink would be expended, how much hot air emitted, how much enthusiasm disseminated. But how many publicists and orators," he wondered, "would we find in the battalions of volunteers?" Few indeed, he implied. It would be the peasantry, Bugeaud stated, which would pay for this urban enthusiasm. Both political Centrism and the general welfare would be injured, he concluded, by any resort to military violence.[11]

In any event, France was quite unprepared for war. "How would one prosecute a war which broke out today," Bugeaud inquired at the height of the agitation produced by rumored events in Belgium, "with 50,000 men in Africa, 20,000 in Paris, 8,000 in Lyons, 12,000 in the Vendée, and 8,000 in the Midi—all of which are places which could not be denuded of troops without imprudence?"[12] He was convinced that there was no possibility of conducting a foreign campaign with the limited forces who were not committed to such duties, and that any attempt to divert additional troops in order to increase their numbers would only expose domestic society to additional challenges from the Jacobin Left.

Perhaps one of the clearest indications of the relationship that Bugeaud perceived between maintenance of the juste milieu and continued French abstention from European conflicts is suggested by the electoral advice which he offered in February of 1839. "I strongly recommend that you vote for conservative supporters of domestic order and international peace," he counseled a correspondent, "and not for the fools who wish to get their country into trouble."[13] Only conservative deputies, Bugeaud believed, could be counted on to safeguard France from internal and continental violence, and to strengthen a political system that would be protective of majoritarian interests at home and pragmatic national interests abroad.

It was the Ottoman Empire, however, which in 1839 confronted French policy with a greater challenge than either the revolt in Poland or the unrest in Belgium. Mehemet Ali, pasha of Egypt since 1806 and long independent of any meaningful control from Constantinople, had in 1838 notified the Porte and the European powers of his intention formally to declare his independence from the empire. Forced to respond to its vassal's action, the Porte in June of 1839 launched an attack, only to be overwhelmed by the Egyptian army in northern Syria. On July 1, Sultan Mahmud II died, and several weeks later the entire Turkish fleet deserted and sailed to Alexandria. France, long a provider of assistance and counsel to

Mehemet Ali, was suddenly confronted with the possibility that both England and Russia might declare war against her as well as against her only-too-successful protégé. Faithful to his opposition to French involvement in war, Bugeaud again, after a brief recantation in August, led the resistance to those who seemed ready to undermine domestic harmony and European peace by their support for the Egyptian pasha.

Bugeaud's temporary repudiation of his antagonism to military adventures abroad suggests both the depth of his commitment to the juste milieu as a political posture and the seriousness of his concern that the monarchy might be unable to continue to sustain a Centrist regime. "It is essential that the government give the nation's agitators something to do," he informed an acquaintance in mid-August, "or that it understand how to restrain them with vigor. I am convinced that it is incapable of the latter, and that is why I rather incline toward war, however dangerous it may be." If victorious, he argued, France would consolidate societal order and the dynasty; without a declaration of war the country would be "killed by journalists and demagogues of all kinds."[14] Such sentiments were only passing disavowals of his basic opposition to foreign and military adventurism. However, they do highlight Bugeaud's continued perception of the sensitivity of domestic political moderation to turbulence, whether at home or abroad. At the same time, they also indicate his nascent acceptance of that governmental or "approved" violence which he soon was fully to embrace overseas. Although without hope for assistance from the ministry for his own efforts to minimize domestic unrest, Bugeaud did continue to consider the politics of the juste milieu as the bedrock upon which foreign policy should be grounded. His brief willingness to contemplate a European war did not reflect his considered opinion concerning the appropriate French reaction to the Levantine imbroglio, and it was contrary to his warnings, prior and subsequent, against military opposition to the expulsion of the Egyptian army from Syria.

Even as he admitted being favorably disposed toward war, Bugeaud warned that war was a "terrible thing for a disunited France to undertake against all of Europe." The uncertainties and possible calamities inherent in any recourse to military violence had totally failed to "open the eyes" of the nation's "bellicose revolutionaries" to the likely results of their propaganda.[15] Urban activists

continued to believe themselves capable of intimidating all the armies of Europe merely by a show of force.[16] In 1839 and 1840
Bugeaud continued to base his opposition to armed support of
Mehemet Ali on the certainty that the cadres which would be called
upon to defend France in the event of war would primarily be levied
from the countryside's peasantry.[17] The traditionalist and agrarian
biases of Bugeaud's thought were as obvious at decade's end as they
had been in the early 1830s.

With no allies and with approximately 54,000 soldiers in Algeria by mid-1839, France faced grim prospects in the event of a
European war. Not only was Bugeaud convinced that the Algerian
campaign had deprived the nation of the continental deterrent which
it had possessed in the early 1830s, but its military commitment
overseas had left even the defense of France's Rhenish frontier in
doubt.[18] "Ah, wretched Africa!" he wrote in a moment of particular
irritation in August. "You have always been an embarrassment, but
right now you constitute an immense danger."[19] Developments within
Europe, now heightened by France's isolation and vulnerability in
Africa, led him during the Syrian crisis to weigh the relative merits
of alliances with Russia and England, and even led him to consider
acquiring certain territory in Europe, which he believed would benefit national security more than would further acquisitions along
the southern or eastern shores of the Mediterranean.

The gravity of the Levantine situation, Bugeaud observed in
early July, made it essential that France negotiate a treaty with
either Russia or England to prevent an anti-French coalition from
forming. An accord with the former, he argued, was to be preferred, because "Russia could grant us more concessions." However, the country was not in a position to adopt that option, he
noted, since the burden of Africa and the power of the English navy
prevented France from making any move which might result in a
blockade of Algeria by the British fleet. "Without Africa," Bugeaud
remarked, "I would lean toward a Russian alliance;" but with it he
felt obliged to recommend a treaty with England.[20] Wistfully, he
itemized the advantages to be gained if France had had the maneu-
verability to "tip the balance" between England and Russia by
forging an alliance with one or the other *according to [its] interests,*" and not according to "political sympathies" or geopolitical
realities.[21] Bugeaud was certain in mid 1839 that France's security in

Europe had hardly been strengthened by its nine-year campaign in Algeria.

The territorial concessions which Bugeaud believed Russia might have granted France, if alliance with France had been possible, lay on the Rhine. "Russia could have persuaded Prussia to cede the Prussian Rhineland to us," he argued in August, "and have indemnified Prussia with the Duchy of Warsaw." This, Bugeaud maintained, would have been a "good deal" for both France and Russia, since the former would have obtained a more defensible border and the latter would have freed itself of a troublesome territory which it now would probably be "obliged to guard with a huge army for centuries."[22] Incorporation of much of the area between Saarbrücken and Cologne would have secured France's northern approaches more effectively than had the neutralization of Belgium and, with the exception of one Bavarian bridgehead, would have enabled the nation to base its defense on the Rhine, from the Alps to the Netherlands.

Bugeaud considered a treaty with Britain acceptable "were [England] to agree to [French] aggrandizement on the Rhine." Since Britain, unlike Russia, could offer no territorial indemnity likely to make the Prussians relinquish the Rhineland, an English commitment of thirty or forty thousand troops to secure the Rhineland for France in the event of war should be the sine qua non of any Anglo-French defense pact. In return, France should promise Britain that it would support "reconstitution" of the Ottoman Empire as a counterweight to Russia.[23] If French security in Europe could not in 1839 be guaranteed by securing the Rhineland through a Russian alliance, Bugeaud was clearly ready to conclude a treaty with England for the same purpose. Soon, however, developments in the Near East removed both the specter of continental war and any urgency to explore seriously Bugeaud's preferred diplomatic alternative.

In early September 1839, British marines and Turkish troops landed on the Syrian coast, and by early November they had captured Acre and destroyed Egyptian power in the Levant. Some three weeks later, with the British navy standing off Alexandria, Mehemet Ali signed a convention renouncing his claims to Syria and agreeing to restore the Ottoman fleet. In return, he was to be recognized as hereditary governor of Egypt. The rapidity of events had spared

Bugeaud from making a public explanation of his support of alliance with England, and spared France the necessity of any major diplomatic or military response. "If we had taken possession of various places in Syria, if we had proclaimed its independence," he later observed, "Europe would unhesitatingly have declared war on us. We were far too deeply involved in Algeria to get bogged down in Syria. The whole idea is absurd."[24] Meanwhile, English operations off the Syrian coast had confirmed Bugeaud's belief in the superiority of British sea power. The threat of isolation of French troops by an English naval blockade had been underscored by the success of the English action in Lebanon. In 1840, he continued to view Africa as a serious obstacle to development of a domestic military capability sufficient to meet any challenge from east of the Rhine.

Always, however, the desire for social peace and the viability of the juste milieu in France were what lay behind Bugeaud's advocacy of diplomatic efforts to solve continental problems. A foreign war, he repeated in 1840, might spark domestic uprisings and enable the Left to plunge the country into civil war. A dispute over control of the Syrian coast ought not to justify France's adoption of policies likely to result in release of the "evil passions" of the nation's metropolises. Only a situation in which great stakes were clearly involved, Bugeaud emphasized, would make acceptable the erosion of political Centrism that war might bring. "[War] is not to be undertaken lightly or without carefully weighing the grounds for it," he observed, and he stressed that this was the fundamental reason why he wanted the government to follow an "opportunistic policy, a policy of armed peace."[25] Far better than any resort to force was a diplomacy whereby one might "dissimulate, wait, negotiate, play one power off against another, and let them get themselves entangled."[26] Military conflict, Bugeaud stated again in late 1840, should be hazarded only in cases of direct European attack on indisputable French interests.[27]

Although he hoped for the maintenance of peace, Bugeaud's belief in the likelihood of war led him to champion the fortification of Paris, the reorganization of French strongpoints along the frontiers, and an increase in the number of soldiers under arms in France. Only with Paris fully encircled by walls and forward strongpoints, with the frontier more effectively secured by new lines of defensive positions, and with both protected by a large metropol-

itan army, Bugeaud believed France would be effectively sheltered
from European dangers. And only then did he think France would
be in a good position to influence European developments in its
own national interests.

Directed by Thiers, then minister of the interior, and by Marshal Soult, the fortification of Paris had been initiated without legislative approval in November 1830. By the summer of 1833, when it
was halted by Republican opposition in the Chamber of Deputies,
4.7 million francs had been spent on the grading of land for a ring
of fourteen forts around the city. In 1838 Bugeaud began efforts to
revive the project. "I am fully convinced," he observed, "that as
long as Paris remains unfortified we will not wield the weight in
Europe to which we are entitled." He argued that France's failure
to erect defensive bulwarks played into the hands of its rivals east of
the Rhine. In his opinion, an unfortified Paris would inevitably
become the principal object of invading troops. A country whose
capital was located only some two hundred miles from a frontier
simply could not avoid the "fundamental necessity" of fortifying it.
"The issue is not one of money," Bugeaud insisted, "but rather one
of security, and 150, 200, or 300 million francs should not enter
into the discussion or influence its direction." The occupation of
Paris some two decades earlier, he recalled, had cost the nation
approximately 2 billion francs.[28] Regardless of price, he believed that
ramparts would prove a bargain in the long run. By the spring of
1839, Bugeaud had no doubt that immediate resumption of construction of the defenses around Paris was imperative for both its
own and the nation's security.

He considered an appropriate defensive system to consist of a
large and unbroken inner wall behind an outer circle of independent forts. Bugeaud estimated that it would take almost a month
for an enemy to breach the outer circle, and that attackers would
thereafter need to get new siege equipment, since what was not
destroyed during the attack on the forts would be insufficient to
breach the inner wall.[29] Completion of the ramparts, he believed in
late 1840, would take at least five or six years even if construction
were to begin at once. Meanwhile, it was essential that Paris be
prepared to mount a defense "similar to that of Saragossa."[30] Clearly,
Bugeaud's recollection of the Peninsular Campaign remained vivid,

and continued to provide him a model for solution of national
security problems.

By the end of 1840, Bugeaud had come to consider the fortification of Paris part of the foundation of the politics of moderation.
"I will indeed be happy if, before leaving for Africa, I have made
even the slightest contribution," he stated in late January of 1841,
"to providing my country with a means of guaranteeing its security
against foreign dangers and its liberty and independence against
domestic threats." At the same time, Bugeaud underscored his conviction that the regime would "kill itself morally, it would commit
suicide" if it were ever to employ the barrier's firepower against the
population of Paris.[31] Thus, his budding violence and moral confusion were still restrained by an awareness of the limits of force and
the perils of compulsion. Destroyed in Algeria, this awareness proved
notably lacking in 1848. In 1841, Odilon Barrot joined Bugeaud in
his admonition, and together they attempted to counter Leftist charges
that the ramparts were being built in preparation for civil war
against the capital's "dangerous classes." Always, Bugeaud couched
his arguments in terms of national security against external dangers, and never suggested that the walls might be independently
useful for control of the city's inhabitants. By 1841, erection of
physical defenses seemed to him as beneficial for maintenance of
political moderation in Paris as election of supporters of domestic
order and international peace had been two years earlier. All of
Bugeaud's efforts were finally rewarded when, in February, the
chamber voted to resume construction of fortifications. Probably,
he departed for Algeria hopeful that France, given enough time,
would succeed in effectively protecting Paris from foreign occupation and any resultant Jacobin upheaval.

The fortification of Paris constituted only part of Bugeaud's
defensive and continentalist military orientation at the end of the
1830s. For such defenses to be strategically effective, a reorganization of France's frontier garrisons and an augmentation of its standing army were essential. To replace the single chain of more than
two hundred undermanned forts strung out along the country's
eastern frontiers, Bugeaud advocated establishing a limited number
of heavily defended garrisons, arranged alternately or irregularly
along two lines. "The first line," he noted, "should be a *ligne*

d'arrêt to slow an enemy offensive"; it would constitute a screen behind which the nation's major forces could concentrate and maneuver. The second line, in addition to its primary purpose of blunting the main force of an invasion, would constitute a "line of withdrawal" to which defenders of the ligne d'arrêt might retreat and await reinforcements.[32] Should the second row of fortresses also be breached, the enemy would still be confronted with a narrow supply and communication corridor, unless it spent time to widen the breakthrough area by capture of adjoining strongpoints. While such operations were being conducted, time would be available to concentrate the main French army near Paris and launch attacks on the advancing columns. These columns would probably be encumbered with siege equipment if the capital was properly fortified. If only France's metropolitan army were larger, Bugeaud maintained, such an invader would probably experience a major military disaster.[33]

During much of the 1830s, however, he little expected that the Algerian quagmire would permit France to increase the size of its home army and thereby augment its defenses against an European invasion sparked by domestic insurrection. "Difficulties within the country may make our neighbors restless," he observed. "From restlessness to war is often only a small step."[34] In 1840, he continued to believe that if France were attacked by the principal European powers it would require an army of 500,000 men, or some two and a half times larger than what was available in that year. Since France had none of the geographical advantages enjoyed by England and America, it could not safely emulate their minimal standing armies. Provision of some of the troops necessary to build a metropolitan standing army of half a million men was to be an important factor in Bugeaud's military and social experiments in North Africa.

Throughout most of the decade Bugeaud remained one of the leading parliamentary critics of the French presence in Algeria. Indeed, personal experience in North Africa only strengthened his continentalism. In mid-1836, Bugeaud had been billeted to Oran as temporary regional commander of the French forces stationed there, and had compiled an enviable military record. In little more than two months he raised an Arab siege of French troops at the mouth of the Tafna River, resupplied the interior city of Tlemcen, and won France's first major battle against the Arab and Berber resistance.

As a result, Bugeaud gained a reputation as almost the only success-ful Algerian commander. Nevertheless, he increased his public op-position to the North African adventure, and continued his effort to redirect parliamentary attention toward the state of French defenses vis-à-vis Europe, and toward needed municipal improvements in rural areas of the Dordogne and elsewhere.

Not surprisingly, Bugeaud's agrarianism had a great deal to do with his negative reaction to his first Algerian experience. In the fall of 1836, he informed Guizot that Africa's soil was uniformly infer-tile, and that its climate would prevent the application there of European agricultural techniques.[35] Two months later he told Thiers that the Regency was simply not cultivable, and that "one way or another it will have to be evacuated sooner or later."[36] In early 1837, Bugeaud denounced those in the Chamber of Deputies who pre-dicted a brilliant economic future for Algeria, replete with produc-tion of "cotton, cochineal, indigo, gold, and ostrich feathers." Rather than pursue such impossible dreams, he urged that they support construction of new roads and canals in backward areas of France itself.[37] Still, the most important reason for Bugeaud's criticism of the Algerian venture was his desire to increase French military security and diplomatic flexibility in Europe itself. Metropolitan national security and continentalism continued to be the fundamental cata-lysts of his thought.

Immediately after his first Algerian campaign, Bugeaud advised Guizot that the government should give careful attention to what maintenance of an army in Africa might mean for France if a Euro-pean war were to erupt. In addition, the ministry should reassess the importance of its several coastal enclaves in the Regency.[38] Bugeaud confessed himself worried about the widespread belief in France that the country could satisfy all of its military requirements by a levée-en-masse, or general conscription.[39] In March 1837, he again was sent to Algeria, this time to direct the military campaign which in May culminated in the signing of the Tafna Treaty. This treaty halted Franco-Muslim warfare for more than two years. Again, Bugeaud apparently had achieved a signal success in Africa, but again he denounced the whole colonial enterprise. For example, he stressed that an ever larger army in Algeria was an "immense dan-ger" for France, and would likely "compromise [French] indepen-dence in Europe" by depriving the nation of emergency use of its most experienced contingents.[40] A year later he stated that Algeria might become for the July Monarchy what Spain had been for the Empire.[41] Even after his formal appointment to the Algerian governor-generalship on December 29, 1840, Bugeaud continued to express concern over the military vulnerabilities and diplomatic problems that resulted from France's involvement abroad. In early 1841, he repeated that the African expedition constituted "an enormous danger, a great disadvantage for our position in Europe." Once more he observed that the country's military commitment overseas weakened its defensive capabilities on the continent,[42] and prevented the nation from "speaking forcefully" to its European neighbors.[43] Therefore, the strongly negative reaction in pro-colonial circles to Bugeaud's selection as supreme commander in Algeria was quite predictable.

So clearly was Bugeaud identified with continentalist opposition to colonialism that the *National* predicted his appointment would "upset the colony and disorganize the army." The *Quotidienne* went further: "Bugeaud's name is the last which should have been presented to the ministers for consideration," it editorialized. "Incompetent in statecraft...[and] maladroit in diplomacy, he has only achieved some consideration for himself in politics by his fire-eating speeches, blustering airs, and typical Limousin peasant harangues, plus a certain combination of provincial dynasticism and Gascon populism."[44] The fact that he continued to be "equally detested"[45] by Legitimists and Republicans only amplified such journalistic opposition. Still, at the heart of the criticism of his appointment was his preoccupation with Europe and his long-standing Perigordin regionalism.

There was, however, another side to the coin. As early as the fall of 1836 Bugeaud observed privately that Algeria might prove a useful training ground for the French army, and might even contribute to preservation of the juste milieu if "anarchists" and other disruptive elements were exiled there.[46] At the beginning of 1837, he stated that since France was so deeply involved in war it could only extricate itself by victory. To win, a commitment of troops sufficient to "strike at the morale of the Arabs everywhere" was required.[47] Four months later, from Algeria, he informed the minister of war that France would achieve nothing but endless war if it continued to be unwilling to commit the forces and pay the expenses necessary to establish itself solidly in the interior of the country. It was, Bugeaud added, "not impossible to subdue the Arabs," and he even stated that if he were assured of an adequate number of troops he would gladly undertake the assignment and was confident he would succeed.[48] In early June, he expressed hope that French settlements might be established in Algeria once the Arab and Berber opposition was crushed.[49] The year 1837, indeed, marked the start of his secret campaign to secure command of all French forces in the Regency.

The roots of that campaign stretched far back in time and deep into the soil of Perigord. Immediately after his return to La Durantie in 1815, Bugeaud had begun to contribute portions of his military pension to the construction and improvement of roads in the Dordogne. In 1824, he started to press for development of a road network over which the Perigordin peasantry could more easily transport its produce to market. This interest led to his appointment in 1826 as inspector of roads in the arrondissement of Nontron. Despite his efforts, little road building was undertaken. In 1830, Bugeaud lamented the lack of local arteries and markets throughout the Department.[50] Finally, a major highway construction program was announced by Prefect Romieu in 1834, and Bugeaud confessed himself "overwhelmed with joy." He hastened to expand on his earlier proposals for improvement in Perigord's transportation system, now advocating construction of one major new route and the repair of a road that "exhausted travelers and ruined vehicles."[51] Throughout these years, Bugeaud continued to make personal contributions for highway construction and by the late 1830s his benefactions totaled 14,300 francs.[52] Nonetheless, in 1837 public funding for road construction still lagged. Consequently, Bugeaud determined to secure in Africa those subsidies for highway construction which continued to prove elusive in metropolitan France.

He wasted no time in putting this decision into effect. Shortly after accepting his second Algerian assignment in 1837, Bugeaud informed his wife that he had "requested that if we negotiate with the emir [Abdel Qadir, commander of the Arab-Berber army], and if he agrees to pay us tribute, the first 100,000 francs will be placed at my disposal for public purposes in my arrondissement."[53] In fact, he had solicited official permission from Foreign Minister Molé to impose a total price of 180,000 francs on Abdel Qadir for any treaty which might be arranged. More than half this amount, Bugeaud made clear, was to be for his discretionary use in encouraging highway construction in Perigord.[54] Molé not only approved this request but promised to defend it against criticism by his colleagues. In Molé's opinion, it was the "most natural proposal in the world." Bugeaud "wanted his native region always to remember the services he had rendered France," Molé later observed.[55] In brief, the possibility of securing funds in Algeria for development of the Dordogne was what persuaded Bugeaud to temper his continentalist opposition to aggrandizement in Africa. It was also a key element in his decision to accept the proffered reassignment overseas.

After a dramatic personal interview between Bugeaud and Abdel Qadir, the Tafna Treaty was signed on May 30, 1837. This document confirmed French control of the five coastal towns of Algiers, Mostaganem, Mazagran, Oran, and Azrew, but recognized Abdel Qadir's authority over the remainder of the provinces of Oran and Titteri. In a secret codicil, Bugeaud pledged to supply Abdel Qadir with 3,000 rifles and a substantial amount of ammunition and to limit or abandon French support of his principal tribal opponents. Bugeaud's attempts to channel this covert assistance through the consul he assigned to Mascara, and his praise for Abdel Qadir in reports to Paris and Algiers, were inspired by his desire to obtain the 100,000-franc highway construction fund, which the Emir had in fact promised him. Nothing, Bugeaud was determined, was to prevent acceptance of the Tafna Treaty in France and payment by Abdel Qadir of the amount agreed upon. "I would not hesitate to grant Abdel Qadir everything he requests," Bugeaud advised the minister of war two days before the Tafna signing, "so profoundly am I convinced that he alone is able to provide security for our farmers." A day later he informed Molé that "what I have learned of the religious and honest character of the emir, as well as of his power over the Arabs, completely convinces me that all of the provisions [of the Treaty] will be perfectly executed." Bugeaud went so far as to pledge himself the "guarantor of the emir," insisting that only because he had complete confidence in Abdel Qadir's word was he willing to accept such responsibility.[56] Perigordin regionalism, not naiveté, explains this remarkably sanguine assessment by a commander with substantial prior experience in Algeria. In addition, such optimism suggests a latent moral myopia which permitted Bugeaud's regional agrarianism to undermine his scrupulous professionalism and the larger national interest. In the spring of 1837, securing of funds for municipal improvements in the Dordogne was obviously of more immediate concern to Bugeaud than was the European balance of power. Two years later, when an Arab attack abrogated the treaty, Bugeaud's enemies did not forget the ardor with which he had once defended it.

In the fall of 1837, opposition within the governing coalition finally forced Molé to abandon his campaign to secure governmental permission for Bugeaud to collect the desired payment from Abdel Qadir. By then the affair had become a scandal, and on October 11 Bugeaud informed the emir of his renunciation of the amount in question. Nevertheless, the events of 1837 were not without benefits, at least for the Dordogne. In fact, 25,000 francs were paid to Bugeaud by other tribal chiefs and delivered in the greatest secrecy to his prefectural collaborator Romieu during the first week of November.

Less than three weeks after his renunciation of the gratuity from Abdel Qadir, Bugeaud informed Romieu that the Dordogne had not thereby been totally deprived of subsidies for road construction. "I told you, my dear prefect," Bugeaud wrote to Romieu from Paris on October 31, "that I would explain to you why I had to renounce the 100,000 francs which I had reserved for my arrondissement. I didn't want to accept this sum without being authorized to do so by the government. I was informed that [such an acceptance] *would give the press too much of an opportunity for carping criticism.* You will appreciate how that increased my love for the journalistic fraternity." Bugeaud hastened to explain that the prefect had no reason for despair. "Obliged to reject so gratifying a deal, I seized upon opportunities to partially indemnify myself. Two gifts were offered to me by tribal chiefs. I accepted them, but only for the benefit of my electoral arrondissement, and you will receive 25,000 francs by mail." Secrecy was essential, Bugeaud reminded Romieu, if he were to escape chastisement and these funds were not also to be blocked by Paris. "Don't go and publicize [what I have told you]," he cautioned the prefect, "for the government would consider me to have exercised bad judgment in accepting funds without its consent. Therefore keep quiet about it." Yet no time should be lost, Bugeaud emphasized, in distributing the booty from Algeria. "While awaiting my arrival, please make 3,000 francs available for the road from Excideuil, or for the bridge, whichever you prefer; 2,000 francs should also be appropriated for the most useful labor in the canton of Saint-Pierre de Chignac."[57] Obviously, Bugeaud's decision to suspend his strategic judgment and mire the *métropole* more deeply in Algeria owed much to his devotion to Perigord. What had proven possible to obtain through a position of secondary authority in Algeria, he had evidently concluded by late 1837, might more easily be secured from a position of absolute power there. During much of the last three years of the decade, therefore, Bugeaud circumspectly attempted to obtain appointment as both governor-general and commander-in-chief of all French forces in Africa.

Apparently, Bugeaud began to contemplate the advantages of supreme authority in Algeria early in 1837. In February, he expressed surprise that the government, having selected him to negotiate peace with Abdel Qadir, had failed to appoint him governor-general.[58] During the spring, conflict with then-governor-general Damrémont over the conduct of the Tafna negotiations deepened Bugeaud's appreciation of the power that the governor-generalship provided. It also increased his determination not to return to Algeria unless he was offered iron-clad guarantees against interference. However, acceleration of his campaign for the governor-generalship did not occur before early 1839. From the beginning, it was directed mainly against Sylvain-Charles Valée, who had succeeded Damrémont as governor-general in late 1837.

The recall of Valée, and the selection of his successor, had become matters of major concern to Bugeaud by midwinter of 1839. "If Valée is removed," he observed to an old friend in February, "a major thorn in the side will thereby be extracted." It seemed likely to him, however, that the next governor-general would be an individual who did not know Africa and had never fought there. Personally, Bugeaud noted, he would not be extremely disappointed if he were not offered the governor-generalship. He nevertheless took pains to emphasize that his background and the "wishes of the army" particularly recommended him for that position.[59] For Bugeaud, whoever succeeded Valée would be required to repudiate Valée's defensive military posture and act to counter the extension of Abdel Qadir's authority over new Arab tribes and into the province of Constantine. "Were I in Marshal Valée's shoes," he observed in

July, "I would tolerate Abdel Qadir's advances less, and I would have fewer dug-in positions and more men available as a result."[60] Indeed, Bugeaud described Valée's strategic immobility as "intolerable and absurd."[61] His desire to replace Valée was probably communicated to the government during the summer or early fall of 1839. With renewal of the African war in November, official consideration was given to dispatching him once more to Algeria.[62] Another year was to pass, however, before Bugeaud again was to see Africa and be allowed to "measure swords anew with Abdel Qadir."[63]

Throughout the next twelve months Bugeaud continued to criticize Valée, increasingly manifesting the ambition again to command French forces fighting the emir. He confessed that he found it "inconceivable" that Valée had been permitted to retain his post "after so much evidence of military incompetence, deception, mistakes, and charlatanism." A new bout with Abdel Qadir was attractive in itself. "Fighting this [latter-day] Jugurtha appeals to my imagination," Bugeaud confessed in July 1840, and requested assistance in communicating this fact.[64] By fall, he had come to believe that he alone was the "man for Africa," and that his destiny was to go and put an end to the Algerian war.[65] He doubtless had no clear notion then of just how soon his aspirations would be put to the test.

While continuing his covert campaign against Valée throughout 1840, Bugeaud publicly reiterated the criticisms of the government's Algerian policy which he had first made three years earlier. Despite the obvious bankruptcy of current strategy, he informed his parliamentary colleagues on January 15, the government still had not proposed a new way of using the 60,000 soldiers then in Africa. The decade-old policy of limited occupation, upon which the Tafna Treaty had been based, Bugeaud now described as a "chimera, a dangerous chimera." France, he insisted, had three options in Algeria: abandonment, control of insignificant coastal enclaves from the sea, or total conquest. It was essential, he emphasized, that one of the three options be adopted immediately, and that strategy be devised that was appropriate to its implementation.[66]

Although withdrawal of all French forces from Africa might have proven popular, particularly in rural areas, Bugeaud did not believe that the nation's press would support such a policy. He therefore dismissed it as impracticable. Control from the Mediterranean of limited areas on the Algerian coast would be feasible if such enclaves were "Gibraltars" which could be retained with 1,200 or 1,500 men and supplied by sea. With 35,000 Frenchmen in Algiers, and with substantial French communities in other coastal towns, this option too was not practicable. "Therefore, in my opinion," Bugeaud concluded, "there remains only the option of absolute domination, of subjugation of the countryside." To his critics, he spoke frankly. "Everyone is well aware that I have always considered Algeria the most baneful legacy which the Restoration left the July revolution. However, since my country is there, I don't want it to act with sterile uncertainty....I believe that great nations, like great men, should err on a grand scale. Yes, the taking of Algiers was in my opinion a mistake; but since you wanted to do it, since it was impossible that you not do it, then you must do it grandly, for that is the only way to get any results."[67] Bugeaud later responded to teasing from the Duke of Orleans with typical rhetorical flourish. "Monseigneur, it is quite pleasant and easy for a man to marry a rich, attractive, fascinating woman with whom he is madly in love. What would be astonishing would be his failure not to treat her well. But what would you say about a man forced to marry a poor, ugly, uncouth woman, whom he could not endure, who nevertheless did not fail to treat her with the utmost consideration? Well, Monseigneur, I [would] be for Algeria this second husband, this new type of lover, and I [would] treat her so well, I [would] overwhelm her with so much attention, so much love, that she [would] have no choice but to again become young, alluring, and handsome."[68] The immediate objective, Bugeaud stated, was the overthrow of the "Arab nation," and the destruction of the power of Abdel Qadir. With only a hint of coyness, he recommended accomplishment of these objectives by concentrating the African army and augmenting its mobility. Four months later he again castigated the government for "doing nothing, absolutely nothing" about Africa, and once more suggested his availability if more energetic measures were decided upon.[69] By the autumn of 1840, Bugeaud's calculated campaign for the governor-generalship must no longer have been a secret to most observers of the French political scene.

During the late 1830s, colonization had become in Bugeaud's mind the instrument by which Algeria might finally be subdued, and the means by which French security in Europe might finally be enhanced. By 1840 Bugeaud had concluded that significant rural settlement was the only way the métropole might destroy the war-making capacity of the Arab tribes, free the bulk of the colonial army from the necessity of occupying Africa, and provide itself the 500,000 soldiers necessary to prevent social upheaval at home and invasion from the continent. The desire to free the bulk of the French army from permanent duty in Algeria was what inspired both his insistence on a massive influx of settlers into the country and the rapidity with which he attempted to end the war against Abdel Qadir in 1841 and 1842. By the time of his appointment as governor-general, he no longer viewed the colonization and conquest of Africa as a repudiation of his long-standing continentalist concerns; instead, he believed that thus alone could they be satisfied. What Bugeaud was doing was far from merely surrendering his diplomatic judgments to personal ambitions; rather, he was attempting to achieve quickly what by late 1840 had come to appear inevitable. Only through such speed could France be made secure both north and south of the Mediterranean.

The possibility of establishing a sizable French settlement in Algeria first occurred to Bugeaud during his second sojourn there in the spring of 1837. In contrast to the previous summer, the countryside was then green and inviting from the winter rains. By mid-1838, he was maintaining that civilian settlement was possible and indeed necessary to prevent France from having to maintain a large army of occupation abroad indefinitely. At least 100,000 soldiers would probably constitute France's open-ended commitment to Africa if some 200,000 to 300,000 *colons* did not "seize the countryside."[70] French security in Europe, Bugeaud suggested both privately and publicly during the next two years, required that France undertake Algerian colonization on a grand scale, and begin in Africa an invasion similar to the one the Franks and Goths had once launched across the Rhine. "Look for colons everywhere," he declaimed in 1840. "Get them, whatever the cost, from the towns, from the countryside, from among your neighbors...." It was crucial that settlers be substituted for soldiers rapidly, since one could not, without great dangers for France, "leave in Algeria for any length of time the effectives it would take to subdue the country."[71] By the time Bugeaud was named governor-general, he obviously believed that official support of colonization was the best way to remove the French army from Algeria and gradually make it available for duty in Europe.

No consideration weighed more heavily on Bugeaud in January of 1841 than the replacement of soldiers by settlers with the greatest speed possible. Without a large number of colonists in Algeria, he warned the minister of war, the French presence in Africa would be at the mercy of events in Europe; in particular, it would be vulnerable to war on the Mediterranean. The current situation had an unfavorable effect on France's entire continental policy, "constrained it in its alliances, and left it no freedom of maneuver." It was "undeniable," he insisted, that it was "essential to colonize at once" if the French enterprise in Africa were not to remain "precarious" and "sterile."[72] The campaign of 1841 only confirmed Bugeaud's conviction concerning the best strategy to retain Algeria and guarantee French security on the continent. Without significant rural settlement there, the nation would "never be strong in Europe," and it would "never have freedom of action" until it withdrew the major part of its colonial army from Africa.[73] Three months later, he repeated that since military involvement in Algeria weakened France in Europe, it was advisable to end the war quickly and begin settlement overseas. Thus alone would the army be freed for metropolitan service, and French defenses against domestic insurrection and foreign invasion be completed.[74]

A decade of calculation of national, provincial, and personal interests thus had left Bugeaud both a confirmed opponent of armed intervention in European disputes and an advocate of the total conquest of Algeria. No more desirous of eroding the politics of Centrism by permanently involving French troops in Africa than he had been of committing them to Poland, Belgium, or the Levant, Bugeaud attempted merely to capitalize on events to benefit Perigord and to practice a profession whose allure had not dimmed with time. Nevertheless, both his nascent character flaws and his regional sentimentalism were highlighted by his first contact with the Regency. The advocacy of settlement in Algeria was by decade's end the strategy by which he attempted to shield the métropole from difficulties inherent in military occupation abroad. With Paris soon, he hoped, to be protected by walls, strengthened frontier garrisons, and an augmented army, with the Dordogne receiving subsidies from Africa, and with himself holding the appointment for which he had campaigned, Bugeaud by late 1841 surely looked toward the future with considerable optimism.

4

Strategy, War,
and the Conquest of Algeria

By the early 1830s, Bugeaud had developed the military strategy which he began immediately to implement upon his arrival in Algeria in 1836. Indeed, most of his major articles on military affairs had been written years earlier and published as pamphlets or in professional journals between 1815 and 1831. During his first years in parliament, however, he had applied his military theories to metropolitan France rather than to North Africa. Resistance in the Vendée to the new juste milieu embodied by Louis Philippe led him to recommend use there of antiguerrilla tactics first developed in Napoleonic Spain. Legitimist Chouannerie in the Vendée, he argued, would prove as vulnerable to antiguerrilla tactics as had Royalist opposition south of the Pyrenees. By 1832, Bugeaud was a recognized critic of the defensive tactics then being employed by most European armies, an advocate of flexible, appropriate strategy in either conventional or partisan warfare, and a strong exponent of the offensive in military operations. Ultimately, his Algerian assignments provided an opportunity to revive the principles of mobility, morale, and leadership, which he considered as applicable to western France as to either Spain or North Africa.

Total pacification of the Vendée, Bugeaud observed in 1832, had not been accomplished by any French government since 1790. By its very nature, guerrilla resistance was exceedingly difficult to crush, and no instantaneous end to Vendéan unrest could be expected. He noted that in Spain partisans had operated behind French lines for six years and had survived all efforts to destroy them. Bugeaud impatiently rejected suggestions that failure to terminate current disturbances in the Vendée resulted from the regime's secret sympathy for Carlism. Again, he insisted that policies that promoted peace abroad and "order" at home were essential in order to weaken revolutionary impulses. Only if such policies were firmly in place, Bugeaud believed, was there hope of success for even the most determined antiguerrilla strategy. Even then, Chouans operating in remote or difficult terrain would pose a challenge to the largest conventional force, which obviously could not permanently occupy every hamlet in regions such as the Vendée. Still, he argued, a combination of "firepower, energy, determination, courage, and especially mobility" could be expected gradually to undermine Vendéan guerrilla strength. Combat would likely be bitter, but only thus did Bugeaud anticipate that gradual pacification of the Vendée might be achieved.

An essential tool for effective action against partisans, Bugeaud stated, was accurate intelligence. Knowledge of all roads, ravines, and streams within a theater of operations was essential for government troops, as was familiarity with all entrances to and exits from it. Careful advance planning was necessary, to assure that every contingent knew its area of operations and where to assemble once a guerrilla band had been sighted. When word was received that a band had appeared in a village, reinforcements should not hurry there by the most direct route. Rather, troops should be concentrated and wait until special detachments could occupy all routes of retreat from the hamlet. Only then should the village itself be attacked. Bugeaud insisted that more could be gained by blocking escape routes and by setting ambushes than by attempting to pursue scattered or fleeing groups of guerrillas. Nevertheless, all troops involved should be mobile enough to assume the offensive at a moment's notice, and should maintain contact with each other by appropriate prearranged signals. Such signals might consist of specified sequences of rifle or cannon shots.[1] He noted that the utility of such communication had been demonstrated during his Alpine campaign in 1815.[2] Fundamentally, Bugeaud believed that antiguerrilla warfare was similar to the hunt. Wherever it might occur, pursuit of the world's "wild beasts" by the forces of order fascinated him. Many of his comments about combat with partisans struck an obvious "sporting" note.

Experience in Spain had exposed Bugeaud to the organizational weaknesses in defenses used by Europe's regular armies. During the late 1820s and early 1830s, he proposed that scouts and rotating patrols be substituted for the tightly linked defensive positions of the day. In addition, he emphasized that morale must be kept high in order for infantrymen to maximize the effect of their fire. By 1832, Bugeaud had developed strategy appropriate to either conventional or antiguerrilla warfare. Actual testing of such strategy was to be limited to colonial operations alone.

Bugeaud was convinced that the current defensive system of closely linked and heavily fortified outposts designed to prevent breakthroughs from surprise attacks had proven generally counterproductive. "I never attempted to capture a detachment [so protected] without succeeding," he remarked.[3] In Spain and elsewhere, dug-in advance positions had occasioned a "multitude of unfortunate developments." The worst of such developments had been encirclement, and Bugeaud maintained that proper deployment of scouts could have prevented such occurrences.[4] In fact, his arguments were well taken. Outside Alicante, lack of an effective early warning system had allowed Suchet to envelop and destroy between 6,000 and 7,000 enemy troops in 1812. In 1813, the French army in Catalonia had suffered grave losses because of its immobile defensive network. And Bugeaud's own encirclement of an enemy corps near Moustier in the Alps on June 26, 1815, clearly was made easier by the stationary outposts employed by the Austrian army. Defensive systems had not improved in the years since. In Bugeaud's opinion, small, mobile scouting units could shadow enemy forces with little risk to themselves and provide intelligence sufficient to prevent any encirclement of major troop concentrations. Such patrols might consist of three or four men during the day, and up to eight men at night. This strategy had general utility. "It is indispensable," he wrote, "for small detached corps, for armies on the defensive, and even for those on the offensive. It is especially when one wishes to avoid combat or when, not fearing it, one has dispersed one's troops to forage or rest that a judicious deployment of scouts is of the highest importance."[5] In 1830, Bugeaud formally advised the minister of war that deployment of such scouts was the best way to assure that French troops would not be surrounded and forced into battles where they were outnumbered.[6]

The primary objective of his proposed special forces was to

collect the intelligence that was needed to guarantee that routes of retreat could not be interrupted. Retreat, indeed, was an option which Bugeaud believed false pride had led French forces to adopt all too seldom. He noted that he had personally ordered retreats four times in his career. His soldiers, "far from blaming [him]," had been delighted that retreat had placed their enemies in front of them once again. It was especially important that retreats not be delayed until an army had sighted an opponent. "*When combat should not be risked,*" Bugeaud insisted, "*it is not necessary to have sighted the enemy before undertaking a retreat.*" By the time an enemy was in view, it was often too late to avoid disaster. He challenged his fellow officers to study French history and learn how frequently the demands of "honor" had led to reverses on the battlefield. Information concerning enemy movements and the possibility of encircle-ment, Bugeaud argued, could easily be provided by properly constituted scouts on patrol. Military commanders required only the prudence to act upon intelligence which such surrogate observers would furnish.[7]

Above all, he sought to end the system of inflexible "chain-link" barriers so impenetrable that "not even a cat" could slip through unobserved.[8] Development of substitute defenses in order to prevent both surprise and encirclement was a problem to which Bugeaud devoted great attention. His recommended solution was assignment of soldiers to patrol a hypothetical circle (*cercle sup-posé*) whose center was identical with the location of the protected detachment. Depending upon circumstances, such rotating patrols might consist of small scouting units, larger contingents of specially designated troops, or a combination of the two. Special forces of this type should never initiate combat. Their objective was always to be restricted to the collection of intelligence. Without exception, their raison d'être was to assure that the major forces they pro-tected could engage an enemy when and where they chose. Com-munication between scouts on the hypothetical circle and the protected contingent was as important for prevention of encirclement in con-ventional warfare, Bugeaud believed, as were appropriate signals for the entrapment of guerrillas in irregular combat. In both cases, communication should be by a prearranged number of shots, as long as "local or atmospheric circumstances" were such that no useful intelligence was simultaneously provided the enemy.[9] In conventional as well as in antiguerrilla warfare, Bugeaud considered knowledge of the theater of operations, plus mobility, to be prerequisites for victory.

The principal objection to Bugeaud's system from his professional colleagues was that isolated patrols would be quickly liquidated. This criticism was not new. "The first time most of the officers with whom I discussed the matter heard about my system of patrols," Bugeaud observed, "they exclaimed that any outposts so remote would soon be destroyed. For those whom I could not convince by rational argument, I employed...the following technique. Several days after the discussion I had them called in one by one and addressed them somewhat as follows: 'Sir, I am informed that the enemy is sending a patrol every night into the forest or near the forest of.... I have selected you to destroy this patrol tonight.' Each officer immediately manifested embarrassment, and responded in roughly these terms: 'But, mon commandant, for me to be able to rub this patrol out I would have to know approximately where it is located. Can't you provide me with any directions, or better yet a local inhabitant who may have seen it?'" Bugeaud replied by reminding his interlocutors that since they had found it "so simple the other day to liquidate the patrols around [my] hypothetical circle," there seemed no reason for them to raise difficulties now. "Each then recognized his error," Bugeaud concluded.[10] He constantly emphasized that small unit actions, intelligence, and communications were just as possible and important for conventional forces as for commandos. Indeed, perhaps Bugeaud's principal contribution to military debate was his insistence that tactics used successfully in guerrilla warfare be incorporated more fully into conventional military doctrine.

Conventional warfare could most effectively be waged, Bugeaud argued, if the *carrés*, or squares, into which European infantrymen had long been organized were reduced from 3,000 to approximately 1,000 men. In adopting this position as early as 1815, he crossed swords with such senior Napoleonic commanders as General Joseph Rogniat. In 1816, Rogniat maintained in his *Considerations sur l'art de la guerre* that squares of 3,000 soldiers were necessary to guarantee sufficient firepower and depth to destroy attacking cavalry. In Bugeaud's opinion, no such firepower was actually provided. Only the first row of such carrés ever fired on an enemy, and most of the squares' troops were uselessly immobilized in their interior reaches. In most cases, no loaded or reloaded rifles were ever passed forward to soldiers firing from the exterior faces. Furthermore, reliance on mass to blunt cavalry charges was for Bugeaud a serious error. In fact, he argued that smaller carrés, with shortened sides as targets for charging horsemen, would make disruption much more difficult. "In diminishing the extent of a square's frontage," Bugeaud insisted, "one reduces in the same proportion the number of horses which can overrun it."[11] As long as a number of such reduced carrés operated as a unit and protected each other, there was no danger that cavalry might encircle one of them.[12] Were a reduction of individual frontage combined with effective and increased firepower, Bugeaud believed that foot soldiers would gain decisive advantages over cavalry.

To maximize firepower, he advised that fire be withheld as long as possible, and attackers be permitted to close in to very short range. Then volleys should be sudden, concentrated, and sustained. Bugeaud criticized firing uncoordinated fusillades before cavalry could come within reasonable range. He noted that such fire was not only ineffective, but often left infantrymen no time to reload before attackers smashed into their midst. Bayonets were useless against horses. To prevent spasmodic volleys, he recommended that infantrymen in the first row fire from one knee and that they alternate shots with those immediately behind them. The latter could best fire from a standing position over the shoulders of their kneeling comrades. Meanwhile, loaded rifles and replacements for casualties should be moved forward from within the square. Thus, fire would be continuous and disciplined, and could be expected to have a deadly effect.[13] As a consequence, counterattacks could be launched more easily and with greater prospects of victory. Bugeaud never forgot that "*every good defensive strategy must be capable of instantaneous transformation into an offensive one.*"[14] He had no doubt, however, that ultimate success of all offensive action would continue to depend on effective leadership and high morale.

To motivate soldiers and raise morale, Bugeaud urged commanders to maximize personal contact with their men and foster solidarity within their units. He emphasized that it was essential for a general to "get to know [his] troops, chat with them frequently about war, and prove that [he] is capable of leading them effectively." He observed pointedly that review of forces at inspections or on parade grounds was not sufficient. "Moral force springs from the confidence one is able to inspire in one's subordinates," Bugeaud stressed. "It is augmented by tact, intelligence, and courage." Such confidence would increase patriotism, military spirit, and a desire for glory and regimental honor. Only through creation of élan could a commander expect an army to fight well on the offensive.[15] From the moment of his arrival in Algeria, Bugeaud attempted to inculcate such morale in his troops.

Given the dreary legacy of French strategy in North Africa, this was no easy task. Indeed, to raise morale and enable French forces successfully to engage Muslim tribesmen, Bugeaud was obliged to alter almost totally the ponderous system of transport and supply in use in Algeria since 1830. That system featured heavy artillery awkwardly transported on campaign, native auxiliaries responsible for baggage and materiel, and relative immobility of both columns and individual infantrymen. Scattered, overmanned forts had begun to proliferate shortly after 1830, and French troops sickened and died in them as rapidly as they did from the rigors of campaigning itself. Equipment, rations, and hospital care were extremely poor and suicides were frequent. No extended stay was necessary for Bugeaud to assess the situation and propose remedies. "The fundamental elements of success in Africa," he observed in July 1836, "are sufficiently manned mobile columns freed of heavy wagons and field artillery. Soldiers should be physically fit, have good morale, and be commanded by young, energetic officers. The transport system should be well organized, and carry four or five days more rations than one expects to need."[16] So accustomed was the Algerian general staff to established practices, however, that initially they strongly opposed Bugeaud's orders.

The existing system had been modeled on the requirements of conventional warfare in Europe, and few adaptations had been made to meet the challenges of a guerrilla war overseas. Despite repeated campaigns along Algeria's trackless coast, French columns of 8,000 to 10,000 men continued to drag as much baggage and artillery mounted on heavy wagons as they would have if they had been moving along a European highway. It was not uncommon for 1,500 men to do nothing but construct a roadway for the passage of such wagons. Of course, generals selected geographical lines of least resistance for the movement of materiel and men, and their location or line of march was therefore quite predictable by the enemy. Detachments were obliged to withdraw along the same routes over which they had advanced, allowing little flexibility in the face of danger. Worse yet, responsibility for the transportation of supplies and the evacuation of wounded was in the hands of Arab or Berber auxiliaries. Such mercenaries were usually hired on the eve of an expedition's departure. Driving their own camels or mules, Muslim "allies" controlled crucial portions of the French military machine. Whether from carelessness or sedition, they often permitted their pack animals to cool themselves in streams, oblivious to damage or destruction of their cargoes. In the face of enemy attacks, native auxillaries frequently ditched supplies in panic, thereby causing great confusion at the worst possible moment. Wounded evacuees typically provided them with excellent sport; they made camels run "to cause the soldiers on them to fall off."[17] Once fallen, they left them where they fell. Before 1836, French strategy was clearly hostage to geography and these indigenous mercenaries, and played directly into the hands of Abdel Qadir.

In addition, such strategy was dependent on overloaded, exploited, and unhealthy foot soldiers. Individual infantrymen were no more mobile than the columns into which they were organized. Treated little better than beasts of burden, they marched carrying rations for seven or eight days, extra ammunition, spare shoes, and pots and other cooking utensils. All provisions were stuffed into one large campaigning bag. "Many succumb under such burdens," Bugeaud observed in June 1836, "and even the strongest must be led so slowly that it is impossible to execute those rapid maneuvers which alone produce results."[18] Attrition was also a problem in the numerous blockhouses in which much of the French army was garrisoned. This was particularly true of forts in the malarial Mitidja Plain south of Algiers. Of course, immobilization of effectives in stockades left all military initiative to the tribesmen, a practice that was disastrous for French morale. Bedding for troops on campaign and on garrison duty was uniformly poor, and soldiers frequently slept on the bare ground. Rations were even worse, the stale bread, poor-quality rice, and salted bacon characteristically producing violent diarrhea and death from dehydration. Hungry soldiers often resorted to eating cats, dogs, and whatever roots were available.

Pure drinking water was unknown in the backcountry, and troops had to make do with water from rivers or any stagnant pools which might be found. Not surprisingly, hospitals were packed. However, they did little but process the dying for burial. Perhaps fearing hospitalization, four or five soldiers usually committed suicide during each expedition. In sum, sickness, psychosis, and despair pervaded the French Algerian army before Bugeaud's arrival. General Théophile Voirol only reflected this situation when he remarked in 1833 that it was "far better to be confronted by 20,000 armed bedouins" than it was to have rampant disease and misery waste one's forces from behind the lines.[19]

In early June 1836, Bugeaud landed at the mouth of the Tafna River to assume command of French troops stationed there. One of his first official actions was to convene his subordinates and inform them that the strategy employed previously would never produce victory. For many years, Bugeaud stated, he had campaigned in Spain against enemies and under conditions similar to those in Africa.[20] Tactics tested during antiguerrilla operations seemed to him especially relevant to the present situation in Algeria. Such tactics, he emphasized, involved the abandonment of heavy artillery, creation of a new system of transport and supply, and constitution of mobile columns able to maintain offensives for substantial periods.[21] "If I had 3,000 of my soldiers from Spain with mules to carry their rations," Bugeaud informed the minister of war, "I would traverse as master the entire province of Oran."[22] Forces currently on the Tafna, despite their recent enfeeblement by bad weather and lack of food, he still believed capable of launching an offensive "so rapid, energetic, and unexpected" that, as in Spain, their morale would be dramatically raised and the enemy thrown into confusion.[23] "An enemy who flees is always pursued," he informed his colleagues. "A force which offers battle is respected, and one which takes the offensive is feared." If they "acted like sheep," the Arabs would batten on them like wolves. "Act like lions," Bugeaud concluded, "and you will be respected." To that end, he ordered that no heavy artillery be used in the upcoming campaign to resupply the defenders of Tlemcen. The absence of artillery would halve the time required for the march, and greatly diminish exhaustion and sickness. Mobility and new esprit would finally enable the French forces to "hurl themselves in any direction from which attacked with that enthusiasm and resolution which are essential for success."[24]

Immediate preparations were therefore made to ship to Oran all wagons, field guns, and gun carriages. Next, Bugeaud ordered formation of special detachments of French soldiers to handle pack animals and supervise evacuation of the wounded. He emphasized that more determined attempts would henceforth be made to live off the countryside.[25] In the future, whatever animals were required would simply be requisitioned, and 80 to 100 mules, each capable of carrying up to 240 pounds, assigned to every 1,000 men. In Bugeaud's opinion, such reorganization would increase the possibility of surprising the enemy, reduce the chances of sabotage, and enable French columns to remain on campaign for at least two weeks. Geography would be made an ally, rather than an opponent, and French forces rendered as "nimble as the Arabs, or at least sufficiently mobile to go anywhere."[26]

Predictably, Bugeaud's directives provoked horrified reactions from officers on the Tafna. Opposition was especially strong to abandonment of heavy artillery. Colonel Combes argued the matter with Bugeaud, insisting that heavy weaponry in fact maintained morale by keeping tribesmen at a distance, and reduced the number of French wounded. Bugeaud responded that Combes was quite in error, and that artillery clearly discouraged French forces from acting effectively in the field. "Do you mean to tell me," he inquired of Combes, "that you would be unable without artillery to fight Arabs who don't have any heavy weapons when you already possess three enormous advantages over them: organization, tactics, and discipline?" If such were the case, Bugeaud noted, it would be as much as to say that French soldiers were inferior to Arab troops. "As for me," he told Combes, "I believe them much superior, especially when commanded by men such as you." Artillery indeed kept enemies at a distance, Bugeaud admitted. However, that was precisely why he desired to eliminate it. Rather than keep hostile forces at bay, Bugeaud stressed that he "wished to give [the enemy] confidence in order to engage [him] in a major battle." He informed Combes that not only did artillery fail to reduce the number of wounded, but in fact it increased attrition by reducing mobility and obliging French troops to endure enemy fire for extended periods.[27] For his part, Combes was impressed by Bugeaud's decisiveness.

Only days later, he informed General Castellane that "Bugeaud understands and makes war well. . . . His talents can only assure us a victory which. . . otherwise would remain uncertain."[28] Among those varied talents was an assiduous concern for detail and a profound solicitude for the welfare of his men. Beginning in 1836, Bugeaud inaugurated a new era in the provisioning, basing, and general maintenance of the French army in Algeria.

When on campaign, foot soldiers in the new-model army which he created carried little but their weapons and a limited amount of ammunition. All else was transported by the new mule corps. Meat was provided by cattle seized in raids, or by the wild game which abounded in North Africa. Soon, French mobility was enhanced. Bugeaud's troops became skillful at uncovering the secret underground granaries constructed by the tribesmen for use by their warriors. Locating such granaries became one of their major preoccupations. Typically, lines of French soldiers, often several miles long, advanced over likely ground, prodding with their bayonets until they struck one of the stone slabs which sealed such granaries. These tactics marked an important military breakthrough, since the granaries contributed greatly to tribal mobility. Bugeaud boasted as early as 1836 that henceforth every operation would be "easy and safe." Generals would no longer be paralyzed by developments in their baggage train, and "[would] be able, should the opportunity present itself, to devote two or three days to pursuit of an enemy no matter where he goes." Should they learn "that a hostile force is located some distance away, they [now] will be able to move against it."[29] No longer would Muslim troops be able to run to ground, or enjoy secure zones of reassembly or recruitment. France's new ability to live off the countryside and hunt its quarry meant that tribesmen no longer would be able to plant, harvest, or graze their flocks without French permission.[30] Consequently, Bugeaud believed it would be unnecessary to retain the existing network of permanent garrisons as base camps and supply depots.

This was a point which he argued with unflagging zeal between 1836 and 1841. "We must. . . renounce useless and compromising positions," he informed Thiers on August 10, 1836, "in order not to paralyze our troops and to have enough of them to traverse the country and subdue it."[31] Once invested with the governor-generalship, he moved quickly to put his convictions into practice. Bemoaning the "unfortunate legacy" which he had inherited,[32] Bugeaud early in 1841 ordered evacuation of all outposts in the Mitidja Plain except those in Blida and Kolea which had special importance as communication centers. Abandonment of some ten garrisons in the vicinity of Philippeville also was initiated.[33] By July, most of the troops stationed in Miliana and Medea had been withdrawn. In August, Bugeaud ordered dismantlement of several blockhouses between Constantine and Sétif.[34] Although some time would pass before he was able to reduce the number of forts to what he regarded as a completely satisfactory level, the policy of retrenchment was well advanced by 1842, and the military initiative firmly in French hands. Bugeaud's boast of 1837 became simple fact during the early 1840s. "I have made myself as much an Arab as you are, more than you are perhaps," he had informed the unsubdued tribes in the province of Oran then, "for I can remain on campaign longer without returning for supplies. Your vast solitudes, your steepest mountains, your crags, your deepest ravines cannot frighten me or stop me for a single moment.... I am as mobile as you are. There is not a single corner of your territory which I cannot reach. Like a river of fire I will scourge it in all directions, today to the south, tomorrow to the east, the day after to the west, then to the north."[35] Such scourging, by means of unceasing, pitiless raids or *rhazzias*, succeeded in ending widespread, organized tribal resistance in most of Algeria by 1843.

Throughout the years between 1836 and 1841, Spain served Bugeaud as the cautionary example against which his strategy for North Africa was developed. If Paris were to recollect the results of proliferation of outposts in Spain during the Peninsular Campaign, he noted in 1836, it might prove useful in avoiding similar errors in Algeria. Establishment of an excessive number of forts in Spain, Bugeaud observed, "perhaps caused the loss of 100,000 men. Let this experience not be forgotten in relation to Africa."[36] He stated in parliament two years later that in Spain France had been dominated by a "fatal mania of fortifying all the towns and district capitals [*gros bourgs*] which it took. When we seized a monastery we put 400, 500 or 600 men in it, depending on its importance; we thought we could control the country because we were covering it with tiny forts, with small, improvised military installations. The result was paralysis of our movements; instead of our controlling others, it was we who were everywhere controlled. Our garrisons were surrounded by the insurgents and their defenders could not escape. More than half the army thus found itself neutralized." Nevertheless, he warned, the same errors were being repeated in Algeria. "Today, at this very moment, in Africa, we are applying the same system. We believe ourselves powerful because we are constructing so many strongpoints; everywhere we are establishing forts, blockhouses, and heavily defended positions, with the result that the army finds itself so reduced in numbers that it cannot act."[37] During 1839 and 1840 Bugeaud continued to adduce Spain as proof of the fundamental error in Algerian strategy, and to insist that no progress could be expected until French commanders freed themselves from the incubus of the Peninsular experience. In the end, his arguments were grudgingly accepted by the French general staff. When Bugeaud undertook to suppress the garrisons in Africa in 1841, he did so with the formal approval of the minister of war.

Thereafter, French troops fared far better in the field than had their predecessors in the early and middle 1830s. In those years soldiers on campaign frequently slept without shelter and on mattresses unworthy of the name. In 1834, Governor-General Drouet d'Erlon urged that this situation be corrected, and accurately described its unfortunate results. "Improvement in bedding is absolutely essential to preserve soldiers' health and diminish the great number of illnesses to which they have been subject up until now," he wrote then. "All men *must* be provided with a good hammock and mattress. Without this precaution fleas and other insects will continue to prevent them from sleeping, and force them to move from one spot to another during the summer nights. During the winter they will continue to be chilled by nighttime humidity and cold, and contract intermittent fevers and intestinal problems. The hammocks provided heretofore have been badly manufactured and of poor quality."[38] Nevertheless, no improvements were made until Bugeaud addressed the problem in March of 1841. Condemning the "sorry state of bedding" furnished troops in North Africa, he ordered manufacture of new and larger wool mattresses which could either be safely placed on the ground or suspended as hammocks. Each of the new mattresses was to be one meter 90 centimeters long and 61 centimeters wide.[39] In addition, Bugeaud insisted that strips of cloth be provided to all soldiers, and that each individual be assigned to a "camping group" of three or four men. Assembled, such cloth strips would make a tent sufficient for each camping group. Henceforth, there would be no need for those huge tents for fifteen or twenty men which typically accompanied expeditions during the 1830s, but often arrived too late to be of any use. Response from the War Ministry in Paris was immediate, and before winter the Algerian expeditionary force had the new bedding and cloth stripping at its disposal.

In short order, Bugeaud also succeeded in upgrading the quality of boots furnished the common soldier and obtaining adequate supplies of drinking water. As early as 1836, he had lamented that many soldiers were quickly incapacitated as a result of poorly made footwear.[40] By 1842, special marching boots had become a standard issue in Africa, and attrition during campaigns consequently reduced. Potable water was by then always carried by the mule corps, thus sparing infantrymen the necessity of drinking from the malarial pools scattered through the countryside. Of course, these reforms also contributed to higher morale and greater mobility among Bugeaud's troops.

Of particular interest to Bugeaud was improvement in the standards of hospital care in Algeria. During the early 1840s, he complained frequently about medical failures and abuses.[41] His concern was not without effect. "The hospitals are much improved since Bugeaud's arrival," one soldier wrote in late 1841. "In several places they have begun to build strong, massive hospitals to replace the wooden sheds; and the frequent personal visits of the Governor-General have done much towards abolishing the prevailing abuses and rough treatment of the surgeons."[42] Suicides began to diminish, and spread of the new élan throughout the African military to accelerate. By 1842, a military legend of Père Bugeaud, planted six years earlier on the Tafna, was clearly beginning to blossom. Thereafter, that legend provided inspiration to generations of French soldiers in Algeria and elsewhere.

As Bugeaud had foreseen, the "enfeebled" troops assigned him on the Tafna, which soon were heavily reinforced, were capable of fighting extremely well during the 1836 campaign to resupply the isolated Koulougli defenders of Tlemcen. The Koulouglis, who were the offspring of unions between Turks and Arabs, had traditionally been discriminated against by both groups. Nevertheless, before

1830 the Turkish ruling caste in Algiers had favored some Koulouglis by granting them police powers in specified inland areas and the authority to collect tribute from the Arab tribes. Detested in the backcountry, they had been threatened with extermination after the collapse of Turkish power. However, they soon found a new patron and, by the early 1830s, had rallied solidly behind the French. In 1836, Abdel Qadir was attempting to capture the Koulougli garrison town of Tlemcen and neutralize Mustapha ben Ismail, the Koulougli commander and Abdel Qadir's most dangerous indigenous rival. Arriving before Tlemcen, Bugeaud scattered the besieging forces of the emir, reestablished contact with the Koulougli army, and decisively, if temporarily, defeated Abdel Qadir on the banks of the Sikkak River on July 6. On the Sikkak, Abdel Qadir mustered some 4,100 cavalrymen and 3,000 Berber footsoldiers. Bugeaud countered with more than 6,000 infantrymen. By evening, approximately 1,200 Algerians lay dead and 130 had been captured, against 32 French dead and 70 wounded. Victory on the Sikkak constituted a truly spectacular debut for Bugeaud in North Africa. Abandoning heavy artillery had indeed encouraged the Muslim army to offer battle, and the result was precisely as Bugeaud had anticipated. However faulty the comprehension of Bugeaud's abilities still was in metropolitan France, his stature within the Algerian army was firmly established by his striking military accomplishments in 1836.

Although his logistical reforms and improvements in materiel and sanitation contributed greatly to morale, Bugeaud's primary contribution was to galvanize soldiers by manifesting in his own person the principles of leadership which he had earlier detailed in France. He won the confidence of his troops by personal conversations and shared privations, and he raised their spirits by his own competence and bravery in combat. On campaign, he "led the life of a common soldier. He was everywhere, kept an eye on everything, and knew how to endure privations and fatigue despite his age. During battle he ordinarily went to the most exposed positions and demonstrated calm courage and fearless daring.... He was an ideal molder of men."[43] Bugeaud dressed like a common soldier, marched on foot with his men, and took particular pleasure in long nighttime conversations with them around the campfire. Frequently, he reduced his own food ration when supplies were short. He could often be observed munching on a roll which he softened, like his troops, by soaking it in water. Whether or not in action, Bugeaud's "restless activity" was remarkable. He slept little, usually gave audience at three in the morning, and "kept everyone on the alert by his continual presence."[44] Bugeaud "ran a school in Algeria," a contemporary remarked. "He loved to explain things, and never let slip an opportunity to do so. His troops responded with an affection which was both respectful and familiar."[45] That affection was perhaps most obviously voiced in the famous marching refrain inspired by Bugeaud's loss of his military cap during an Arab attack:

> As-tu vu
> La casquette
> La casquette?
>
> As-tu vu
> La casquette
> Du père Bugeaud?

By the force of example, Bugeaud succeeded in infusing the Algerian army with a spirit it had never previously known. That accomplished, a major obstacle to French ascendancy in North Africa was removed. By the early 1840s, Bugeaud expected that the time was ripe for significant metropolitan colonization in the Regency, and the ultimate return of most of the overseas army to service in Europe.

The strategy Bugeaud had first learned in Europe, properly adjusted, obviously assisted him in conquering Algeria. Since Muslim troops never attempted to overrun French forces in European fashion, carrés proved unnecessary in North Africa. No danger of liquidation from encirclement by large native armies existed after 1836, and there consequently was little need for the rotating patrols he had favored in France. Still, it remained difficult even for Bugeaud's own lieutenants always to distinguish between conventional warfare and antiguerrilla actions. "We must forget those orchestrated and dramatic battles which civilized peoples fight against one another," Bugeaud felt compelled to remark as late as 1842, "and realize that unconventional tactics are the soul of this war."[46] Of course, the superiority of mobile, highly motivated, and offensively minded troops had by then become as obvious in Africa as it appeared in retrospect in Spain. "Perhaps never before," a military colleague of Bugeaud's related, "has an army commander been able, by his benevolence and moral authority, to obtain so much from his soldiers. [Bugeaud] could have led them to the ends of the earth, or made them walk on hot coals."[47] Nonetheless, the submission of Algeria, however exacting, proved to require less exalted leadership and fewer sacrifices.

5

The 1840s
Algeria and the Bases
of Colonial Rule

Throughout 1841 and early 1842, Bugeaud advocated construction of a massive barrier to protect the Mitidja Plain. However, by late 1842 he had repudiated that project, arguing that such defenses were unnecessary and that there was no alternative to subjugation of the entire littoral and backcountry. So rapidly had military efforts progressed, and so numerous had capitulating tribes become by the second year of his governor-generalship that Bugeaud began increasingly to stress the conditions of tribal submission, and the development of durable methods of native control. During much of the 1840s, he attempted to rule the indigenous population through its traditional authorities, and he endeavored to sanction this system of indirect rule by severe penalties, unprecedented since 1830. Although his feelings toward totally defeated tribes and their established elites were paternalistic and even admiring, he believed that the French presence in Algeria could ultimately be guaranteed only by the assimilation of Muslim to French society. In order to begin the process of assimilation, Bugeaud undertook efforts to promote Franco-Arab commerce, to undermine and destroy the Algerian Jewish community, and to immobilize selected tribes by settling them in villages constructed or subsidized by Europeans.

In the countryside, the French profited from the severe winter of 1841-42, which followed hard upon the heavy military losses suffered by the Muslim alliance in 1841. Record cold and deep snow killed tribesmen and herds alike, and by winter's end tribal morale had been seriously eroded. By the spring or early summer of 1842 most Arab tribes on the Chéliff River, and many Berber tribes in the mountains between Tenès and the Mediterranean, had surrendered. Meanwhile, French troops occupied or destroyed such interior villages as Mascara, Tlemcen, Taza, Tegdempt, Boghar, and Nedroma, and seized many supply centers and arms caches. "The system of mobility and unremitting warfare is triumphing over the tenacity, fanaticism, and cunning agility of the Arabs," Bugeaud reported to Adolphe Thiers on June 27, 1842. "Abdel Qadir's forces are shattered, the tribes are submitting everywhere, the serious war is over. The [emir] is only an inconsequential guerrilla with nowhere to lay his head. He will yet hurl a few bolts of lightning, as does a storm which is ending and whose thunder is no longer heard, [but] he is no longer to be feared."[1] By autumn, France had effective control of the mountains between Tlemcen and Constantine, and at year's end its first raiding parties were sent into the northern fringes of the Sahara.

Nevertheless, Bugeaud harbored no illusions about the bitterness of the resistance, which he believed was likely to continue. Until well into 1842, he was so concerned with the Arab threat to European settlements in the Mitidja Plain that he advocated construction of an immense ditch and earthworks to protect its western, southern, and eastern edges. He did not regard the valley's size (some ten by sixty miles) as a deterrent to erection of such defenses. His memories remained vivid of the Arab incursion into the Mitidja in early November 1839, which had cost the lives of more than a hundred settlers and ended the peace he had negotiated on the Tafna. Bugeaud was determined that it not be repeated. Sheltered behind a barrier strong enough to block tribal raids, new villages might be rapidly established in the vast and potentially fertile lowland behind Algiers. In this way, he hoped to begin a process by which Africa would finally be subdued without compromise of French security in Europe. For at least a year after his arrival in Algeria as governor-general, Bugeaud gave as much attention to completion of the Mitidjan ramparts as he did to military subjugation of the countryside.

Construction of these defenses had been initiated by France's military Engineering Corps in 1840. The project had been endorsed by Marshal Valée and strongly recommended by General Rogniat, who detailed its importance in his *De la colonisation de l'Algérie et des fortifications propres à garantir les colons des incursions des tribus africaines*. For Alexis de Tocqueville, who made a brief visit to Algeria in 1841, the wall's advantages were several. "This is the only type of defense which can succeed against the Arabs," he observed. "It would be more effective and less expensive to implement than people think.... What would not halt a European force for a single instant is impregnable for an Arab army. In addition, the natives will always be very hesitant to get themselves inside [such] an enclosure because they will never be certain of being able to get out of it with their horses and booty." A year later, Tocqueville repeated that "*security* means the *barrier*. It will provide complete security by day.... Traversing it will be possible at night but difficult.... One cannot burn crops at *night*. [The Arabs] will therefore destroy neither trees nor bridges."[2] To Bugeaud, such defenses seemed the most effective way to renew colonization, solder a French presence on Algeria, and maximize the uses to which the overseas army might be put.

To promote vigorous French settlement was high among the new governor-general's priorities. On February 22, 1841, he declared it to be among his principal objectives in an official proclamation to the city of Algiers. Six months later, Bugeaud explained that construction of a Mitidjan barrier would enable France to "settle quickly" that portion of the valley where lack of security had previously discouraged settlement, and contribute to the mobility of colonial forces.[3] In December 1841, he assured his subordinates that "colonization outside of Algiers is at last going to begin to develop within the shelter provided by the rampart presently being built."[4] By then, construction of two fortified villages just inside the new barricade was well advanced. "Once [such defenses] enable this area to be settled," Bugeaud maintained, "it will be capable of providing the army with a great deal of fruit and vegetables, and especially with the means of transportation necessary for expeditions beyond it."[5] In his opinion, fortified villages inhabited by European farmers would both buttress the Mitidjan wall and hasten the day when a large standing army would no longer be needed to maintain security. Bugeaud's efforts deeply impressed Clemens Lamping, a German member of the French expeditionary force. "The completion of this eighth wonder of the world is much to be desired," he observed, "for the protection of the lives and properties of the unfortunate colonists in the plain and as an inducement to others to settle there." Like Tocqueville, Lamping believed that "this work will very much impede, if it does not totally prevent, the nocturnal forays of the Bedouins. It will, at any rate, put a stop to their coming on horseback and in great numbers. If a few should steal in on foot between the blockhouses, they would not be able to drive away their prey, such as cattle, etc., which is their chief object."[6] For Bugeaud, the Mitidjan defenses clearly meant that French forces could be used with greater confidence elsewhere in Algeria or even be transferred to Europe if conditions demanded.

A barricaded valley, Bugeaud informed the minister of war, would also guarantee the army of fodder for its animals and make it easier to establish a storage depot west of Algiers. In addition, it would enable France to offer secure asylum to surrendering tribes and provide Europeans near Algiers with ample grazing land for their flocks. Perhaps most importantly, it would free the army from the distraction of police duty.[7] Therefore, the governor-general marshaled all available resources to push the project forward. "We are working on the *obstacle* with all the means at our disposal," he reported in November 1841. "I have left elsewhere only what is absolutely necessary for essential services. Work is going forward reasonably quickly as a result of the plows being used to dig the ditch, a consequence of which is that soldiers have little need to wield pickaxes. I am currently convinced that I shall be able to complete the western section during December and January."[8] By year's end, a scar some ten feet deep by twenty feet wide angled along western approaches to the Mitidja, buttressed by an interior talus approximately ten feet high. Observation towers or blockhouses protruded from the talus every thousand yards. Early in 1842, Bugeaud broached the possibility of employing Arab or Berber labor to speed up construction.[9] By then, a consensus existed within the French military that the governor-general's laborers soon would succeed in ending tribal forays into western portions of the valley. In General Rumigny's opinion, the barricade would be especially useful in ending the incursions of the Hadjout tribe into the Mitidja between Kolea and Blida.[10] In fact, however, the recall of the laborers and denunciation by Bugeaud of the entire effort was then only months away.

Despite his enthusiasm for the great wall, Bugeaud always

maintained that a wall was no substitute for active prosecution of
the military effort. In November 1841, when his support for the
barricade was perhaps at its zenith, he carefully delineated one of
his major differences with General Berthois, director of the Engineering Corps involved in actual construction. "According to him,"
Bugeaud stated, "*the obstacle is the most important requirement in
Algeria and everything must be subordinated to it.* . . .; while in my
opinion, the most pressing need is to terminate the current bitter
war which began before I arrived and which I believe I have energetically prosecuted."[11] During 1842, the unexpectedly sudden collapse of organized tribal resistance convinced Bugeaud that completion
of the wall was no longer necessary. By midyear, he had concluded
that there was no sense in "enclosing a portion of Algeria to make it
a kind of *île française* for establishment of colonies sheltered from
enemy attacks."[12] General Berthois's laborers soon were shifted to
other duties, and French forces guarding the ditch withdrawn. Bugeaud
again began to emphasize during the second summer of his governor-
generalship that the requirements of French diplomacy in Europe
could tolerate nothing less than complete subjugation of Algeria.
With characteristic decisiveness, if not candor, Bugeaud by fall was
denouncing the barrier which he had endorsed so heartily less than
a year before.

In September 1842, he reminded the minister of war that even
the most heavily defended earthwork could not achieve its purpose
without the support of offensive operations. "It would prove vain
to hope that, thanks to the barrier, one might be spared the necessity of making war throughout the country." He added that any
suggestion of passivity on the part of the French would only provide the enemy time to rebuild forces sufficient to overrun the
French defenses. He believed that if France was serious in its intention to root itself in Africa, there was simply no substitute for
sustained offensive warfare. Repeating arguments he had made in
the Chamber of Deputies two years earlier, Bugeaud insisted that
there was "no middle way. Either we must withdraw to the coast
and have only insignificant, well-fortified trading posts defended by
a few men, or we must subdue the Arabs." The difficulties of man-
ning an extensive barricade now seemed to him overwhelming.
"One cannot thus guard a significant area effectively." He noted
that even if one temporarily managed to do so, such bulwarks

would "absorb a large division," and, in an area like the Mitidja, would enable illness to claim 5,000 or 6,000 soldiers annually. In his opinion, it was better to use troops to conquer the country than to permit them to perish of "boredom and fever" within the "detestable" Mitidjan defenses. In fact, the governor-general now went so far as to insist that he had "never been a supporter of this system."[13] His disillusionment, however, was not shared by all of his military colleagues. Pressures to continue work on the wall remained strong enough during the balance of 1842 to oblige him to permit trees and hedges to be planted along sections of the ditch still lacking an interior talus. In early 1843, all work finally was suspended, leaving the barricade in various stages of completion between the Mediterranean and Blida. Work had not yet been started on the Mitidja's eastern side, where its precise route had long been a subject of dispute. By then, Bugeaud's conviction that colonization could only be assured by an active and aggressive military establishment had been reinforced by new military victories.

From the beginning of his tenure as governor-general, Bugeaud had been faced with the problem of relocating and governing the surrendering Muslims. Early in 1840, individual Arabs and Berbers who offered submission had first been permitted to settle in parts of the Mitidja. Security problems resulting from this influx, plus friction between newly arrived Muslims and the European community in Algiers, persuaded Bugeaud to initiate a new program of native administration. It rejected any but tribal surrenders and established the principle that Muslim chiefs were to bear original responsibility for the behavior of the tribes they led. Developed and formalized during the capitulations in and after 1842, the governor-general's system of indirect rule was enforced by measures of a rigor which his prior career had only hinted at. Solicitous of the welfare of natives once they had demonstrated the sincerity of their surrender, Bugeaud throughout the 1840s sought improved relationships between conquerors and conquered, which he believed were essential for reduction of tribal hostility and assimilation of Muslim into French society.

On March 6, 1841, Bugeaud issued an edict intended to reduce the immediate problems of security in the Mitidja. For the most part, the difficulties there involved the theft of crops or livestock of European settlers. He ordered that all Muslims already in the plain be relocated ten miles east of Algiers between the mouth of the Harrach River and an old Turkish fort which the French had renamed the *maison carrée*. Henceforth, only entire tribes pledging submission would be allowed to settle near the fort or in other designated areas. Tribal chiefs alone, Bugeaud specified, were to be recognized as legitimate brokers of such submissions. After surrender, all tribes would be placed under chiefs selected or approved by French authorities.[14] Thus did Bugeaud act on the advice he had given Thiers five years earlier. "Select the most influential [natives] to govern in our name," he had counseled them, "[but] don't give them enough power to become dangerous. . . ."[15] Thus, resettlement of tribes on the orders of France, and investiture of indigenous authorities with initial responsibility for their followers, dated from the earliest days of his governor-generalship.

In his March edict, Bugeaud also specified that European hiring of laborers from the new Arab reserve was to be done only through the appropriate tribal chiefs. These chiefs were to be responsible for maintenance of a list of all natives so retained. In addition, chiefs alone were to have authority to certify native laborers by granting official medallions (*médaillons*) that authorized temporary departure from the tribal reserve. Such médaillons were to be hexagons of white iron, and were to be hung around the wearers' necks. Each médaillon was to have a number identical to one on the responsible chief's list, and the inscription *arabe soumis* ("conquered Arab") in both French and Arabic. At sundown, each chief was expected to collect the médaillons from returning workers. Thus, a combination of indirect rule with employment of Muslims by Frenchmen was established. This system, greatly elaborated as the years passed, constituted the basis of Franco-Arab relations throughout the next three decades.

A new commercial relationship between Muslims and Europeans also was outlined in Bugeaud's proclamation of early March. The edict decreed that a native market should be held weekly near the maison carrée and that French settlers be encouraged to trade with tribesmen. Six weeks later, Thursdays from sunrise until noon were designated as official market days. In the event, this *suq* was never successfully organized. However, this early effort by Bugeaud to promote Franco-Arab trade is evidence of a technique he soon employed more widely to encourage assimilation of Muslims by Europeans.

His program of native relocation, Bugeaud specified in the March edict, would be enforced by dire punishment of Arabs without médaillons who were apprehended outside the native reserve. Unarmed tribesmen so observed by day were to be brought before their *caid*, or chief, fined ten francs, and given some form of corporal punishment. The colonial administration alone, however, was granted authority to impose penalties of from one to five years of imprisonment on armed Arabs who were illegally abroad during the daytime, five to ten years of hard labor on tribesmen without weapons who were outside the reserve at night, and death to those with arms who were apprehended after dark. When an individual repeated one of the lesser offenses, French military authorities were to impose the immediately higher punishment. All judgments would be rendered and penalties inflicted by a council of war. Thus, after March of 1841 there was little doubt as to the source and significance of sanctions upon which all native authority rested. These severe penalties, which were immediately criticized in France and were to some extent moderated by Paris, were grimly defended by Bugeaud.

"We have neither the time nor the means," the governor-general informed the minister of war in late April, "to observe metropolitan legal procedures." He now maintained that his March proclamation had been occasioned by a "succession of murders" which, "stimulated by the weakness of repression," had led the European community to "understand only too well that it is necessary to renounce the delays, the half-measures, the legal niceties ignored or scorned by the Arabs."[16] According to Bugeaud, many settlers had come to believe that summary execution was the only answer to harassment by Muslim neighbors. He insisted that his March decree had been enthusiastically received by all Europeans in Algeria.[17] As long as major outrages were not "immediately followed by severe punishment," he claimed, the tribal population would believe France neither just nor powerful. The Arabs were accustomed to arbitrary harshness, and this was what Abdel Qadir himself employed. "As Africa requires different military tactics from those required in Europe," Bugeaud concluded, "so also does it require different administrative measures and a different kind of legality."[18] Evidence of a growing gap between colonial and metropolitan values, and of the beginning of Bugeaud's personal withdrawal from the juste milieu, is surely suggested by his edict of March 6, 1841.

As tribal surrenders multiplied and increasing numbers of Muslims accepted French protection, applying a system of indirect rule more generally became unavoidable. Clearly, France lacked the resources to rule the indigenous population directly. "Each day I become more aware of the necessity of governing Arabs by Arabs," Bugeaud informed a fellow officer in the fall of 1842, "and of finding able chiefs who may serve as intermediaries between us and the Muslim population. Let us meddle as little as possible in the administration of these chiefs. Our role, for the present, is to support the chiefs we have selected, maintain tranquillity in the country, and promote commerce."[19] Two years later he repeated that it was essential for France to "avail itself of [Arabs] having influence over the tribes," and he observed that any immediate reduction of the traditional prerogatives of tribal aristocracies would only augment the number of the métropole's enemies.[20] In 1846, he explained the thinking behind these sentiments in more detail. "Even the most savage nations have their elites, which they are accustomed to obey. If foreigners are substituted for these leaders such peoples will show little obedience, since their traditional authorities, their ambitions unsatisfied, will be constantly inciting them to revolt. If one does not have [such elites] on one's side, if they are not made part of the administration and their amour propre and interests satisfied, they will be enemies. They will be far more dangerous outside than inside our camp, for they will be able to boast of not having bent their knee before the foreigner, before the Christian, and they will be perceived as representatives of the purest nationalism, patriotism, and religious fundamentalism. If this prestige is removed by associating them with our endeavor, religious and nationalist fanatics will regard them as renegades, but the masses will obey them from habit. These leaders will not be sufficiently powerful to cause harm but will retain, in order to serve us, a large part of their former authority."[21] For Bugeaud, control of the colony could best be maintained by a pyramid of authority whose apex was represented by the French commanders-in-chief of the territorial subdivisions. Day-to-day relations with the tribes would be handled by the appropriate Arab Bureaus, reestablished in 1841 for this purpose. As overseers and collectors of intelligence regarding the indigenous population, the bureaus constituted one of the key instruments by which all governors-general attempted to control Algerian Muslims during the next two decades. Firmly supervised from above, the native hierarchies which the bureaus protected came to serve France well. In Bugeaud's opinion, political collaboration between Muslims and Frenchmen was essential in order for trade between the two communities gradually to increase.

The usual testaments of tribal submission were simple enough. After a chief had surrendered and agreed to assist French troops on campaign, to fight with France against Abdel Qadir if requested to do so, and generally to "govern for France," he was required to visit Algiers to be invested. He was also obliged to deliver specified tax payments there or to another urban center twice annually. Excise taxes, normally payable in kind, were levied on flocks and wheat crops and tailored to a tribe's ability to pay. Imposition of other duties without the governor-general's specific permission was forbidden. Indeed, payment of taxes soon became the basic indicator of a tribe's loyalty to the European administration, and symbolized acceptance by the tribal chiefs of their role as surrogate rulers and military allies of France. Surrender necessarily remained "totally without meaning," as Bugeaud reminded one of his field commanders on July 4, 1842, unless excise taxes were paid.[22]

A corollary of this arrangement, Bugeaud maintained throughout the 1840s, was that each tribe bore collective responsibility for the security of travelers and roads within its territories, and for the punishment of all crimes committed therein. He insisted upon these points in a letter to General Négrier as early as March 19, 1841.[23] "This fundamental principle, laid down with the first submissions, was among the conditions imposed on the Kabyle tribes in 1847, a few days before the governor's departure," one historian of Algeria observes. "It was a constant of Bugeaud's policy concerning surrenders. By this means, he undoubtedly wished to guarantee order within native society and enhance the security of commerce."[24] On the well-founded assumption that the author of almost any outrage was usually known or readily discoverable in a traditional society, and that failure to reveal or punish the guilty was an act of insubordination, the governor-general endorsed heavy fines on any allied tribe that failed to police itself. This penalty, however, was only a pale reflection of what he recommended for tribes that refused to submit to French hegemony, or tribes guilty of revolt after offering submission. The darker, distinctively colonial values, encouraged by the Algerian war, that Bugeaud increasingly absorbed, were exemplified by his endorsement of tribal or mass deportation late in the second and third years of his governor-generalship.

Although he consistently opposed the taking of hostages, by fall of 1842 Bugeaud was advocating other and more drastic measures to obtain tribal obedience. "I have issued a proclamation to the Arabs," he advised the minister of war on September 20, "in which I threaten [with deportation] those tribes which, having once surrendered, revolt anew, or which fail to use force to resist Abdel Qadir when he appears in their territories." Bugeaud stated that all men, women, and children belonging to tribes which had violated their "sworn loyalty" should suffer this "most severe of punishments." A few such examples, he was convinced, would greatly solidify French control.[25] A year later he requested official approval to deport to Martinique, Guadeloupe, or the Marquesas Islands all tribes "incorrigibly hostile" to France, or which had rejoined Abdel Qadir after pledging loyalty to the métropole. He maintained that such tribes should be thrown on their own and challenged to survive without outside assistance. Of course, the governor-general was aware that this would probably result in the death of most of their members. Such rigor, however, had irresistible attractions. It would, Bugeaud claimed, "terrorize Muslims who believed France would not exterminate them," and would probably prove as effective in advancing pacification as had the Turkish practice of decapitating hostages.[26] By 1843, attempts to implement that "different kind of legality" which Bugeaud believed Algeria required had lessened his opposition to extremisms far worse than those he had once condemned as inimical to the juste milieu. These attempts underlay his endorsement of mass murder in the Dahra caves in 1845.

Nevertheless, Bugeaud insisted that loyal Arabs be treated with respect and that their legitimate interests be protected. He argued throughout the 1840s that firm but benevolent paternalism would have positive political and economic consequences. If combined with medical ministrations to the indigenous population, such paternalism could be expected to hasten that assimilation which alone could finally secure Algeria for France. The fact that real empathy existed between Bugeaud and several of his most significant vassal chiefs made it all the easier for Bugeaud to attempt to implement the harsh policies which he believed the character of Algerian society demanded.

In mid-1843, at the same time he was recommending deportation as a means of tribal pacification, Bugeaud inserted an announcement in the principal newspaper of Algiers that condemned colon violence toward conquered Arabs and threatened to arrest and jail Europeans responsible for such excesses. He observed that "serious political setbacks" might result from mistreatment of Muslims, and that such abuse would certainly hinder rapprochement between Arabs and Frenchmen.[27] In March 1844, Bugeaud interrupted a morning's shave to intervene personally in an altercation between a European and an Arab. Hearing shouts in the street below his residence in Algiers, he glanced out a window and saw what proved to be a Maltese "brutally beating" an Arab. Without taking time to put on his clothes he "hurried downstairs, his face still covered with soap, called the watch, and had the Maltese arrested and taken to the police station."[28] Infuriated, he ordered all newspapers to carry the following notice: "The Governor-General commands all officers and officials to immediately arrest and take to the nearest post any individual beating a native."[29] This notice was translated into Arabic and distributed among the tribes. In addition, Bugeaud created the position of Muslim public defender, who was a French lawyer in Algiers charged with representing indigent Arabs and Berbers. In September, he repeated his general order to detain anyone mistreating Muslims.[30] "We have formally promised natives that we would protect their lives, property, religion, and customs," he emphasized. "We owe them and we owe ourselves the keeping of our word in every respect."[31] Thus, Bugeaud restated the importance for tribal control of what he had described in 1836 as "fidelity to one's word" plus "firmness, justice, and honesty."[32] In 1847, on the eve of his resignation of the Algerian command, the governor-general summarized the distinctions which, he insisted, had guided his native policy during the previous six years. "When the Arabs are subdued," he observed, "I give them the best possible treatment . . . and rule them with humanity. I have daily defended them against all who desire that they be ignored or scorned. . . ."[33] Only obdurate resistance, he implied, had evoked severe reaction on his part. Although Bugeaud's sentiments evidently were sincere, his attempts to shield vanquished Arabs from colon exploitation had by the late 1840s generally failed. By then, gradual, peaceful absorption of Algeria by France must have seemed increasingly unlikely to him.

The benevolent firmness with which he believed allied Muslims should be governed constituted the foundation of Bugeaud's decade-long campaign to encourage assimilation of the indigenous population. Making modern medical care available to non-Europeans, he noted in late 1843, would also promote that goal. Eye ailments, fevers of various sorts, and syphilis were rampant in the backcountry, and only through effective remedial action might French "political and financial interests"[34] be forwarded, and the tribes gradually persuaded to "identify with us in such a way as to form but one people governed paternalistically by the french king."[35] Meanwhile, there was no substitute for considerate treatment of those allied chiefs who made Bugeaud "feel like a father in the midst of his children."[36] (Or perhaps like a prominent French provincial among an affectionate peasantry.) In 1844, he assured his indigenous collaborators that French troops would increasingly concentrate on the construction of "roads, dams, and bridges," and that he himself would strive to improve native agriculture.[37] Enlightened paternalism encouraged Bugeaud to defer to tribal leaders, to defend native chiefs against criticism from Europe, and even personally to subsidize one chief who had been threatened with imprisonment for debt. Nevertheless, toleration of Muslim authority did not conflict with his conviction that only through assimilation could the native problem finally be solved.

In fact, employment of the stick and the carrot were for Bugeaud only provisional tactics until direct governance of the Arabs became possible. "In the long run it is good policy to replace the great Arab chiefs by French officers," he advised the minister of war in the summer of 1843. Otherwise, France would inevitably suffer "disappointments," since no early change in the "traditional tendencies" of an "entire nation" could realistically be expected.[38] A year later he reemphasized the necessity of "gradually modifying" indigenous society.[39] "We must attempt by all possible means gradually to alter their customs and assimilate the Arabs," he repeated in 1846. "We cannot hope for their friendship at least for several generations. In rendering our sway bearable, however, we will greatly weaken that spirit of revolt which has animated them under all their rulers."[40] Direct trade between Europeans and Muslims was basic to reduction of tribal bellicosity and to an acceptance of colonial domination, Bugeaud insisted.

From the beginning of his governor-generalship Bugeaud made great efforts to enhance French power by promoting commerce. Early in 1841, he did sanction a halt to trade with Muslims bearing arms against France. However, this prohibition soon gave way to support of more selective economic warfare designed to erode enemy morale and fragment Abdel Qadir's coalition. In his edict of March 6, 1841, Bugeaud endorsed trade with Arabs or Berbers who had pledged to cease all acts of war. By the spring of 1842, the governor-general was urging that official efforts be made to establish economic relations with every capitulating tribe.[41] "It was alcohol which vanquished the [American] Indians," he observed later in that year, "and it will be trade which subdues the Arabs." Force might temporarily deprive them of their war-making capacity, but commerce alone could bind them to France. "We must therefore trade as much as possible with the Arabs. Every Arab who enriches himself will become our supporter; this will mean one enemy less and one ally more." One prerequisite to such exchange was roads which might be traveled in safety throughout the country, he noted.[42] Another means of increasing commerce and realizing its strategic dividends, Bugeaud insisted, was to end the role traditionally played by Algerian Jews as intermediaries between Europeans and Muslims.

Relations between Jews, foreigners, and the non-Jewish native population in North Africa had historically been good. Jewish relations with the Muslim majority before 1830 had not been without storms. However, these occasional attacks against Jews were not religiously motivated and ordinarily represented only expressions of protest against oppressive political or social conditions by the most wretched of the Muslim population. "There was never at any time in the Muslim Maghreb a philosophy and tradition of anti-Semitism such as existed in Europe down to modern times," André Chouraqui correctly observes. During most periods of history, the Jews of North Africa were "happier than those in most parts of Europe, where they were objects of unrelenting hate; such extreme sentiments did not exist in the Maghreb [because of] a way of life intimately shared. Even the haughtiest Muslim noble would not have hesitated to recognize that he was the brother of the humblest Jewish peddler and...would have expressed the great truth that Jews and Muslims in the Maghreb were both grafts on the original Berber trunk...."[43] After 1830, French policy ruptured the network of understandings upon which such tolerance had been built.

Sizable Jewish communities had long existed in Algeria's coastal towns. In 1838, Algiers counted 6,065 Jews and 12,322 Muslims. Mostaganem contained 698 Jews and 1,413 Muslims. Oran was a predominantly Jewish city (5,637 Jews out of a total—native plus European—population of 9,978).[44] In the mid-1830s, there were eight synagogues in use in Algiers.[45] With Muslim Africa to the south and the Mediterranean and Europe to the north, Jewish entrepreneurs were ideally situated to become brokers of trade within and beyond Algeria. In fact, Jews dominated Algeria's commerce at the time of the French occupation.[46] In the early 1830s, Jewish speculators sold many of the abandoned houses in Algiers, and even houses and land in or near Blida and other towns in the Mitidja, to Europeans.[47] Jewish monopolization of trade in woolens, cloth, wheat, and sugar continued without interruption after the French conquest. Their role as middlemen was enhanced by their proficiency in Algeria's *langue franque*, a mixture of Spanish and Arabic long used by Muslims to communicate with foreigners, and their increasing fluency in French. By decade's end, Jews had extended their economic power to the point that they were able to dictate the currency acceptable in trade between Muslims and Europeans, insisting that Spanish, not French, currency was to be legal tender. After 1840, the Jewish community increasingly adopted French customs. The colony's civilian administrators ostentatiously favored Jews over Arabs. Consequently, Muslim disapproval of Jews, which had first surfaced during the 1830s, deepened. Bugeaud considered the Jews to be obstructing direct business relations between settlers and Arabs. Thus, they were a major hindrance to development of the trade that was essential in order to assimilate the conquered. It was on these pragmatic grounds that he denounced the African Jewish community, that he opposed the Jews on the currency question, and that he finally argued that all Jews should ideally be deported from Algeria.

As early as 1832, Muslim resentment of Jewish collaboration with the Christian administration and Jewish mediation of Franco-Arab contacts began to surface. "We have been offended by the power that you have granted to several Jews in your government," an Arab chief informed the French military in September. "If we consent to be ruled by you we do not want the Jews to serve as intermediaries between us in any way at all."[48] Three years later a former member of the Turkish military in Oran suggested that peace and commerce might be restored by "overturning the obstacles which the intrigue and greed of one part of the population interposes between the Arabs and French authority."[49] The heavy involvement of the Jewish Busnach family in negotiating both the Desmichels Treaty (1834) and the Tafna agreement increased Muslim antagonism. Arabs suspected Judah and Haim ben Durand, who controlled the grain trade with Abdel Qadir and were key participants in all Franco-Arab negotiations before 1838, of taking money under false pretenses from both sides. However, what "most contributed to making [France] fall in Arab opinion," Bugeaud insisted in 1837, was its policy of "dealing with the Jews as equals."[50] After 1840, the tendency of Jews to ape members of the European community and abuse Muslims served only to deepen the animosity. Therefore, from the time of his return to Algeria as governor-general, Bugeaud denounced the French administration's favoritism toward Jews and proposed specific measures to end Jewish control of financial relations with the Arab population.

By that time, French sponsorship of Algerian Jewry had contributed to striking changes in Jewish life. Jewish women had generally abandoned the veil, young Jews frequently wore western clothes, and wealthy Jewish women often attended dances given by the French elite. Almost all municipal bureaucrats in Algiers and interpreters of Arabic were Jewish. After 1841, the rapid progress of French military efforts made Muslims acutely aware of contrasts between the privileged status of Algerian Jewry and their own position as vassals of Africa's new masters. In Bugeaud's opinion, the civilian administration had made a "major error in immediately raising the Jews to [our] level." He noted that no such mistake had been made inland, where the military was responsible for governing the countryside. There the Jews were "treated the same as the Arabs. They are both subject to military jurisdiction, and the Arab is not humiliated by that contrast—so shocking to him—of seeing a Jew, whom he scorns, enjoying all the legal protections of our system of jurisprudence... while he receives Arab justice—cudgeling—for the slight-

est infraction. This comparison, you will agree, is quite upsetting to
an Arab warrior...." Continuation of such favoritism of Jews,
Bugeaud argued, would make it much more difficult to lessen Arab
dislike of their Christian rulers; it would probably spark new tribal
revolts and certainly inhibit direct Franco-Arab trade. "The Arab
suffers and is indignant," the governor-general observed. "He stokes
his hate in order to vent it, as he says, in better times." With some
bitterness, he observed that Jews controlled the "better part of the
commerce, which French nationals could conduct very well."[51] Bugeaud clearly opposed the civilian administration's policy toward
Jews in the late 1830s and 1840s. In 1848, his opposition even led
him to warn against appointing as governor-general an individual
who had been formerly married to a Jewish woman.[52]

For Bugeaud, the most immediate obstacle to the development
of Franco-Arab commerce was the Jewish veto on trade in all but
Spanish currency. Long obligated to purchase Spanish money at
high rates from Jews in Oran in order to do business in Algeria,
both the colons and the military regime had helped enhance the role
of Jews as commercial middlemen. Jews usually refused to accept
other than Spanish money from their Muslim customers, in order to
be able to resell those funds to the French. French currency had "no
general circulation among the natives, the Spanish dollar being the
principal currency," Moritz Wagner reported in 1841.[53] Spanish
funds entered the Regency mainly through Oran, a former Spanish
presidio whose 2,073 Spaniards were outnumbered in 1838 only by
the city's Jews.[54] Jews "made a double profit," as Bugeaud noted, for
they "gained both on merchandise sold [to the Muslims] and on the
money which paid for it." Only substitution of the French franc for
Spanish currency could begin to terminate Jewish economic hegemony, he maintained, and destroy the "parasites" which stood between France and the Arab market. In May of 1842, the governor-
general requested permission from Paris to prohibit Jews, on pain
of expulsion from the towns they inhabited, from dealing in other
than French funds.[55] Obviously, he considered banishment of re-
fractory Jews as appropriate a penalty as he did deportation of
insubordinate Muslims.

In fact, Bugeaud's petition to Paris was based on convictions
which he had long held. "It would have been wise to have expelled
[the Jews] from towns under our control as soon as we arrived in

Africa," he had written in July 1837. "This would be even more prudent today, it seems to me, for this race is the greatest obstacle to a rapprochement between Arabs and Frenchmen. The Jews insert themselves between the two groups to deceive both. As they speak the language and understand the customs of the country, they impose themselves as commercial arbiters and only very rarely permit an Arab to deal directly with a Frenchman."[56] Five years later, it is not surprising to find Bugeaud urging General Bedeau in Tlemcen to "accustom the Arabs little by little to take our money and *oblige the Jews, under threat of punishment*, to deal only in French currency." In May 1842, he ordered Bedeau to "call [the Jews] together and tell them that if they accept Spanish money for their goods you will expel them from the town. Make however many examples of such expulsion as are necessary to force them to submit."[57] Shortly thereafter, he emphasized to the minister of war that severity with the Jews was essential if Muslims, who currently "make almost all their purchases from that community," were to accept French currency and indeed to begin to demand it.[58] Despite the vigor with which it was pressed, metropolitan France refused to sanction such severity. Nevertheless, the governor-general pushed ahead on his own with efforts to achieve the desired results.

Early in July, Bugeaud lectured his commanders in Medea and Miliana on the importance of replacing Spanish by French currency, and instructed them to issue the "most severe orders" to accomplish this. "Inform the Jews," he commanded, "that every infraction will be punished by 150 blows with the cudgel and whatever fine you think is appropriate." Were the first infractions "severely chastised," circulation of French money would soon be "soldered to the practices of the country."[59] Two weeks later he wrote in similar fashion to General Lamoricière, commander-in-chief of the province of Oran, and emphasized the necessity of preventing Jewish speculation in the colonial money market. "Call together the [Jewish] merchants and tell them my wishes in this matter," Bugeaud ordered. "Inform them that any infraction will be punished by fifteen days in prison plus a fine to be determined by you, and that any repetition will entail doubling of the length of the jail sentence and the amount of the fine."[60] In the event, Bugeaud's orders were never executed. Despite growing French commerce with Muslims, significant Jewish economic influence continued throughout the remainder of the decade.

For the governor-general, permitting Jews to remain anywhere in Algeria seriously compromised French authority and Muslim assimilation. In his opinion, ideally the French should adopt a policy "considerably more far-reaching and severe, but also much more useful and politically advantageous" than that of local expulsions or occasional fines and imprisonments. That policy was one of "complete deportation" of all Jews in Africa to France or elsewhere. "When one wants to effect or maintain the conquest of a country like Algeria," Bugeaud advised the minister of war, "when one has spent a billion francs to that end and sacrificed 150,000 of the youth of France, one should not recoil at employment of [such] a measure...." He recommended, however, that Jews be given a two- or three-year grace period before deportation. In order that they not be despoiled by "greedy speculators," Bugeaud advised that an estimate be made of the value of the property they owned and that France compensate them in that amount if, when the time for their departure arrived, they had not sold it at a better price. He anticipated that the French administration would resell such properties to Europeans and thus assist in "swapping a troublesome, onerous, detrimental population...for Frenchmen."[61] The mechanics of this plan were remarkably similar to those in a proposal for removing Jews from Algeria which Bugeaud had submitted in 1837.[62] However, as a realist, the governor-general never entertained real hope that his recommendations would win approval in Paris.

His advice, Bugeaud conceded, was alien to the spirit of a century in which "far-reaching and significant decisions" were no longer taken. The basic problem with deporting up to thirty thousand North African Jews, he admitted in late 1843, was in getting such a policy approved in the métropole. The difficulties were "not of a material kind," but rather inhered in the "whole complex of ideas dominating certain intellectuals in France."[63] Jewish deportation would certainly appear "hideous" or "unconscionable" to metropolitan "softheads" (*philanthropes*) and "scrupulous legalists."[64] Thus, Bugeaud again criticized from Africa those European values which he had first scored in 1837. "The problem [with expelling Jews from Algeria]," he had argued then, "is that it will produce much objection [in France] on the grounds of its injustice and barbarity...."[65] In late 1843, an explicit endorsement of moderation from War Minister Soult finally ended Bugeaud's advocacy of general Jewish deportation. Soult told Bugeaud flatly that his proposals were much too extreme and suggested that with time Jewish economic hegemony could be expected to decline. "To attempt to get rid of Jews by radical means and subject them to deportation," Soult emphasized, "would be to provoke a storm, and public opinion [in France] would certainly manifest the most vehement disapproval."[66] Thereafter, Bugeaud looked elsewhere for the means to promote that assimilation of Muslim Algeria which he continued to believe essential.

By the end of his third year as governor-general, the colony already was clearly becoming estranged from the métropole. Whether directed against Arab tribes or Jewish merchants, the deportations Bugeaud urged were rejected by a France still wedded to softer values. Indeed, the very Centrism which Bugeaud had tried so hard to strengthen during the 1830s surely contributed to metropolitan opposition to the extraordinary measures which he was now recommending from Africa. In 1845, Bugeaud's renewed commendation of a peculiarly African legality was to make the evolution of his own extremism even more obvious and contribute further to alienation of colonial from French values.[67]

The settlement of Arab tribes in agricultural villages, an idea that was endorsed by the governor-general in 1841 and undertaken by the Arab Bureaus in the late 1840s, had been envisioned by Bugeaud as early as 1836. From Algeria in July of that year, he announced that several Arab prisoners would be dispatched to Marseilles and expressed hope that they might be sent on to Perigueux or to Excideuil where they could be taught farming and provided "good ideas to take back to their country."[68] Shortly thereafter, he informed Abdel Qadir that prisoners recently taken were to learn farming in France in order to familiarize themselves with that "pleasant, sedentary life [which is] infinitely preferable to the wandering and uncertain existence which you seek to perpetuate."[69] To Thiers, Bugeaud argued that only by settlement of Muslims in rural hamlets in Algeria would it be possible to anticipate the gradual assimilation of indigenous society.[70] He advised Guizot that whenever Arab tribes were acquired as allies France should construct houses for their members and assign European agronomists to teach them how to grow cotton and indigo.[71] In January 1837, Bugeaud stated in parliament that he favored establishment of Arab farming communities in Algeria, since it was only by "settling a part of the [native] population" that France would best be able to govern it. Such communities would provide Arabs with "tastes which will nourish [our] commerce" and generally encourage them to behave less aggressively.[72] Six months later, after more experience in Africa, he was more emphatic. "Settling the Arabs in houses," he argued, "would in my opinion be the best policy we could adopt...." By being immobilized on specific parcels of land they would become "less ferocious and warlike" and they could be defeated more easily in case of revolt.[73] Development of a nascent Muslim peasantry, Bugeaud continued to believe in 1840, was one of the best ways to increase French security and tribal assimilation. Thus, from the beginning of his governor-generalship, he advocated creation in Africa of a class similar to that of whose importance he was so convinced in France.

In November 1841, Bugeaud again endorsed the employment by Europeans of Muslim day laborers, and he repeated his conviction that only through more general settlement of Arab tribes was native assimilation conceivable. Widespread settlement would make Arabs both wealthier and more vulnerable, and it would enable the métropole more effectively to "modify and render [them] less warlike."[74] Seventeen months later he remarked that construction of villages for native habitation would tend to "attach [the Arabs] to the soil and provide those permanent and fixed interests which would make them much less disposed to revolt."[75] To Adolphe Blanqui, he wrote that he wished to give Muslims "a taste for buildings and regular cultivation by annually constructing several villages for them, and by encouraging them to build such settlements for themselves."[76] However, it was not until well after his proposals to eliminate the Algerian Jewish community were finally rejected that Bugeaud began seriously to attempt to immobilize portions of the tribal population.

Of course, for a policy of settlement to be successful required that Arab Algeria accept the supposed advantages to be gained therefrom, and required clear evidence that the French were willing to assist the transformation of nomads into peasants. In a homily as paternalistic as any he ever delivered in Perigord, Bugeaud in mid-1845 pledged that he would support tribesmen wishing to "get actively and intelligently involved in agriculture and commerce. Establish villages, build good stone houses with tile roofs in order not to suffer from the rains and cold of winter or the heat of summer," he urged his Muslim listeners only six days before decreeing construction of Algeria's first native hamlet. "Plant nice gardens and fruit trees of all kinds.... Olive trees and mulberry bushes will enable you to sell oil and silk for good prices, and you will thus procure everything you require in the way of clothes and furnishings for your homes. Store up straw and hay to feed your animals during the winter. Construct sheds to shelter your flocks against the rains and snows which cause you losses. Geld calves and lambs except those to be used for breeding.... [Such gelded animals] sell better because their meat is of higher quality. Improve your plows. Do one or two preliminary plowings each year on the land you want to plant: the first in February or March, the second in May. This will reduce the amount of weeds.... With land thus prepared you will be able to plant with the first fall rains, and your wheat will no longer be threatened by a lack of rain in May.... I cannot too strongly recommend that you not destroy your forests as you are currently doing. A time will come, I predict, when they will be a source of great wealth for you.... You will be able to sell wood for construction and heating at a good price."[77] Money, however, was required to get the process started, and in 1846 the governor-general requested that the métropole designate specific funds for the purpose of village construction. Were Paris also to give financial priority to the building of roads, mosques, and religious shrines, Bugeaud suggested, the government could realistically anticipate assimilation of the developing native peasantry.[78] With such backing, he was confident that commerce with Europeans could not but increase, and the probability of native revolts diminish. In fact, substantial funds for construction of Arab settlements were provided after 1847, and throughout the subsequent decade the Arab Bureaus supervised the building of homes for Muslims.

In 1850, sixty Europeans and 140 Arabs were at work building houses for natives in the military region of which Miliana was the capital. Between 1851 and 1856 the number of such homes rose from 365 to 546. Similar progress was made elsewhere, but primarily within the province of Oran. Nevertheless, little permanent settlement was achieved. No more than 11 percent of the indigenous population ever lived even briefly in any of the buildings constructed. Apparently, Muslim women spearheaded opposition to a non-nomadic lifestyle.[79] At midcentury, a German adventurer who had campaigned in Algeria observed that "General Bugeaud tried to settle the tribes allied with France in fixed villages. He gave them building material, and sappers and miners began to erect houses for them. But the half-built cottages were soon deserted. Most [Arabs] would rather have gone over to Abdel Qadir than have become fixed to the soil...."[80] Still, by 1860, the consequences of the efforts which Bugeaud had initiated were having an unfavorable impact on the cohesiveness of tribal society. Policies that were subsequently adopted by Napoleon III heightened the unfortunate effects of his policy.

If his early campaign to complete the Mitidjan barricade suggests the sincerity of Bugeaud's desire to renew European colonization in Algeria, his later advocacy of tribal settlement illustrates the seriousness of his attempt to implant in Algeria a societal ideal forged in rural France. Assimilation of Arabs by a secure European peasantry, the governor-general believed, would over time enable French soldiers to be reassigned to that continental theater of primary importance. For Bugeaud, indirect rule of Algerian tribes and unrestricted trade with them constituted the means whereby cooperation and self-interest might gradually be substituted for military rule in Africa. Despite the sincerity of his attempts to shelter conquered Muslims from European exploitation, the violence Bugeaud showed toward unsubdued Arabs and Jewish financiers indicates how far he had distanced himself from his earlier metropolitan moderation. Soon, such alienation came to symbolize a personal and colonial *durcissement* which ultimately made realization of both his assimilationist and continentalist visions impossible.

6

Military Organization, Militarism, and the Death of the Juste Milieu

The system of army recruitment, instruction, and use which Bugeaud advocated in the 1830s foreshadowed his withdrawal after 1840 from political moderation, his defense from abroad of African atrocities, and his assault on Centrism in France itself in 1848. Throughout his first ten years in parliament, Bugeaud defended the long-term, professional army against military reformers, and particularly against those on the Left who recommended reliance on a levée-en-masse. His advocacy of an independent, internally cohesive army encouraged military particularism in Algeria, and especially the hostility of colonial officers to metropolitan values. Indeed, it was fundamental to his own contemplation of a coup d'état in France. Stung by domestic criticism of methods used to conquer Algeria, Bugeaud concluded in 1848 that only harsh employment of the army could purge and regenerate French society. A new military ideal, incorporating values learned in Spain and applied in Africa, had by midcentury replaced the juste milieu as the basis on which Bugeaud and other Africains proposed that France should be ruled.

During the 1830s, debate concerning the best type of military organization focused on the accomplishments of the French nation in arms during the early 1790s. Bugeaud disagreed with the allegation of many on the Left that the levée-en-masse had been responsible for French victories in 1792 and 1793. Rather, he believed that discipline, training, and experience in combat were what enabled revolutionary France to gain the ascendancy over its opponents. The undirected enthusiasm of untrained masses of soldiers no more explained the successes of French arms during the early revolutionary period than it promised to assist France should war break out anew. "People know the history of the Medes and Persians better than they do that of '93 and '94," he remarked sarcastically to an old friend in 1839.[1] In Bugeaud's opinion, all the "histrionics of Danton" and the fervor of the Jacobin clubs would have availed France little without a reassertion of military professionalism. Infuriating the parliamentary Left, he insisted that the Marseillaise should never be sung during combat. On the contrary, silence and firm self-discipline, essential for victory, should be demanded of all troops in action.[2] Discussion of military affairs after 1830 was part of a larger ideological debate over issues first raised four decades earlier. In that debate, Bugeaud expressed unqualified opposition to the liberal romanticism of Republican opinion. "M. Lafayette once remarked that it is not the war of tactics and of strategy which must be waged," he observed, "but the war of propaganda and of liberty. My response to him would be that the war of propaganda and of liberty is resolved by battles, and to win battles one requires well-organized battalions and cavalry squadrons, and carefully drawn-up plans. There is a tendency to rely heavily on the sympathy of foreign peoples. . . . I, who have learned what the sympathy of the foreign masses is really like in the various countries where I have campaigned, have little confidence in this approach."[3] On matters at hand, Bugeaud maintained that no change was desirable in the existing system of recruitment of soldiers for a minimum service period of seven years.

For Bugeaud, quality, rather than quantity, was the touchstone of military effectiveness. History demonstrated the validity of this conclusion. "Napoleon, with 45,000 men, all that was left of an army of 400,000," he asserted, "kept all of Europe at bay for four months around Paris. Thus does one see what small armies can do when they are good and decisively commanded."[4] High quality, Bugeaud argued, could not be maintained if military reforms led to shorter terms of enlistment. Since 1818, conscription in France had been accomplished by an annual lottery in which those drawing "bad numbers" were technically subject to seven-year tours of duty. He strongly opposed proposals to reduce this period of service from seven to five or three years and to increase the size of reserve forces.

Repeatedly, Bugeaud deplored the disorganization that he believed shorter terms of enlistment would occasion, and the difficul-

ties that constant turnover would cause officers seeking to know
their soldiers personally. In his opinion, a civilian could become an
excellent soldier in three years but would not do so if he knew he
would remain in the army for only that period. "Draftees who
know that they will bear arms only for three years will perceive
themselves to be in a temporary situation, a sort of exile," Bugeaud
wrote. "They will count the hours, the minutes which separate
them from the paternal hearth. There will be little competition to
rise in ranks they are soon to leave." Maintenance of combat readiness could not be achieved by reliance on reservists, nor could
morale be sustained by periodic retraining of veterans who had
been reintegrated into civilian society. Reservists would "rapidly
lose whatever military abilities they acquired during their three
brief years of service," and would get married and assume normal
civilian responsibilities. Bugeaud insisted that even in a national
emergency most would return to their units with reluctance, and
many would refuse to report at all. "Modern war requires that
armies be well organized from the moment of a war's outbreak," he
emphasized. "One engagement today is almost always critical to
the success or failure of a campaign. Warfare moves quickly; one
has little time to recover [from defeat] and take revenge." To substitute reservists for soldiers on active duty would be to leave the
country vulnerable to hasty improvisation at the worst possible
moment.[5] Therefore, Bugeaud stressed his preference for a professional army of 150,000 men rather than for the force of 500,000
citizen-soldiers which proponents of a reserve system insisted it
would supply.[6] Clearly, re-creation of an army which drew upon
reserve contingents and thereby reactivated a form of levée-en-masse
held no attraction for him.

   Maintenance of professional troops, Bugeaud argued throughout the 1830s, was impossible without rigorous discipline and training. Only thus could soldiers be expected to perform effectively in
battle and the abilities of their commanders be provided scope for
operation. Discipline was what distinguished an army from a mob,
and Bugeaud lauded Napoleon's contributions to that new military
professionalism forged during his Italian campaign and especially
during his encampment at Boulogne.[7] Thorough training was a sine
qua non of success in battle. "There is an absolute difference between a seasoned, disciplined, trained army," he observed, "and a

force which has these salutary characteristics only to a very slight extent, or not at all, such as spontaneous or revolutionary crowds."[8] However, professional training was only a prerequisite for that comprehensive military education which he believed necessary for every soldier, and which in his opinion could be furnished only through many years of military service.

Indeed, education in military values constituted the wellspring of Bugeaud's defense of seven-year enlistments and the basis of his advocacy of re-creation in the army of that cohesive societal unit which remained elusive in France as a whole. Training alone was insufficient to mold a true soldier. It was "not enough to know how to fall into place in a company, march in step, load a gun...or drill other troops."[9] Whatever a soldier's competence in such matters, he might still lack that "spirit" and "love of the profession" which were far more important than formal training. The military education of recruits consisted in their instruction in a congeries of values that produced a desire for glory and a veneration of their unit's flag. Bugeaud believed that it was only when such sentiments were held in common that "real regiments" might exist. Education in the traditions, usages, and self-images of the military alone could infuse troops with confidence in their officers, and create a community wherein "every soldier knows, respects, and loves every other soldier."[10] Only through the cohesiveness which such education might provide could troops be expected to remain under fire for several hours without cracking or manifest that stability and self-control necessary to emerge from battle victorious. In fact, Bugeaud believed the strongest argument for seven-year military service was the necessity of a distinctively military education.[11] Fundamentally, he perceived the "love of fatherland and king" by an army "united in body and soul"[12] to be one realizable example of that societal ideal which he unceasingly pursued.

Bugeaud argued that such an army might itself be able to recreate the agrarianism he had long extolled. Soldiers could be assigned to "colonize the vast unexploited lands in Brittany and around Bordeaux," and be so organized as to divide their time between farming and military training.[13] They might begin to clear and improve land whose uncultivated state was a "shame and a loss to the country."[14] Bugeaud considered cavalrymen good candidates for such colonization, since the manure of their horses could be used as fertilizer and the horses themselves could be used as draft animals. Large tracts of undeveloped state land in Limousin, Auvergne, Perigord, and elsewhere should be leased to the army for five years to enable it to begin such settlement, and to demonstrate that rural life would prove more "satisfying" than residence in traditional barracks. Taking part in common tasks would lead to common aspirations, and both would contribute to a sense of communion.[15] Unification of plow with sword, Bugeaud was convinced, would result in creation of communities with both peasant and military values, and thereby provide an alternative model of the good society to that afforded by the rest of France. Indeed, national salvation might even spring, he had apparently concluded before his departure for Algeria in 1841, from military settlements rooted in the soil, schooled in their collective responsibilities, and isolated from civilians.

Gradually, however, Bugeaud lost faith that salvation of the larger society could be achieved entirely through the power of example. In 1840, he hinted that national redemption might ultimately be brought about only by employment of the army against civilian France. In fact, the alienation of army from nation which was soon to assume palpable form in Africa and later to foster militarism in France was underway well before Bugeaud's arrival in Algiers in 1841. Despite his continuing support of political Centrism, Bugeaud by the late 1830s had already set foot on a path that would lead him far from the juste milieu which he had once defended.

Whatever positive effects he may have hoped that a fully professional, long-service army of peasant soldiers might ultimately have on civilian France, Bugeaud urged no proselytization of military values in the country as a whole. On the contrary, he insisted that soldiers terminate all contact with the world beyond their units and divest themselves of all attachments to civilian life which prevented them from substituting their "regimental flag" for the "steeple of their village church."[16] Since the country seemed to lack generally recognized moral principles and tended to "destroy any conception of what [was] true and righteous," Bugeaud concluded that the army could accomplish little by missionary activity and had no choice but to withdraw from the rest of the nation. By 1840, he had come to perceive the army as a repository of superior values, values that were clearly threatened by civilian society. So serious did he believe the situation was becoming that he confided that "it may be up to us, men supportive of order and true patriotism, to save the nation."[17] The unrestricted use of military force in Algeria prepared him to advocate military action publicly against France in the late 1840s.

Nevertheless, Bugeaud's fundamental allegiance to political moderation did survive the 1830s. He consistently opposed the thesis that military crises required substitution of a regime of despotic terror for one of political temperance. What he feared fully as much as any foreign enemy, Bugeaud stated in late 1840, were assertions that the country could not be defended with the current governmental system.[18] The "horrible maxim" of some military reformers and Leftists that an invasion could not be successfully countered except by terror and tyranny he denounced as a "deadly and monstrous error."[19] On the eve of his third assignment in Algeria, Bugeaud was still committed to that congeries of political values to which he had adhered since at least 1815.

His antipathy to extremism, however, did not survive renewed exposure to African warfare. In the spring of 1841, that sustained and total war which Bugeaud had contemplated earlier finally began. Never before had systematic devastation of native crops and orchards been undertaken. "Until Bugeaud's assumption of responsibility," a contemporary observed, "burning of grain and cutting down of trees had been done only sporadically."[20] Thereafter, such destruction became official policy. Throughout the early and middle 1840s, the governor-general relentlessly pursued a military strategy aimed at severing the taproot of native society. By 1845, he had largely destroyed Muslim agriculture and seriously undermined tribal cohesion. At the same time, he had nourished an ethical disorientation within the French expeditionary force which in time contributed to erosion of political stability in the métropole. By defending massacre in the Dahra caves, Bugeaud revealed the degree of his own moral deformation. Nascent in the 1830s, it had finally come to the fore. After 1845, his personal durcissement encouraged his subordinates to engage in additional massacres. By decade's end, estranged soldiers and an estranged commander-in-chief returned to confront an almost foreign homeland.

Bugeaud initiated the rhazzia during the first two weeks of May 1841. Leaving behind a trail of devastation, columns under his command resupplied the French garrison in Miliana and marched across much of the plain of the upper Chéliff. They chopped down fruit trees, burned settlements and crops, and seized livestock. Few of the region's numerous Arab villages escaped destruction. What once had been hillsides "teeming with rich crops" were transformed into blackened wasteland.[21] By midsummer, most of the old Turkish province of Titteri had been subdued, and Abdel Qadir's influence had been confined to the Ouarensenis and Dahra mountains and the province of Oran.

As French forces advanced during those days in May when the Muslim population ordinarily began to harvest its wheat, they "burned the crops as they went," Clemens Lamping reported. "We did not, like Samson, set fire to the corn fields of the Philistines by driving into them 300 foxes with burning torches tied to their tails," he commented. "We had the advantage of the experience of ages, and the noble inventions of modern times over the Israelite hero."[22] In scorching heat, enveloped in the smoke and flames of the burning grain, Bugeaud and his troops endeavored to deprive their enemies of all means of subsistence. Soon, the entire valley resembled a "sea of fire." Everywhere, native flocks were driven off by the French columns.[23] Similar tactics were employed elsewhere by the governor-general's lieutenants during the balance of 1841. This "different kind of legality," congruent with that which Bugeaud had recently recommended to the minister of war and already initiated in the Mitidja plain, was imposed on all of western Algeria over the next several years. The soldiers Bugeaud commanded proved apt pupils of the new colonial legitimacy.

During 1842 and 1843, the governor-general's retreat from the values of the juste milieu, and the maturation of an African military outlook isolated from civilian influences, became increasingly obvious. Bugeaud's conduct at a dinner he and his wife gave for Canrobert, Négrier, and several other generals in 1842 reflected this durcissement. Throughout the meal, Bugeaud "told stories that raised the hair on one's head," Canrobert reported. "Several times his wife said to him: 'Robert, Robert . . . really, this is just too much.' And he calmly replied: 'But my dear wife, I am not saying anything bad.'"[24] In the field, Bugeaud's attempts to destroy all means of native livelihood became ever more indiscriminate, and he removed all sanctions against excesses by his lieutenants. In denouncing the lack of understanding in France of the necessity for the rhazzia, of the nature of African warfare, and of the sensibilities of colonial troops, the governor-general became the principal symbol of an overseas army which had come to act with untrammeled ferocity. His equating of present atrocities with future beneficence demonstrated how total colonial rejection of moderation had become by 1845. Having repeatedly voiced the African military's objections to censure by politicians and intellectuals in France, Bugeaud and his colleagues were ill-prepared to communicate effectively with the parliamentary fact-finding commission which arrived in the country in 1846. Triumphant extremism had made almost total strangers of the Africains encountered by Tocqueville and his fellow commissioners six years after Bugeaud's appointment as governor-general.

From outside Cherchell early in 1842, Bugeaud lamented that the Beni Menacer tribe had succeeded in fleeing into the mountains and thus had spared itself the sight of the destruction of its possessions.[25] General Saint-Arnaud reported that the tribe's territory had been "superb," one of the richest he had seen in Africa.[26] Orchards had dotted the countryside, and villages had been unusually close together. One had boasted some three hundred buildings. For the French, such wealth offered good kindling. Throughout the winter and early spring, villages and orchards were indiscriminately set ablaze. Everywhere French columns "demolished, thrashed, pummeled, plundered, scourged, ravaged, and shattered" the tribal population, a participant reported. It was "impossible to imagine to what extremity we reduced these wretched people," he confessed. "During the past months we seized all their wheat and barley. We took their flocks, their tents, their carpets, all their household furniture, in brief, everything they owned."[27] Many women and children fled to the mountains and died of cold and hunger. Nevertheless, the Beni Menacer soon rose against the French again, and they were joined by several other tribes elsewhere in the province of Oran.

During late 1842 and early 1843, Bugeaud directed new campaigns against the Muslim population. General Saint-Arnaud provides a picture of what typically transpired. "Here I am with my small army in the center of the territory of the Brazès," he reported on October 5, 1842, "burning the tents and huts of these unsubdued tribesmen, driving off their flocks, emptying their granaries, and sending to Miliana all the barley and wheat that I can.... I shall

leave them no peace until they submit."[28] Six days later he wrote that
he had laid waste and burned everything the Brazès possessed, and
that he was proceeding to do the same on a "grand scale" to the
Sindgès. "A few [Sindgès] tribesmen brought in their horses as
tokens of submission," he noted. "I refused because I wanted a
general submission and began burning once more...."[29] In January
1843, he reported that he had received orders from General Changarnier to follow the Chéliff "ravaging and destroying" everything
he encountered.[30] Three weeks later he noted that he had "reached
Haimda, destroyed the pretty village, and burned everything in [his]
path," and that he had subsequently come upon "heaps of bodies
huddled together, frozen to death during the night." These victims,
he observed, had been members of the Beni-Naaseur tribe "whose
villages and huts I had burned and whom I had driven before me."[31]
Never before had western Algeria suffered such devastation, Bugeaud
advised the Ministry of War in April. "Not a single house remains
standing. Our troops have taken a vast amount of booty, 3,000
head of cattle, and 120 prisoners."[32] "Grass no longer grows where
the French army has set foot," Lucien-François de Montagnac added.
"We have ravaged the countryside, killed, burned, carved up, and
chopped down, all for the best in this best of all possible worlds."[33]
By the summer of 1843, Muslim Algeria, formerly so "warlike and
fanatical," was "as meek as a lamb."[34] To encourage continued tranquillity in the countryside, Bugeaud in November went so far as to
order the head of Abdel Qadir's principal lieutenant paraded from
Oran to Algiers, and exhibited for three days in Miliana. By then,
official sanction of unrestricted violence surely was obvious to every
French soldier in Africa.

Perhaps the young Montagnac, who had arrived in Algeria as a
captain in 1836 and been promoted to chef de bataillon in 1841,[35]
best voiced what this sanction implied. "Kill all the men over the
age of fifteen," he recommended early in 1843, "and put all the
women and children aboard ships bound for the Marquesas Islands
or elsewhere. In a word, annihilate everyone who does not crawl at
our feet like dogs."[36] This warrior clearly practiced what he preached.
"I personally inform all the soldiers I have the honor to command,"
he stated, "that if they return bringing me an Arab still alive they
will receive a beating with the flat of a sword." His midnight visions indicated a pathology different only in degree from that shared

by his colleagues. "Always alone, like the polar bear, I dream a lot. I have truly monstrous dreams. Inside my four white walls I make horrible plans of campaign. I scour Algeria from north to south, from east to west, and, like one inspired or possessed I imagine that to me alone belongs the power to put an end to every last Arab in Africa."[37] The rhazzia provided every opportunity for him to indulge his "inclination to scourge human flesh."[38] By 1843, scourging of human flesh was not likely to be reprimanded by senior officers in Algeria. Not surprising, therefore, is the "fear and hatred" with which those considered "wild beasts" by such officers as Montagnac and Saint-Arnaud regarded their French pursuers.[39]

At year's end, Bugeaud's public defense of the rhazzia demonstrated how far his *durcissement* had progressed and reflected the accelerating alienation from metropolitan France of the African expeditionary corps. "Were the rhazzias necessary?" he inquired in Algiers's *Moniteur algérien* on December 25, 1843. "*Was this war inevitable?*" For the governor-general, those questions allowed only one answer. Bugeaud did not hesitate to boast that, to subdue an Arab population in arms, French troops overseas had made themselves "even more Arab" than their enemies. With particular impatience, he rejected accusations that the Algerian army was engaged in unnecessary operations designed to enhance its prestige, or facilitate the careerism of certain of its members.[40]

The rhazzia was unavoidable, Bugeaud maintained, because Africa, unlike Europe, lacked any of those economic, demographic, or political centers the capture of which ordinarily resulted in surrender of an enemy. "It is by taking control of all vital interests that one makes nations capitulate," he stated. "That is the purpose of war." However, no such interests existed in Algeria: the littoral had "no roads, no navigation, no capital, no key points." Destruction of the "agricultural interest," the governor-general therefore argued, alone offered a possibility of bringing native society to heel. Moderation during the 1830s had failed to achieve that end, or even to prevent massacre of settlers in the Mitidja in 1839. The success of the rhazzia he believed its sufficient justification, and a satisfactory response to those who argued that it was employed only to produce information for military bulletins or to obtain "promotions and decorations" for Algerian campaigners.[41] "Softheads" in the métropole erred badly, Bugeaud insisted, in charging that the overseas army could have limited and more rapidly ended the recent war of mass destruction.[42] Protective and increasingly defensive concerning France's colonial troops, Bugeaud offered no apology for even the most outrageous actions of his subordinates. By the end of 1843, such actions had become barbarous enough to "make the hair on the head of an honest bourgeois stand straight up."[43] During the next two years, the new-model army which Bugeaud defended increasingly engaged in the torture of French soldiers (for infractions of discipline) and Muslim prisoners. Early in 1845, the governor-general reminded General Bourjolly that treatment of all "insurgents" should be sufficient to "make the entire countryside tremble from afar."[44] By then, colonial military esprit had become even more remote from the values still characteristic of metropolitan France.

In June 1845, the execution by fire of a large part of the Oulad Riah tribe revealed most dramatically the hiatus which had opened between the African army and its metropolitan overseers. On June 19, a column under the command of Colonel Amable Pélissier trapped a portion of the Oulad Riah in a cave in the coastal mountains north of the Chéliff. After desultory efforts to negotiate surrender, the French army ignited a fire at the cave's mouth and killed by asphyxiation some five hundred Arab men, women, and children. Colonel Pélissier could not resist the temptation, as General Canrobert later observed, to describe the action in excruciating detail. His official report was "evocative and realistic" concerning the suffering of the victims. He depicted how the cave, crowded with corpses, looked to soldiers entering with lanterns, and complaisantly expatiated on the number of the dead, the hideous contortions of the bodies, and the agonies which those wretched people must have endured.[45] Bugeaud, who was absent from Algiers when the report arrived, was unable to prevent its being forwarded to Paris. War Minister Soult, whose differences with Bugeaud had become profound, immediately released the statement to the Chamber of Peers. Denunciations of the French expeditionary corps—and of the governor-general personally—erupted throughout France, and assumed a stridency seldom heard in the past. For Bugeaud, the furor was merely one additional example of metropolitan softheadedness, and further evidence of French ignorance concerning the realities of colonial rule.

In fact, the govenor-general quickly endorsed the atrocity; he had himself recommended similar action in cases of "extreme urgency."[46] He informed Soult that the Dahra episode had been precipitated by the Oulad Riah, who, by "taking refuge in caverns where they believed themselves impregnable," had compelled Pélissier to resort to extreme measures. In Bugeaud's opinion, what was worthy of discussion was the effect the event would likely have on tribes still bearing arms. "This example will have a terrible impact throughout all these mountains," he insisted, "and will be productive of salutary results." Only through the sort of unrestricted violence by which tribes could be made most "rudely to feel the evils of war" could permanent victory be achieved. Indeed, so far was the governor-general from feeling remorse for Pélissier's action that he urged Soult to have his formal defense of Pélissier published in the Parisian press.[47] Any "loyal soldier," Bugeaud argued, would have acted the same as Pélissier.[48] The African army backed its commander to the hilt. "Every one of us would have done the same as Pélissier," Canrobert agreed, "if we had happened to find ourselves in the same position." The army was "shocked," he noted, "by the abuse which was heaped upon its devotion, sacrifices, and even its successes."[49] By 1845, metropolitan and colonial France were obviously different worlds, and communication between the two had become almost impossible.

Still, Soult made an attempt to reason with Bugeaud. From Paris on July 9, he informed him that he was unable to believe that he had ordered commanders to resort to such liquidations even in the most exceptional of circumstances. Mass executions, Soult maintained, would prove more counterproductive than helpful as far as pacification was concerned, and would bequeath to the Muslim population a hatred of France which would endure for generations. Such violence he believed "dangerous," and likely to result only in temporary capitulations, which would be repudiated at the earliest opportunity. "Why should such submissions last any longer than the terror which produced them?" he inquired of Bugeaud. "Will not such people revolt at every opportunity which presents itself?"[50] His effort at persuasion was unsuccessful. To circumvent Soult's prohibition of publication in France of his formal defense of the Dahra affair, the governor-general inserted it in the *Moniteur algérien*. Thereby, he formally issued a declaration of war on those values of morality and moderation he had once defended.

All "ignorant attacks" on the African army, Bugeaud informed Soult, demonstrated the métropole's incomprehension of colonial warfare, and the "inevitable rigors to which the [overseas] army is forced to resort." Greater understanding should be forthcoming of the reason he had "ordered Colonel Pélissier, before leaving him at Orleansville, to employ such violence in situations of the direst extremity."[51] However, the Governor-General had little confidence that such could be expected. "Very few people in France," he maintained, were "capable of understanding the cruel necessities of total war,"[52] or the indispensability of employing the rhazzia against opponents who understood only the language of force. Among those most resistant to enlightenment, he now believed, were his parliamentary colleagues. Consequently, he urged Soult to strive to "impress upon the noble chambers the cruel requirements of war and politics which I have so often explained to you."[53] From Algiers on July 15, 1845, Bugeaud addressed a detailed reply in the *Moniteur algérien* to specific charges then being made against Colonel Pélissier and the entire African expeditionary force.

He argued that, in an undeveloped country, employment of the most extreme measures was unavoidable and should not cause horror or astonishment. What would have proven counterproductive would have been a withdrawal by Pélissier, which would have left the Oulad Riah in command of the cavern in which it had taken refuge. "The political consequences [of any such action] would have been fatal," Bugeaud stated, "for [tribal] confidence in caves would have greatly increased." The tribesmen's hatred of the French was for him a fact of life, and likely to continue whether or not such incidents as that in the Dahra occurred. That event could "hardly increase [Arab] hatred," but rather would "inspire a salutary terror" which would hasten the end of the war. Far from being ineffective or dangerous, such liquidations would finally convince the natives that they had no choice but to "accept the yoke of conquest" and to devote themselves to that "agriculture and commerce which rapidly heal the ravages of combat." Only indecisiveness and moderation in the current war, congruent with the "ill-advised notions of the softheads," would encourage future upheavals in the countryside. If France was unwilling to confront "war and its necessary consequences," Bugeaud concluded, it should somehow infuse Muslim Algeria with a "yearning for eternal peace."[54] In the meantime, observers in France and elsewhere should leave the waging of colonial warfare to those who understood its requirements.

Despite such convictions, Bugeaud attempted to persuade Soult that the values of the foreign military community were not any baser than those of the majority of metropolitan Frenchmen. "Is it not indicative of an enormous spiritual aberration," he wrote from the darkest shadows of the Dahra affair, "to imagine that such a group of men does not possess the same sentiments of humanity and civilization as does the rest of France?" That army of "*enfants de la France*" presently serving in Algeria was commanded by officers belonging to the "highest classes in society," who boasted an education "not the least inferior to that of the most civilized men in our country."[55] Resentment at being rejected by the métropole was more forcefully expressed by two of the individuals whom Bugeaud had recommended to the minister of war. "I am both disgusted and shocked," Saint-Arnaud commented on July 26. "How now! Here we are in Africa, ruining our health, risking our lives, working for the glory of France, and the most uninformed observer can insult us and slander our intentions, imputing to us criminal feelings which are not of this century and which cannot belong to a soldier. Be off with you, public revilers."[56] Montagnac was even more explicit, denouncing the "prize-winning idiocies of French newspapers," and observing that it was "*sentimental measures*" which had to be employed to satisfy them. "*Bunch of pigs!*" he added. "If I found myself in a situation similar to that of Colonel Pélissier I would really give them something to shout about. Oh, to please you who indulge yourselves at home... the poor devils who break their necks and pour out their blood here must even let themselves be devoured by wild beasts instead of destroying them. That much is necessary to satisfy the requirements of your stupid philanthropy... It is just incredible."[57] By 1845, Bugeaud and his fellow officers obviously were suffering from a "psychosis that it was they who were being wronged and misrepresented," and had created an image of themselves "as the victims of those in France who wanted the fruits of victory but were too self-seeking and cowardly to do more than criticize the men who bore the brunt of the fighting."[58] The governor-general's justification of the Dahra massacre as an act of humanitarianism further illustrated the incomprehension of France which had taken root within the African military, and the extent to which colonial psychology had transformed the greatest of excesses into the most salient of virtues.

An appreciation of Pélissier's action, Bugeaud explained in the *Moniteur algérien*, required an understanding of how important it was "*from the point of view of benevolence*" everywhere to destroy the confidence of Muslims in the impregnability of mountain caves. Benevolence required that "all measures, however drastic they may be, be employed in order to reach one's goal as promptly as possible." Only thus could the "interests of compassion be served," since wars prolonged by the use of less than energetic measures were those which "ruin nations and multiply victims." If French "indulgence" permitted the "spirit of revolt" to perpetuate itself, the colonial army would continually be required to put down uprisings in which "much more money would be spent and many more soldiers consumed" than if Arab tribes were dealt with severely from the beginning.[59] Moderation could only render the African war eternal and prevent realization of the benefits of peace by everyone.[60] "The Arabs will seek to throw off our yoke all the more frequently if repression is compassionate," Bugeaud repeated two days later. "The disastrous episode of the caves will prevent the shedding of much blood in the future."[61] To hasten the day when the benefits of peace might begin to be enjoyed, the governor-general in mid-July 1845 reissued his order that Muslims refusing to abandon caves be incinerated.

"It is certainly to be presumed that the Sbéah will not withdraw into caves," he advised Saint-Arnaud on July 20. "If against all expectations they do...it is necessary to have resolved to employ, in a crisis and as a last resort, the tactic used by Colonel Pélissier."[62] His lieutenant, who had evidently expected such instructions, already had indicated that he would soon "lay seige to the grottoes of the Sbéahs in the fashion of Pélissier." Tribal liquidation did not offend the sensibilities of this experienced Algerian campaigner. "I would have done and I would do what Pélissier did," Saint-Arnaud observed on July 26. "Should I happen to find myself in the same situation...I would act like a military man and wipe out as many of the enemy as possible in order to spare myself losses. My soldiers above all."[63] Two weeks later he was as good as his word. "On August 8 I reconnoitered the grottoes or caverns [in which Sbéahs had taken refuge]," he reported, "and was welcomed by shots. . . . On the ninth we began the siege, tunneling, detonating explosions, appealing, entreating and pleading [with the tribesmen] to come out and surrender. Response: insults, curses, shots. . . . The same thing on the tenth and eleventh. . . . On the twelfth I had all the outlets of the cave hermetically sealed and made of it a vast cemetery. The earth will cover forevermore the bodies of these fanatics. No one went into the cavern and nobody but I knows that there are 500 brigands down there who will never again butcher Frenchmen." Saint-Arnaud added that his conscience bothered him not at all, and that he had "done [his] duty as an officer and would begin again tomorrow."[64] Generals Cavaignac and Canrobert similarly liquidated tribes during the next two years, and this technique continued to be employed until conquest of the littoral was completed in 1847.

A visit to Algeria in October 1846 by a parliamentary delegation of four headed by Tocqueville and representing the Chamber of Deputies' Committee on Algerian Affairs served only to impress upon the métropole how intense the ferocious alienation of the African army had become. Bugeaud, desirous of convincing the Parisians of the necessity of military initiatives for Algerian development, personally led them on a tour through Blida, Medea, Miliana, and Mostaganem. Results, however, were quite other than he had anticipated. The delegation was insulted by a petty officer, deluged with complaints by civilians concerning the severity of military authority, and treated to an announcement by Saint-Arnaud at a formal dinner that for causing trouble he had colonists "put head first into a grain pit."[65] The delegates returned to France to denounce the colonial regime, and to recommend that the moderation and liberties of the metropole be established in North Africa for all. Tocqueville later described the Algerian army as "imbecilic,"[66] a sentiment which was reciprocated by colonial officers. It was obvious that attitudes forged in the pitiless war which had raged in Algeria since 1841 no longer permitted understanding between France and its overseas army.

By 1846 collective, comprehensive, and sustained violence had produced soldiers so Africanized that discussion or even recognition of the most fundamental principles of the juste milieu had been rendered impossible. Repudiation of modernity, so evident in Bugeaud's prescriptions for the good society in the two decades before 1840, had become widely shared. It assumed novel forms within the colonial expeditionary corps during the years of his command. Disgusted with metropolitan opposition to his military and colonial policies, Bugeaud finally resigned the governor-generalship in June 1847 and returned to Perigord. There, his political mandate had become considerably less certain than it had been on his departure for Algeria six years before.

Throughout his years in Africa, Bugeaud had retained his seat as Excideuil's representative in the Chamber of Deputies. Absence abroad, however, made political fence-mending difficult, and after 1842 he began to encounter significant opposition for the first time in a decade. That opposition was led by the mayor of Excideuil, Dr. Jean Chavoix, Bugeaud's former friend and personal physician. The master of La Durantie had shattered the good doctor's glasses in the town's main street during a quarrel in the late 1830s, and thereby transformed Chavoix from a confidant into a determined political opponent. In the election of 1842, the mayor ran for Bugeaud's seat and received 107 votes against the governor-general's 178. Chavoix charged Bugeaud's supporters with illegally manipulating voting lists to enfranchise pro-Bugeaud voters from distant parts of the Department. The following year, Bugeaud again defeated Chavoix, this time by 169 votes to 101. The balloting was so irregular that 60 of the electors joined Chavoix in addressing a formal protest to the Chamber of Deputies, again accusing Bugeaud of orchestrating the casting of illegal votes. Although the chamber took no action to change the results, the protest was supported by solid evidence of fraud. In 1846, Bugeaud defeated Chavoix by only 37 votes, winning 168 to 131. The 1846 slippage occurred despite a whirlwind tour by the Governor-General through his district only a month before the election. Chavoix's party filed a second protest against what it described as "open, long-standing corruption," but once more the protest was ignored by the president of the Chamber of Deputies.[67] In 1847, Bugeaud again narrowly defeated Chavoix. To Thiers, the marshal complained that his absence in Africa had not permitted him to "corrupt as many electors as were willing to be corrupted." He lamented that the death of certain electors, the departure of others, and especially the way Chavoix had "exploited the invective of the press" had cost him "many votes."[68] From Algeria, the marshal's endorsement of corruption was seconded by General Saint-Arnaud. In Saint-Arnaud's opinion, it was an "eternal shame" that Chavoix seriously threatened Bugeaud's seat in the chamber. It was indicative, he said, of the fact that Excideuil's voters had become nothing but "grocers" lacking any "patriotic spirit."[69] Clearly, Africa encouraged little respect for metropolitan political niceties. When Bugeaud was appointed commander of the Paris military garrison in February 1848, he was offered his first opportunity to begin to infuse the new élan of the Algerian army into French society.

From the beginning of 1848, Bugeaud had been in Paris, deeply concerned with rising popular discontent. Indeed, launching by the Left of the political banquet campaign convinced him that revolution could not be far distant. On January 14, he requested a copy of the Gérard Plan (a blueprint for military takeover of the city of Paris) from War Minister Trézel, and hinted that if revolution did break out he would expect to be invested with the authority to repress it. In mid-February, he assured supporters in the Chamber of Deputies that he would surely be "called to the bedside of the patient, when the condition of the sufferer becomes critical."[70] Early in the afternoon of February 23, with the uprising he had feared well underway, Bugeaud informed the minister of public works of his "amazement" at not yet having been given command of troops in Paris.[71] At 5:00 P.M. he spoke personally with the king at the Tuileries, and repeated his readiness to undertake the reestablishment of order. Although he declined Bugeaud's offer, Louis Philippe invited him to dinner. When the marshal departed in early evening, irritated by the desultory mealtime conversation and lack of any sense of urgency on the part of the king and his entourage,[72] the fusillade on the Boulevard des Capucines was perhaps an hour away.

Between 8:00 and 9:00 P.M. on February 23, troops protecting the Ministry of Foreign Affairs in the Boulevard des Capucines panicked and fired on a large crowd of lightly armed National Guardsmen and citizens, killing 52 and wounding 74. Grotesquely illuminated by torches, the corpses were paraded through the streets by demonstrators, and barricades thrown up throughout the city. Early in the morning of February 24, Louis Philippe finally summoned Bugeaud and appointed him commander-in-chief of all army units stationed in Paris. During the next several hours the marshal with great effort organized available forces, attempted to clear rioters from the streets, and decisively put down the insurrection. Although betrayed by General Bedeau and opposed by elements of the middle class, he finally ceased his efforts primarily because of repeated orders from the king.

About 2:00 A.M. on February 24, Bugeaud arrived at the Place du Carrousel, to which most commanders had withdrawn their troops. There he discovered demoralization and total confusion, and found nobody capable of furnishing him reliable information. Worse yet, soldiers were exhausted and horses unfed. Nevertheless, by 6:00 A.M. the marshal had succeeded in dispatching three major and two minor columns to dismantle barricades and occupy objectives in various parts of the city. The orders given these forces were as severe as many of those upon which rhazzias had been based in Algeria, an indication that Bugeaud was as determined to destroy revolution in the nation's capital as he had been to repress partisan resistance abroad.

He had "decided to employ extreme measures to reestablish order,"[73] Bugeaud informed Thiers shortly before dawn, and looked forward with "pleasure" to the "killing of many of this *canaille*, [which] is worth something."[74] His charge to the commanders of the departing columns left no doubt of what the marshal intended. "We must make an end to the revolutionaries," he stated. "You know that in such circumstances I have never been defeated. You certainly do not wish to make me lose my virginity."[75] No quarter was to be given. "You are to attack *energetically* the crowds and barricades you encounter on your march," Bugeaud ordered. "If buildings are occupied by the enemy, you will send one detachment past them on the right, firing into the windows from the left, and another past the buildings on the left, firing into the windows from the right." To as great a degree as possible, such volleys were to be made at point-blank range.[76] All evidence suggests that as his columns departed at dawn, Bugeaud anticipated a "vigorous offensive, one without compromises and without indecision."[77]

Only the column led by Bedeau failed to reach its objective. Disobeying Bugeaud's orders, Bedeau allowed himself to be drawn into negotiations with crowds on the Boulevard Poissonière and to be persuaded that violence would only exacerbate the situation. After considerable delay, he sent to Bugeaud for new directives while National Guardsmen arrived and the crowd pressed in among his soldiers. The marshal's response was unequivocal. "Order the crowd to disband, and if you are not obeyed use force and act as I told you in my instructions."[78] Orders given and repeated by the marshal indeed were "quite explicit," and it seems difficult, as General Rébillot later maintained, "to excuse those who, having received them, negotiated with the rioters."[79] Bedeau's insubordination, and the failure of others to master the situation in localities to which they had been sent were not, however, decisive in convincing Bugeaud to call off the offensive and order all troops to withdraw to barracks.

Around 7:30 A.M. a delegation of middle-class Parisians arrived at the Carrousel to implore Bugeaud to halt military action and leave the calming of the insurrection to the National Guard. Thiers and Odilon Barrot now seconded them, arguing that further violence would be counterproductive, since news of the fall of Guizot and the formation of a liberal ministry was at last reaching the streets and should suffice to quiet the crowds. "I was trying to make them understand all that was dangerous in the advice they were giving me," Bugeaud reported, "when... I received the order from the king to recall the troops and to use only the National Guard." Even then Bugeaud refused to countermand his earlier instructions, and continued to argue with his solicitors. "An extraordinary combination of circumstances paralyzed me," he later related. "I was unable to make use of my experience and the military abilities with which nature had endowed me. I had... only the shadow of command. The ministers, the king, the princes, the bourgeoisie, everything hindered me. How much I wished, at that moment, that the court and government were at Vincennes!"[80] Finally, when the Duc de Nemours arrived with a second order from Louis Philippe to terminate military action and withdraw all soldiers, Bugeaud decided to obey. He could "no longer assume the responsibility for prosecuting an offensive which the king had twice ordered halted."[81] However, his outrage at what he perceived as Louis Philippe's cowardice knew no bounds. "Everything could still be saved," Bugeaud protested bitterly. "[The king] does not desire such salvation. Royalty is f[expletive deleted]."[82] Recall of the army was quickly followed by the replacement of Bugeaud with the aged Marshal Gérard, the abdication of the king, and the collapse of all resistance to the revolution. Although the royal commands apparently were what caused Bugeaud to cancel his rhazzia, evidence exists that Thiers may have encouraged this decision by suggesting that moderation could lead to Bugeaud's appointment as minister of war in a new government.

The marshal was desirous of such an appointment, and made this clear to Thiers in the early hours of February 24. "I do not know whether you really want to include me in your cabinet," he observed. "However, I could provide you with support from a fairly large proportion of the conservatives." Bugeaud added that he was reluctant to advise Thiers to dissolve the chamber, "especially were [he] to include [him] in his cabinet" and were it possible for him to assume a seat in parliament as a ministerial spokesman.[83] In subsequent days it was said that Bugeaud had ended military action because of an "assurance" from Thiers that he would be named war minister, a post which he believed might enable him to "implement in Algeria . . . his highly controversial projects."[84] Whatever encouragement his hopes may have been given, no such responsibility was forthcoming, and the marshal soon accepted a republic which he had concluded was opposed to "anarchic passions" and committed to the "great principles of social order."[85]

That acceptance was compromised in mid-May by an attempted attack on La Durantie by rioters marching out from Lanouaille. Rumor had it that Louis Philippe, before his flight, had given Bugeaud 35 million francs which the marshal had buried in the cellar of his estate. The result, so it was said, was imposition of the highly unpopular 45 centime surtax. The 200 marchers intended to "seize the money, burn the farm . . . and execute the vengeance of the nation."[86] Bugeaud's household servants and sharecroppers immediately rallied to his defense. They were reinforced by métayers from other nearby farms. When the mob arrived at La Durantie, it was confronted by at least 40 well-armed men. For his personal use, the Marshal had reserved five rifles and four pistols.[87] This show of force prevented bloodshed. The crowd, its ardor cooled by the two-mile march from Lanouaille, dispersed peacefully after considerable shouting. Nevertheless, denunciations and threats against Bugeaud continued, and obliged him to remain in a state of seige for more than two months. Homesick for Africa, this stranger in France soon was to repudiate again a republic which apparently produced only insurrection and societal disintegration.

Early in July, Bugeaud expressed his nostalgia for the land of his greatest triumphs and for the values of the army which he had left there. "Goodbye, my dear Colonel," he wrote sadly to an officer in Algeria on July fourth. "I consider you fortunate to be in Africa, far from these sad debates between civilization and barbarism. Remember me to our brave army; I carry it in my heart and am profoundly sorry to have left it." As for France, he advocated measures of the "greatest vigor" to extirpate the "Red Republic" which had threatened during the June days. However, he saw little likelihood of their adoption.[88] Despite the ferocious excesses of troops commanded by Cavaignac, a veteran of sixteen years of Algerian warfare, Bugeaud was convinced that the metropolitan army had "not stuck hard or widely enough" during the June days.[89] Flirting briefly with the possibility of entering his name in the presidential election of December 1848, the marshal by autumn was contemplating employing the army to overthrow the republic and the parliamentary system.

"When one observes the stupid selfishness and cowardice of a part of the bourgeoisie, one is tempted to become a demagogue in one's own turn," he informed Genty de Bussy on September twenty-third. It was "shameful," he maintained, that the "Red Republic" was being accorded victory without opposition in Paris. "O wretched France, where are you going and who will save you," he inquired, "you who lack the might to help yourself?"[90] By fall, Bugeaud was considering offering himself as that savior, and was receiving considerable encouragement in military circles to stage a coup d'état. General Changarnier urged him to lead "liberating troops" into Paris, and Colonel Gramont sought to impress upon him the "impatience" in the Army of the Alps to move against the capital. The marshal at length decided to repair to Lyons in the disguise of a peasant, and there take command of forces capable of seizing power in Paris. However, the size of Louis Napoleon's victory in the December elections persuaded him to try to convince Bonaparte to proclaim military rule, rather than to attempt to impose it himself. Whatever violence was necessary to support such a proclamation, Bugeaud asserted, should be employed without hesitation.[91] Thus, use of military force, to which Louis Napoleon would have recourse in 1851, was endorsed by Bugeaud three years earlier.

At the end of 1848, the government invested Bugeaud with command of the Army of the Alps, headquartered in Lyons. Authorities in Paris, still fearful of new upheavals, considered Bugeaud a useful weapon to hold in reserve. For his part, Bugeaud made no secret of his readiness to conquer the nation's capital with troops based in the provinces. "I have made up my mind," he told his military subordinates on February 6, 1849, "that if the Red Republic were to triumph in Paris for even a single day I would immediately put myself at the head of all those who were willing to follow me in order to go and defend society. I will have my eyes continually fixed on Paris; and should it be necessary for me to enter it at the head of the provincial National Guard, let us hope that this time, with God's help, order will be reestablished, not just for a brief period as has happened in the past, but forevermore."[92] A week later he expressed satisfaction with the "excellent [military] instrument" under his control, and indicated that he had made plans for its deployment.[93] By spring, he evidently desired nothing more than to regenerate France by leading a rhazzia against Paris. "When I wanted to force submissions [in Algeria], I began by attacking the strongest and most warlike tribes. When I had defeated them, the others surrendered readily enough."[94] Indeed, he now advocated that "open warfare begin between society on one side and its demolishers on the other."[95] Establishment of the good society, in France as in Africa, seemed to Bugeaud by early 1849 to require the immediate unleashing of unrestricted violence.

Bugeaud's total rejection of the politics of Centrism and the extent of his alienation from metropolitan values were even more obviously demonstrated in an essay he completed early in 1849 on how the army might best be employed in urban warfare.[96] His *Traité de la guerre des rues*, whose "audacity" shocked even his closest associates,[97] was suppressed by a committee consisting of Decazes, Molé, and Thiers. Most copies of it were destroyed, and it was never published in later years. Bugeaud's most detailed endorsement of a cohesive military as the only effective instrument of societal regeneration, it evidently supported the legitimacy of even its worst excesses. So estranged from Centrism had Bugeaud become by 1849, however, that he was unable to understand the inappropriateness of printing and widely distributing his essay. "I don't see how this treatise can hurt my reputation—quite the contrary," he protested in early February. "It can only fill to overflowing the anarchists' hatred of me—but is their hatred not already as great as it can be?"[98] Of 6,500 copies which he had requested be reserved for his personal disposition, he asked that 200 be forwarded to Lyons for distribution to officers of the garrison there, 30 sent to each of the five divisions of the Army of the Alps deployed outside Lyons, and two copies each mailed to the president of the Republic, minister of war, and the *préfet de police*, in addition to generals Changarnier, Baraguey d'Hilliers, Lebreton, Tartas, Bedeau, Bar, Rapatel, Gourgaud, Lauriston, Regnaud de Saint-Jean-d'Angely, and "all generals having a command in Paris."[99] Such distribution would have made the pamphlet available to the entire French officer corps. Apparently, he wished to establish beyond question that unlimited violence should be substituted for the juste milieu as the animator of government and society in France.

If the widespread rhazzias he initiated in 1841 soon became the norm in African warfare, the generalized ferocity which Bugeaud inspired abroad had by 1850 made significant inroads into French society. Saint-Arnaud's comments on the Parisian upheaval of June 1848 only echoed the sentiments of his former commander. "Let the torrent flow and finish with this once and for all." Months later he asserted that *Montagnards* could only be eliminated with a "gun in one's hand." He, like his Algerian mentor, had become "consumed by a hatred of revolutions," and favored merciless warfare against all "assassins and savages" in the nation's capital. His condemnation of the press and the Chamber of Deputies only reiterated convictions shared by Bugeaud and expressed by Montagnac as early as 1844. When Saint-Arnaud endorsed Cavaignac as "dictator" in 1848, he merely reflected the durcissement and demand for order of former Algerian campaigners.[100] Echoing his colleagues, he bluntly insisted in mid-1849 that "the army alone can save France."[101] Military action was imperative, the Africains believed, if all metropolitan *indigènes* were to be crushed. When Saint-Arnaud as minister of war enforced Louis Napoleon's proclamation of total power on December 4, 1851, he demonstrated how successfully the rhazzia had served as a "school for the coup d'état" in France.[102] Algerian legitimacy was thereby engrafted upon the métropole, and an alien military violence infused into French political life. African legitimacy continued to exacerbate tensions in France in subsequent years, and accelerated the army's metamorphosis from an entity popularly associated with liberation into one identified with reaction. Nevertheless, it was Bugeaud himself who constituted the primary and "critical link in the chain connecting the guerrilla war in Spain under Bonaparte with Algeria, the repressions of 1848 and 1851, and the Paris Commune."[103] For a soldier who once had agonized over the theft of chickens and firewood by soldiers on campaign, this was no mean transformation.

7

The Good Society
From Collectivism in Algeria to Private Property and Individualism in France

Throughout the 1840s, Bugeaud attempted to promote European colonization in Algeria. In addition to augmenting French authority in Africa and security in Europe, he believed that governmental sponsorship of settlements abroad would contribute to evolution overseas of the cohesive society which he had endorsed in France during the 1830s. In the early 1840s, Bugeaud was convinced that civilian and military colonies ought to be patterned on Utopian socialist lines. Establishment of rural values in communities of cooperating peasants, and discouragement of concentration of foreign immigrants in Algerian coastal towns, demonstrated the renewal after 1840 of his campaign to lay the agrarian foundations of a good society. Anti-urbanism and antimodernism, so basic to his thought in earlier years, he reasserted from Algeria. Although realization in military form of the socialistic model of his societal ideal proved a mirage, Bugeaud continued to believe that a traditional peasantry was essential to general social health. Rejecting socialistic proposals and insisting on individual initiative, private property, and personal inequality at decade's end, Bugeaud remained certain that only a rural community unaffected by modernity could provide a foundation for moderate human progress.

European colonization in Algeria, Bugeaud maintained, should be of two basic types and should be encouraged in two separate areas. Settlement of civilians should be restricted to a coastal strip extending no more than forty or fifty miles inland, and colonization solely by soldiers permitted in the rest of the country. This approach won him the strong support of Prosper Enfantin, who had sojourned in Algeria from 1839 to 1841 and traveled as widely as the military situation had then permitted. Beyond the coastal mountains, colonization by the army seemed to Bugeaud the only way to increase French control of the more distant tribes, prevent raids from the desert on civilian settlements to the north, and maximize the mobility of the African expeditionary corps. In Bugeaud's opinion, encouragement of civilian and military settlement in appropriate zones was the best way to extend French power in Algeria and profit, as he remarked in the middle 1840s, "from the present state of peace to establish something strong enough to survive all eventualities."[1] However, most of his specific proposals focused on military colonization. By 1847, opposition by Bugeaud and the Arab Bureaus to unrestricted civilian settlement had become a major source of conflict between the overseas military and the colon population.

Bugeaud argued that civilian colonization south of the Atlas would expose Europeans to challenges of the harshest kind. The distance from the Mediterranean alone would render it extremely tenuous and expensive. However, the basic reason why he believed civilian settlement should be limited to the coast was the problem of defending settlers against hostile and incompletely subdued tribesmen. "Direct and immediate protection," Bugeaud stated in 1845, "would be so utterly impossible that it should not even be considered."[2] Two years later he was even blunter. "God alone would be able to protect a mob lacking any collective strength and made up for the most part of old men, women, and children. I'm sorry," he sarcastically corrected himself, "the public liberties of France, which will have been given to them, will protect them."[3] On the other hand, colonists with military training would be able to defend themselves and might even gain the respect of the tribes. "The Arabs are much less offended by military takeover of an area," Bugeaud maintained in 1842, "than they are by the coming of civilians, who are generally untrustworthy and unenergetic. Arabs respect the former more; they recognize in their coming a right of war which has already been exercised. . . . They scorn the latter, and consider settlement by them a theft."[4] In addition, settlers knowledgeable about military tactics would provide a buffer against attacks on Europeans closer to the Mediterranean. Strategically, zonal colonization would prevent "immobilization of the entire [African] army" in attempts to guard immigrants,[5] and thereby leave it free to respond to exigencies in Algeria and in Europe. Despite the persistence with which Bugeaud advocated these two types of colonization, a métropole increasingly estranged from its overseas army delayed and finally refused approval of any widespread military settlement in Africa. Indeed, French rejection of his proposals was a major reason why Bugeaud ultimately resigned from the governor-generalship.

In 1841 and 1842, Bugeaud experimented with settlement by soldiers in Ain Fouka, Beni Mered, and Mahelma on his own authority. The socialistic organization which he attempted to provide these Mitidjan villages subsumed principles of state-sponsored civilian colonization that he continued to endorse until his resignation in 1847. Official, bureaucratic, and corporate implementation of colon agriculture was to be paralleled by military settlements in which labor was prescribed from above and land collectively worked. Echoing Enfantin, Bugeaud maintained that "individualism is fatal, for it produces weakness and one can only survive in Africa by force." In fact, during the early 1840s both Bugeaud and Enfantin deplored the absence of the kind of official direction that had previously been given colonization, arguing that a task as enormous as the settlement of Algeria could not succeed unless "vigorously and even despotically directed by government." They agreed that state intervention was an "imperious necessity." Both were convinced that the "triumph of individualism" was a cause of weakness in contemporary society, and that a principle of authority had to be restored. They believed that isolated actions by people with no "material or ethical bond" would inevitably founder. Both argued that state sponsorship of colonization was essential to "discipline energies and associate efforts."[6] However, experience soon led Bugeaud, unlike Enfantin, to repent of such convictions.

Even before his arrival in Algeria in 1841, Bugeaud had informed the minister of war that civilian colonists should be neither unorganized nor totally lacking in military capacity. "It is not sufficient to collect people and families and dump them into Africa," he stated. "Only after every preparation has been made to receive them on African soil should they be sent across the sea. They should be so placed and supported as to be able to begin farming immediately and resist the Arabs." Such colonization should be organized in as military a fashion as possible, and all villages be of a size sufficient to prevent successful tribal raids.[7] Soult, mindful of criticisms Governor-General Valée had made of unorganized civilian colonization, gave Bugeaud carte blanche to regulate all settlement by civilians. Specifically, the new commander-in-chief was accorded authority to oversee "organization, direction and regulation of colonization by the state, or by the army."[8] *Étatisme* became basic to Bugeaud's campaign to establish civilians in Algeria during the next several years, and constituted part of the African version of his long-standing ideal of progress through use of both plow and sword.

Emphasizing that the Algerian situation no longer permitted new settlements to be established "without the intervention of higher authority," Bugeaud issued a decree on April 18, 1841, outlining how civilian settlement was to be prepared by the colonial administration and subsidized by the métropole. Before departure from France, every prospective colon was to be allotted building material, animals, seeds and farming equipment, and assigned a plot of land between four and twelve hectares in size. Thereby, Bugeaud terminated policies of the previous decade, which had countenanced acquisition by European speculators of properties between 500 and 4,000 hectares. Title to the new, smaller plots was to be granted upon completion of governmentally specified improvements. The cost of transportation of settlers to Africa was to be borne by the national government in Paris. Overseas officialdom was accorded all authority to determine where colonists should be located.[9] In fact, after 1841 civilian settlers were "entirely under the thumb of the Algerian administration," but benefited from very substantial support from the métropole.[10] In 1842, official colonization began in a serious fashion with the establishment of nine pilot villages. Bugeaud gave the effort his careful attention. Typical of the welcome accorded French immigrants was the reception given twenty-nine families in Algiers on October 16. The governor-general ordered a ranking bureaucrat to greet each family in person. Vehicles furnished by the administration transported the newcomers to the hamlets to which they had been assigned. Lots were then drawn to determine which families would inhabit which houses. Probably, governmentally sponsored settlement started that process of concentration of productive land in European hands which later accounted for much of the intractability of the Algerian dilemma.

Somewhat ironically, Bugeaud staunchly defended the virtues

of small landholding. He insisted that properties not exceeding twelve hectares would encourage that spirit of cooperation and community essential both to frontier agriculture and to the militias which he planned to organize in every settlement. Plots of that size he believed "sufficient for the prosperity of a family working with its hands." He maintained that proliferation of large estates would encourage growth of a rural proletariat, thereby creating a population with no attachment to the soil or any internal cohesion, one which would "depart at the first sign of danger or dissatisfaction."[11] In 1846, Bugeaud repeated his view that development of large tracts by private investors would not prove more conducive to successful colonization than would distribution and financing of much smaller holdings by the state. "In investigating all factors involved in action by capitalists, in comparing their means to those of the state, one perceives quite conclusively that it is impossible for them to do as well....In summary, I think [private developers] cannot realize that vigorous, solid colonization rooted for all time in the soil which France requires to consolidate its conquest; and that to perform this truly gigantic task the power of the government is essential...."[12] Clearly, he had no desire to encourage creation of properties in Algeria rivaling those that he himself possessed in the Dordogne.

Still, Bugeaud emphasized that more was required to guarantee successful colonization than state-sanctioned small ownership. Only if the surrounding territory were able to produce crops adequate to make European villages self-sufficient, Bugeaud believed, could an irreversible process of settlement be assured. In his opinion, agricultural development of the countryside was in the "forefront of colonial necessities." Hence, he pledged that his administration would strive to provide immigrants with "completely constructed settlements surrounded by fertile fields protected against unexpected attacks by the enemy."[13] Only in this way did he expect that an overseas peasantry could be created and "attached to the soil forevermore."[14] An agrarianism modeled on that which he had attempted to actualize in Perigord constituted the basis for the cohesive society which Bugeaud proposed to realize in Africa.

To excise all "individuality" and "unfettered independence" from that society, he sought to transform a portion of the population in the colony's coastal cities into a controlled peasantry settled in villages whose economies were as overwhelmingly agricultural as those of most hamlets in the Dordogne. Unchecked growth of a "confusion of Jews, Spaniards, Maltese, Italians, Germans, and Frenchmen" in the coastal towns was for him as undesirable as concentration of the metropolitan population in urban areas. For Bugeaud, an ethnic potpourri made creation of a homogeneous and rural society almost impossible, and afforded no source from which military recruits might be levied in an emergency.[15] Algeria's urban demography suggests the reasons for his concern. Population statistics as of January 1, 1841, for the non-Muslim and foreign communities in towns where Jews and Europeans were most numerous break down as follows:

	Algiers	Oran	Bone	Philippeville
Jews	6,160	3,192	406	118
Spaniards	5,043	2,178	104	140
Italians	1,024	550	622	369
Germans	931	416	82	136
Frenchmen	7,316	1,492	1,343	1,541

A year later, the Spanish and French communities in Algiers and Oran had increased by 10 and 13 percent respectively, and comparable increases had occurred for all other groups except the Jews.[16] Clearly, the trends seemed to indicate that in the future a larger population would be almost as fragmented.

Sporadically, Bugeaud cast about for ways to resettle such urban "idlers and speculators" in the backcountry, and to create a new commonality of values. He had no illusions concerning the difficulty of the task. Apparently, most urbanites desired nothing more than to "do a little gardening around the large towns."[17] Ultimately, his attempt to relocate foreigners in Africa proved as fruitless as his efforts to discipline new immigrants, train them in war and agriculture, and establish them in farming villages inland. Although by 1847 the European population had swelled to more than 100,000, only some 15,000 lived anywhere except in the old coastal towns. To the governor-general's great regret, foreign residents in those towns had become four times as numerous as they had been in 1841.

Other examples of the agrarianism and anti-urbanism Bugeaud demonstrated in Africa present themselves. Outside Mascara in the summer of 1841, he encountered a shortage of barley. To feed horses and men, Bugeaud organized troops to harvest grain planted by their Arab enemies. Each day, some soldiers were detailed to cut the barley, others to thresh it. Predictably, the governor-general harangued his military harvesters, and extolled the benefits of agriculture:

Bugeaud: What is your trade?

Response: I'm a tailor, sir.

Bugeaud: There are all too many people making shoddy clothes today. Thresh grain, my friend, and both you and the public will be better off. And you there, what do you do?

Response: I'm a student, sir.

Bugeaud: Everybody knows students don't study. Take up the scythe.

Throughout, Bugeaud took great pleasure in giving lessons in farming. He constantly corrected his laborers. "No, no, you don't do it that way, you don't understand anything.... Give me a mallet.... Look, you start like this... and gradually build up to a crescendo."[18] In the autumn, he convened prominent colonial bureaucrats and officers near the maison carrée, lectured them on how a flourishing agriculture constituted the backbone of society, and proceeded personally to demonstrate how to handle a plow.[19] Small wonder that he soon was nicknamed the "Great Head Gardener." In 1843, Bugeaud reemphasized his conviction that cities were socially and morally destructive, insisting that Europeans in Algiers were guilty of more crimes than Muslims in all the rest of the country.[20] After his return to France in 1847, he was to reassert his antipathy to cities in considerably greater detail.

Until 1843, Bugeaud argued that military colonies organized along socialist lines offered the most promising way to encourage settlement, increase security, and promote militarization of society. He believed that colonization by soldiers in farming villages near the Mitidjan barrier would strengthen defenses against tribal attacks, and provide an example of a disciplined and traditional agrarianism. However, the colonists' dislike of socialism in Ain Fouka, Beni Mered, and Mahelma persuaded Bugeaud to terminate his experiment in September 1843, and release all land and property to individual ownership. The totality of this failure profoundly influenced his recommendations for realization of the good society at decade's end.

In December 1841, the governor-general offered to make building materials, agricultural implements, and financial assistance available to any of 800 soldiers then being discharged in the Algiers area who were willing to remain in Africa. They were to labor cooperatively to erect a village for their future habitation, and to commit themselves to three days of work weekly on the community's common lands. In "emergencies" the number of days was to be increased to six. Jobs were to be assigned by former officers in conjunction with the African general staff, and profits distributed equally among community members. Despite Bugeaud's personal exhortations, only sixty-three men accepted this offer. With help from a small number of Foreign Legionaires, they began construction in early 1842 of a settlement for approximately seventy-five persons at Ain Fouka, some three miles northwest of Kolea and a half mile from the sea.

The immediate objective of Ain Fouka, Bugeaud emphasized, was to "establish right along the Mitidjan wall" the first of several villages which, being "made up exclusively of discharged soldiers," would be capable of mounting an "energetic resistance against the enemy."[21] Indeed, the selection of Ain Fouka was not determined primarily by the quality of the soil, which was mediocre, but by its location near the point where the Mitidjan rampart began. During the first half of 1842, much of the soldiers' time was spent working on the wall rather than on the village or the surrounding fields. Halting of work on the barrier later in the year did not lessen Bugeaud's enthusiasm for the settlement. In January 1843, he reported that "great progress" continued to be made on Ain Fouka, and that the new colonists were involved both in building the town and in reclaiming land nearby.[22] Bugeaud also announced that efforts were underway to establish similar villages at Beni Mered and Mahelma. In fact, the number of laborers at Ain Fouka had by then been considerably reduced by desertions, and the only thing preventing complete collapse of the settlement was an influx of civilians experienced and interested in farming. Bugeaud's attempt to salvage his experiment by providing wives for the former soldiers only made its ultimate failure more striking.

Hoping to domesticate his settlers and retain them on the land, Bugeaud requested the mayor of Toulon to find women willing to marry them and settle in Ain Fouka. Twenty women accepted this proposal and were married to the Africains in Toulon with great fanfare. Most of the brides were maids from Toulon. Nonetheless, official interest in the weddings was such that the Toulon city council voted each woman a dowry of 200 francs. All transportation costs were assumed by the national government, and each of the couples was granted a subsidy of 500 francs. Unfortunately, in most cases marital harmony did not survive the brides' arrival in Africa. Most of the women reacted to Ain Fouka with consternation. The half-built houses scattered through the underbrush, and the brutish behavior of the soldiers, caused them to "huddle together like terrified sheep." Few of the marriages lasted any length of time. Indeed, rumor soon had it that the women devoted most of their energy to servicing the military garrison in Kolea.[23] Nevertheless, Bugeaud attempted to increase the number of such marriages. These efforts came to nothing, and the steady disintegration of the community as a military settlement continued throughout the spring and summer of 1843.[24]

Undaunted, the governor-general proceeded to establish additional military colonies at Beni Mered and Mahelma during the first half of 1843. Both of these settlements were also located near the incomplete, abandoned Mitidjan wall. The colonists consisted of unmarried soldiers with three years of active duty remaining. To avoid the turnover in population and erosion of discipline characteristic of Ain Fouka, Bugeaud made his new colons fully subject to military authority. He "applied to colonization a military organization in which not the slightest changes had been made. Thus, he preserved the basis of military power—absolute respect for authority, hierarchy, discipline, and also an esprit de corps...."[25] One hundred and twenty one soldiers were assigned to Beni Mered and Mahelma, provided with agricultural tools and subsidies as in Ain Fouka, and required to work the land collectively. Results were identical—the settlers soon petitioned their officers for release from collective labor and requested that all property be distributed to private ownership. When Bugeaud visited the settlements in September 1843,[26] he was deluged with complaints from the disaffected soldiers, and was finally persuaded to accede to their demands.

"Back from an extended expedition," he reported years later, "I went to visit my three tiny colonies, beginning with Beni Mered. Ordinarily I was greeted with joy by the military colonists who considered me their patron and called me Father. This time—it was a Sunday—I found them downcast and almost impolite. They were leaning against their doors and didn't bother to gather around me as they usually did. I saw that something extraordinary had occurred. Since the commanding officer whom I had called was absent, I asked a sergeant what the causes were of the discouragement whose symptoms I had just noticed." The following dialogue then ensued:

Sergeant: My men have good reason to be unhappy, for they are losing most of their crop. They attribute this to collective labor; they have had enough of this system and request that it be ended.

Bugeaud: But how are they losing their crop, for they planted during the first days of June and we are now at the end of September? The harvest should have been in the barn long ago.

Sergeant: You are right, *mon gouveneur*, that should be the situation. But nobody works, and we have not yet threshed a third of either the barley or wheat. Assuming that the good weather would continue as usual we failed to take precautions...; the two recent storms soaked our ricks and all our grain has begun to germinate.

A personal inspection revealed that the grain had indeed begun to sprout, the bins being totally covered with plant life. Bugeaud thereupon assembled the settlers to question them directly concerning the disaster.

Bugeaud: How is this, my friends, that having sown in June you have yet to thresh at the end of September?

Settlers: Because we don't work.

Bugeaud: And why don't you work?

Settlers: Because everybody relies on someone else, nobody wants to do more than anyone else, and thus *everyone ends up on the level of the laziest*. Don't you think, *mon gouveneur*, that if each of us had owned a portion of this wheat it would have been threshed long ago? We could already have done more than twice this amount. Things can't go on like this any longer; we request that the collective system be ended.

Universal assent greeted these observations, Bugeaud related, "even from the laziest." In hopes of reviving some élan in the community, he reminded the colonists that they had all been drawn from the same regiment, had agreed to become farmers, and were all young and robust. "In a sense you form a family of brothers," he observed, "and yet you still do not know how to live and to work together without thinking about who is doing more work than whom?" "Mon gouverneur," came the response, "we like each other very much, and despite this there is no desire to work; one does not feel he is working for himself when he works collectively with others...." The settlers then showed him their private gardens, on which they had been spending only one day a week. Convinced that they were producing more there in one day than in five days of collective labor, Bugeaud granted their request and pronounced the current regime ended. However, he informed them that the tools and subsidies which they had been receiving would be withdrawn. This declaration was greeted with "unanimous assent."[27]

The next day Bugeaud proceeded to Ain Fouka and Mahelma and discovered the same aversion for collective labor. Opposition was expressed in much the same terms and similar reasons for it adduced. Therefore, he ordered all funds and animals that were held corporately distributed among the colonists, and pronounced the system of collective work terminated. From that moment a rebirth of prosperity began, Bugeaud reported, and by the end of 1845 the three villages were "easily the most prosperous" in the region.[28] A visitor to Beni Mered in October 1846 seconded Bugeaud's judgment, recalling that he had been deeply impressed by the settlement's affluence.[29] Despite its failure, the governor-general's experiment with military étatisme did symbolize a "turning backward," perhaps a "retreat of several centuries" into the past. "If this was not a move backward in time," Demontès adds, "it was so in space, away from that Western Europe which is the mother of contemporary civilization. One did not then encounter [military settlements] outside Austria or the Russian steppes. Was it necessary that Frenchmen, masters of Algeria, transform themselves into Magyars or Cossacks?"[30] Military colonization, alienation and durcissement, it seems, fed each upon the other. Bugeaud's dislike of modernity resurfaced in his eulogies to rural life at decade's end.

Although he continued until 1847 to approve official assistance to civilian colonists in Algeria, Bugeaud never qualified his opposition to socialism in labor and property. After the mid-1840s, he viewed socialism as "deplorable," and expressed consternation that "petty officers and soldiers go openly to socialist banquets and their commanders close their eyes to it,...laugh or shrug their shoulders."[31] To improve agriculture, he argued in France following resignation of his colonial command, individual and undirected labor for private gain was essential. Only voluntary associations of persons with common values and varying capacities, he had become convinced, could advance agriculture, contribute to social progress, and stiffen resistance to modernity. However, without transfer of much of the urban population to the countryside he did not expect the nation as a whole to develop along such lines.

Transfer of urbanites to rural areas seemed to Bugeaud of particular urgency during the early months of 1848. "It is essential," he argued in June of that year, "to set to work at once, energetically and without interruption, to remove from our cities the glut of workers who exploit the Republic twice, because they are paid but do not produce. We must redirect this excess urban population to agriculture as promptly as possible."[32] To proposals that new farming communities be modeled on the "economic system of the phalanstery" he expressed strong opposition. Primarily to highlight the supposed advantages of agrarianism and to counter urbanization, Bugeaud published his *Veillées d'une chaumière de la Vendée* in 1849.

In this brochure, he argued that if people were made to better appreciate rural life, they would remain in their villages rather than crowd into the large cities. Bugeaud maintained that although farming involved harder work and paid lower salaries than did jobs in metropolitan centers, it offered a "freer and more secure life independent of political and financial crises." Furthermore, there was so much that needed to be done in rural France. "I groan when I see such large numbers of people—even young workers—walking around in our large towns with nothing to do," he wrote, "while in the countryside we observe a distressing solitude." In his opinion, many of the agricultural techniques still used there were misguided, and much that was practicable had not yet been attempted. Farming might usefully employ two or three times the people currently involved in it, and provide enough food for a nation of 100 million. Bugeaud criticized the lack of exploitation of vast tracts of potentially fertile land, and extolled the results of which rural industry could be productive. In Berry, Limousin, Auvergne, Perigord, Poitou, Sologne, Creuse, and many other regions there was a "rich mine indeed to be exploited for the welfare of the nation."[33] By wide distribution of his pamphlet, he suggested shortly before his death, support for individual initiative and agrarian traditionalism might be increased, and flight from the countryside slowed.[34] Such might be particularly true, he evidently believed, if all of society understood the moral degeneration of the urban populace.

In 1849, Bugeaud remained convinced that urban misery resulted primarily from the immoral, undisciplined life-style prevalent in cities. "Vices are what produce impoverishment," he maintained. "Those who act in an ethical fashion and are parsimonious always make out all right."[35] Were urbanites governed by a "spirit of sobriety, by true family solidarity," their sufferings would largely disappear. However, such virtues could hardly be expected in places where cabarets and other diversions were readily available.[36] Laziness, prostitution, and drunkenness were ubiquitous in urban centers, and little could be anticipated from efforts to improve the behavior of the city population. At best, the dissemination of virtue was a slow process, although "Christian charity" and the establishment of pension plans by private employers might have positive long-term effects.[37] Bugeaud believed that the moral miasma characteristic of the larger towns, if rightly understood, would suffice to discourage peasants from migrating into them.

To this critique, he now added a detailed condemnation of socialism. Only personal initiative and sustained labor could produce economic progress for individuals and improve the condition of the masses. Bugeaud described private property as almost as fundamental to human existence as the family itself. Attempts to organize, direct, or control society, he asserted, must founder on the rock of natural inequality. Order and respect for authority he considered essential for France. Bugeaud emphasized that any betterment in material conditions depended on improvements in agriculture and a reassertion of the traditional values of rural life.

In 1848, he stated that "soft-headed dreamers and demagogues in all ages and countries seem to have believed that somewhere there is a great mass of wealth provided by God and sufficient for the needs of everyone, if only a handful of aristocrats had not seized it with an unyielding selfishness." This "axiom of the socialist catechism" was based, he said, on the fallacious notion that there existed "innate riches prior in existence to labor." For Bugeaud, such wealth did not exist, and certainly had not been monopolized by the upper classes. "Are there aristocrats," he inquired, "who control the hundred and forty million hectoliters of all sorts of grain, or the forty million hectoliters of wine, wool, hemp, flax, meat, oil, etc., which France will consume in 1849? Are there other aristocrats who control the resources and materials which France requires during a year's time? No, all of this must be produced by the unremitting labor of everyone, or almost everyone. Were work to halt even for three months, the nation would starve to death and be destitute, for it does not have stocks adequate to make up for any such stoppage." Insisting that all prosperity was a consequence of individual effort, he argued that economic redistribution would be a "theft of labor, intelligence, and thrift." It would be equivalent to the "hornet pillaging the hive of the industrious bee."[38] During the last months of his life, Bugeaud thought of little else but the socialist danger.

In 1849, he repeated that God had not created wealth but merely provided the materials whereby it might be earned. Individual intelligence, wisdom, and enterprise, plus earth, air, fire, and water constituted the limits of divine beneficence. All material improvement was the result of the "sweat of one's brow." No riches were preexistent to labor, and therefore nothing could be shared except labor itself. Moreover, the vast wealth which some insisted should be redistributed really existed only in "disordered imaginations." The means to economic advancement were shared daily, Bugeaud stated, on the basis of individual energy and talent. Those who accumulated substantial funds could only continue to augment their capital by plowing it back into society. Redistribution of the wealth of a few would impoverish, rather than enrich, the many, and render any proclamation of equality meaningless. Even if all such wealth were confiscated, it would not support the populace

for even three months. However, the rich would "no longer consume, goods would remain in stores...and capital would no longer
renew itself through sales." National bankruptcy would ensue "despite all the might of the sovereign people." Collapse of the previous year's experiment with redistribution (that is, the national work-
shops) ought to have demonstrated the folly of such schemes. "Your
provisional government experimented with the right to work,"
Bugeaud told readers. "Despite the absolute power which it possessed, all it was able to accomplish was to assign 120,000 or
130,000 idlers to the construction of earthworks which they never
built but for which they were well paid. If they didn't construct
these earthworks it was not because they judged them useless but
because they claimed that the state owed them a living without
them having to do anything. They played *bouchon* and cards, smoked
pipes or cigars, established clubs in the open air, and discussed
great affairs of state while the poor peasants payed the 45 centime
tax to compensate these excellent laborers." Individual effort was
the source of everything, he emphasized, and the only means whereby
ownership of property could be increased and modest progress
encouraged.[39]

"I would ask [socialists] who have the incredible audacity to
proclaim that property is theft," Bugeaud asserted, "whether what
a simple laborer earns in a week or month is not something sacred.
They will respond 'certainly, there is nothing more sacred on earth.'
Well! The work of months, of years, of centuries which has established property in its contemporary form, is this not as worthy of
respect as the labor of one week or month? Cease therefore your
blasphemies against property; rather than saying that the first individual who fenced and cleared a field was insane or a criminal, bless
him, honor him, respect his work; for without it, the human race
would have perished...or be plunged in the most profound misery."[40] Only the gradual accumulation of property in private hands
could keep peasants on the land, provide everyone an easier existence, and augment social stability. The integrity of the rural family, he emphasized, depended on distribution of clear titles to specific
parcels of land to each of its adult members. "The links of blood
and filial piety are often insufficient to maintain collective labor
within a family. In those areas farmed by sharecroppers one sees
sons and sons-in-law separate themselves every day from their par-

ents and relations; . . . almost always these separations are provoked by the fact that vigorous men no longer wish to wear themselves out and endure privations to feed old people and young children. The generosity of the human heart is rarely large enough to allow proceeds from the most difficult labor to be used for the feeding of someone else; one only tolerates such sharing with his own wife and children."[41] It was the "communists" (*communistes*), however, whom Bugeaud regarded as the most dangerous enemies of individual ownership and societal cohesion, and against whom he directed his most unrestrained denunciations.

"Communists wish to push us immediately to the goal to which socialists would bring us gradually," he observed. "This is absolute intellectual and emotional frenzy, it is chaos, it is death. Can human intelligence conceive of the collective administration of the entire wealth of a civilized nation? If one wishes to establish equality . . . it would not only be necessary to seize land and buildings on behalf of the community; it would also be essential to expropriate all types of wealth produced by the arts, sciences, commerce, industry, literature, public service, and the professions—in a word, everything. Who then would administer this disparate assemblage? Who would distribute the proceeds? I do not believe God himself would be able to do so. In truth, it is both shameful and vexing to have to discuss such monstrosities; but how can one refrain from it when communism, in one form or another, is infiltrating into the highest echelons of society and threatens to be written into law?" His opinion of the collectivists, Bugeaud noted, could be expected to produce lengthy polemics on their part. "I warn them in advance that I will not respond," he emphasized. "In addition to the fact that I have little taste for disputation, I am very poorly located to involve myself in it. Living in the country some 120 leagues from Paris I read very few periodicals; most of the time I will be unaware of the criticisms which will be made of this rapid survey of the vicious doctrines which have caused Paris and France so much woe. Let my silence therefore not be taken for acquiescence."[42] Socialism, whether in its reformist or revolutionary variety, was obviously anathema to the marshal, and inimical to his enduring vision of the good society.

Fundamentally, Bugeaud believed that all collectivistic schemes were utopian because of innate differences between human beings. The fact that workers had a "great repugnance" for socialism was due to their understanding of this "inequality in human capacities." Coins could be collected and each treated the same because every piece was identical to its fellow and the value of all precisely known. Mankind, however, varied in "strength, intelligence, energy, and wisdom,"[43] and, unlike coins, lacked any absolute measure by which the cumulative worth of its members might be calculated. "If God had so desired He could have squeezed all men out of the same mold," Bugeaud remarked. "They would all have had the same strength, the same build, the same intelligence, the same tastes, the same economic capacities. Instead of that, He made them very unequal in every respect." To drive the point home, he evoked the example of a hypothetical cousin Nicholas "who, rather than working from dawn to dark as I do, spends most of his time in a cabaret."[44] Inequalities "wound the pride and excite the cupidity of those remaining in the rear and who, although stupid, lazy, and vicious, have a say in the government. From this come the troubles and incessant upheavals which often lead to the triumph of the multitude and rule by ignorance, which must in turn lead to decadence and a return to barbarism...."[45] In sum, the relative value and various abilities of men simply could never be standardized. Even if such standardization were somehow temporarily achieved, property and capital would soon begin flowing back into the "most energetic and intelligent hands." Shortly, and for the "benefit of everyone," society would have employers and investors once more. In Bugeaud's opinion, the ineradicable diversity of humanity constituted the strongest barrier against egalitarianism, and against any socialistic imposition of a "common misery" on the nation.[46]

Bugeaud considered a commitment to order and deference to authority essential to a cohesive community. It was a "grave error" to assert that social order protected only the wealthy, for order was "even more necessary to simple laborers than to large employers." In 1848, the rich had been able to ride out the storm without undue distress, he argued, while vast numbers of the poor had been thrown out of work and had suffered greatly. Were laborers but to "respect the laws" and be "good," their material well-being and that of society as a whole would best be protected.[47] That the "*majority of mankind needs to be led*"[48] he had no doubt, and he hoped that recent upheavals would convince the masses of the importance of honest labor and the rejection of socialistic utopias. Only by individual effort did he believe a commonality of values might be forged, limited material progress attained, and modernity vitiated.

In 1847, Bugeaud had returned to farming on his own property in Perigord, and had again turned his attention to advancement of the agricultural revolution which he had helped to initiate three decades earlier. His fable in 1849 concerning a rural revolution effected by one Jean Carrier in the Vendée was largely autobiographical. "It was Carrier," Bugeaud related, "who introduced cabbage and turnips into that area," and whose "natural good sense" led him to increase the average weight of the region's cattle and the size of its herds. "In three years," Bugeaud stated, "[Carrier] succeeded in tripling his livestock."[49] The marshal emphasized that although better farming techniques offered hope of raising living standards, no radical change in the human condition could be anticipated. He saw no reason after 1847 to alter his judgment of earlier years. Broad or general progress still was "not as easy as people think," as he had put it in 1840. "Labor, which is a necessity for most of the population, does not permit any significant spread of enlightenment. Only those who have money and leisure can progress. This is not possible for the multitude which is condemned, by forces which I deplore, to work from dawn to dark to obtain the means of existence. Let us not count, therefore, on any great improvements."[50] Meaningful progress could only be expected in the fields, in that "great factory which employs some 24 million workers and which, in prospering, causes all other industries to prosper."[51] In "cabbage and turnips" there was a "thousand times more possibility of real progress than in all the theories of the Proudhons, Blancs, and Considerants."[52] An agrarianism resistant to both the economic and political dimensions of modernity, Bugeaud was convinced, alone could buttress the good society.

The incipient collectivism which had once led him to procure state subsidies for comices agricoles in France no longer received Bugeaud's endorsement after his return from Algeria. In the discussions in 1848 of how best to solve the problems created by mass migration into Paris and other cities, Bugeaud was led by his experiences in Africa to reject governmental financing of rural resettlement, and to denounce suggestions that rural hamlets be organized socialistically. However, anti-urbanism and a conviction that only through agricultural improvement could progress toward a good society be achieved remained as characteristic of his thought in the late 1840s as they had been years earlier. If by 1848 Bugeaud's paternalism had hardened into uncompromising authoritarianism, his advocacy of agrarian values continued unchanged. Buttressed by the sword as never before, the plow remained the fundamental implement by which he believed that modernity might yet be checked and advances toward a better society made.

8

Conclusion

And so, in the end, what assessment can be made of Bugeaud? What was the nature and scope of his influence? To what degree did he succeed in proselytizing his political vision? What specific commonalities did he share with other spokesmen of the juste milieu? What was the extent of Bugeaud's contribution to military thought and practice, domestic and foreign? How did his system of colonial conquest and administration influence later architects of the French empire overseas? What impact did Bugeaud's original commitment to corporatism and strictures against North African Jewry have in Algeria and in France? How successful was he in revolutionizing agriculture in the Dordogne, and what role did he play in the nineteenth- and twentieth- century French "peasantist" tradition? Finally, what has Bugeaud's place been in recent French political debate?

During the 1831-41 period, Bugeaud delivered over a hundred major speeches in the Chamber of Deputies. That figure, however, is misleading. In fact, he addressed his colleagues considerably more frequently, often rising to expand or clarify points already made or to controvert criticisms. Unfortunately, his manner of presentation frequently undermined the matter of his discourse. Whether the subject was the press, electoral reform, or the juste milieu, Bugeaud's rhetorical overkill and rustic verbiage restricted his influence. Indeed, he gradually adopted something of a role as the chamber's public entertainer. However clearly his merits as military strategist and agricultural innovator were recognized, Bugeaud's parliamentary strictures on government and politics were generally ignored.

An illustration of his characteristic hyperbole and lack of political subtlety occurred during a debate in 1834 on freedom of the press. Utilizing premodern rhetoric, Bugeaud challenged the government to prove its "courage" by imposing rigorous censorship on the media. Immediately, he was interrupted by shouts of "That's not the issue," and informed that "bravery" was irrelevant to a problem of relations between press and government. Bugeaud was proof against all persuasion, and angrily refused either to end his speech or alter his argument. In fact, he totally lost his temper and screamed that interruptions would not prevent him from continuing. A supporter advised him that stubbornness would only "provoke the chamber," and Bugeaud's subsequent sallies were indeed greeted with increasing impatience.[1] If anything, the effect of his expostulations was probably to extend, rather than diminish, the limits of tolerable press criticism of the regime.

More typically, Bugeaud's addresses evoked mirth rather than irritation. In 1835, his bluff recounting (sprinkled with Perigordin patois) of recent exchanges with newspaper editors produced uproarious laughter. Clearly, he enjoyed providing good theater. Bugeaud simply could not resist playing the clown, even when the issues were those about which he cared deeply. In this role, he was a success. Throughout the 1830s, the reports of his speeches reveal that they were laced with interruptions from "prolonged laughter." For example, he was stopped by hilarity three times while denouncing liberalization of the franchise early in 1835. His jeremiads concerning the threat of democratization to Centrism were described by Garnier-Pagès as "bizarre," and considered unworthy of formal refutation.[2] Then and later, Bugeaud obviously was not an individual whose opinions were taken seriously on political questions.

However unpersuasive to his colleagues, Bugeaud's speeches before 1841 were fully consistent with "middling" ideology. Like other defenders of the juste milieu, Bugeaud neither accepted nor rejected the Revolution in entirety. In a society profoundly rent by faction, he and others strove to defend prudential politics against competing extremisms. All doctrinaires opposed foreign adventures, believing that such would threaten the Settlement of 1815 in Europe and political moderation in France. The Centrism of Bugeaud, Guizot and Royer-Collard was rooted in the notion of property as an inalienable right, and as the foundation of ordered government and the good society. Broad political participation, in their view, was inimical to the viability of state and community. Each opposed extension of the franchise. All were convinced that a small, homogeneous elite of wealth might effectively represent the interests of the larger society. Most doctrinaires were protectionist, and joined Bugeaud in opposition to exposing France to the vicissitudes of foreign competition in grain and livestock. And despite the praise of bourgeois values by others than Bugeaud, the majority remained profoundly agrarian. "No one," Guizot insisted, "is more a friend that I of the influence of landed property, of the preponderance of the agricultural interest within a great country. I am convinced that it is on this interest that the prosperity and security of the social state rests."[3] Surely it is not surprising that Guizot found no difficulty in collaborating with France's leading exponent of traditional mores. Obviously, the bucolic and holistic character of Bugeaud's social thought reflected broader middling ideology. Probably, doctrinaire theory owed much to the organic, anti-atomistic political philosophy of Edmund Burke.[4]

If Bugeaud's political influence was limited, his impact on military thought and practice was immense. He never persuaded the contemporary Left to abandon its military interventionism, or convinced anyone in France of the potential contributions of rural military settlements to domestic agricultural reform. However, Bugeaud's counsel did hasten the start of construction of walls around Paris. In fact, it was largely the plan of Bugeaud and Thiers, who pushed the project forward both as minister of foreign affairs and chairman of an ad hoc committee in the Chamber of Deputies, which was put into effect. Between 1841 and 1844, a rampart twenty-four miles long, with seventeen supporting forts, was erected around the capital. In the event, these defenses never proved necessary. They may even have assisted the Prussian blockade of Paris in 1870-71. In fact, the wall may have been the "single most useless expenditure of a French government in the 19th century."[5] If so, Bugeaud must share a portion of the blame for this misjudgment. Still, he clearly helped to engraft upon Paris an architectural spectacular which was not demolished until after World War I. If hindsight suggests that the project was ill-conceived, it surely was an error made in the grand style.

Bugeaud's single most influential commentary on military problems was his *Aperçus sur quelques détails de la guerre*, published in 1832. This collection of essays was printed in pocket-book size, probably to facilitate use while in the field. It addressed the most pragmatic problems of strategy, maneuvers, organization, and discipline, and included criticism of his arguments by other professionals. The book was republished in 1846, 1860 and 1873, the last two printings with remarks appended by a *général de division*. Obviously, Bugeaud's views on the military were regarded as important by his peers, and remained a subject of debate until well after the Franco-Prussian War. As interpreted and amplified by Ardant du Picq and Louis Jules Trochu, they continued to influence French military thought throughout the rest of the century.

Both du Picq and Trochu owed much of their military outlook to Bugeaud. Born in Perigueux in 1831, du Picq became France's leading military theorist during the 1860s. He made no secret of his discipleship to Bugeaud. Like his mentor, du Picq argued that high morale and spiritual cohesion were essential to victory. Following Bugeaud, he denounced the levée-en-masse, and defended the long-service professional army. In fact, du Picq's emphasis on élan and professionalism served to link the military thought of Bugeaud with that of Marshal Foch. Similarly, General Trochu helped to popularize Bugeaud's ideas in France. Trochu served under Bugeaud in Algeria, and became his aide-de-camp in 1844. He remained a close associate thereafter, and fought with Bugeaud in Paris in February 1848. In his *L'Armée française en 1867* and *Oeuvres posthumes* (1896), the influence of Bugeaud is ubiquitous. The first book is dedicated to the marshal, and in the latter Trochu states that in moments of crisis he always asked himself what Bugeaud would have done in a similar situation.[6] So close did Trochu remain to the Bugeaud family that he was given a study at La Durantie and did much of his serious writing there. He consciously attempted to instruct a new generation of Frenchmen in his master's military thought. Together, du Picq and Trochu assured Bugeaud's continuing authority within the French military for at least half a century after his death.

In Africa, Bugeaud's influence on the French military was profound. During the early 1840s, he transformed a demoralized army into a formidable fighting machine, and remained a brooding presence there until his statues were toppled by Algerian crowds celebrating independence in 1962. Still, the strategy which he implemented so successfully had precedents other than those in Napoleonic Spain, and was not solely conceived by Bugeaud. For example, native control of draft animals had been a problem for French forces in Egypt and the Levant in 1798 and 1799, and had been solved in a fashion similar to that employed later by Bugeaud. Even in Algeria, Bugeaud was not the first to propose direct French control of mules and camels. General Rovigo had made a similar recommendation as early as 1832.[7] Much of Bugeaud's philosophy of mobility and self-sufficiency was shared by Governor-General Clauzel, and attempts at implementation were made in the mid-1830s. Alone among the early governors-general of Algeria, however, Bugeaud possessed the confidence of the king, the full support of the government, and an army of sufficient size to prosecute the war effectively. By 1841, a decision had been taken in Paris to invest whatever resources were necessary to conquer the country. Between 1834 and 1836, French troop strength had been little more than 30,000. Although that number had increased to 54,000 by 1839, the major influx of men occurred only after 1840. In·1841, Bugeaud had almost 80,000 soldiers at his disposal, and by 1846 that figure had grown to nearly 110,000. His requests for boots, bedding, and improved rations were met with alacrity, rather than ignored as had been those of Governor-General Drouet d'Erlon and other of his predecessors. Nevertheless, there is no warrant for the argument that "all of the earlier governors-general, with perhaps one exception, could have achieved more or less the same results [as Bugeaud] if they had had the same support."[8] None of the other supreme commanders equaled Bugeaud in determination and imagination, and none developed detailed plans of campaign and tribal control. None fully comprehended that the Algerian tribes were not classically nomadic, and that agriculture bulked as large in Muslim society as national capitals and military installations did in Europe. Bugeaud's predecessors' leadership in battle was mediocre at best. Favored by circumstances, Bugeaud nonetheless needed personal and military abilities of a high order to convert a losing war of attrition into a spectacular military victory.

In most of the standard works on France and colonial history, Bugeaud is adduced as the first in a series of French soldier-administrators who erected France's African and Asian empire during the century after 1815. Some forty years ago, Jean Gottmann attributed to Bugeaud great influence on the military tactics employed by Joseph Gallieni (1849-1916) and Louis Hubert Lyautey (1854-1934) in Southeast Asia, Madagascar, and Morocco.[9] Lyautey, indeed, did recognize Bugeaud as one of the "glorious initiators" of the French empire,[10] and, with Gallieni, endorsed Bugeaud's emphasis on mobility as fundamental to success in colonial warfare. Following Bugeaud, both he and Gallieni strove to limit the number of permanent French blockhouses in areas under their command, and stressed the importance of Franco-native commerce in attaining lasting French control. Gallieni, especially, emulated Bugeaud by employing soldiers as both settlers and builders. In the early 1930s General Huré, supreme commander of the final French military operations in Morocco, credited Bugeaud with providing him the tactical keys to rapid victory. Principles outlined by the marshal on mountain warfare, Huré maintained, proved as useful in the Moroccan Atlas as they had almost a century earlier in the rugged Algerian fastnesses against Berber tribes.[11] Nevertheless, the success obtained by later colonial commanders largely depended on the extent to which they repudiated Bugeaud's uncompromising guerre à outrance and adopted new techniques of subduing and dominating indigenous populations. Whatever tactical elements of Bugeaud's oeuvre were adopted by his successors, their general military and administrative strategies differed markedly from his. In fact, new approaches to colonial rule were evident less than a decade after Bugeaud's death in the spirit of governance regnant in Senegal under Louis Léon César Faidherbe.

Faidherbe (1818-89) belonged to both the past and the future. As an Algérien he was fully schooled in the rigors of the rhazzia. A member of the Third Company of Engineers stationed in Mostaganeum from mid-1844 to mid-1846, he had ample opportunity to observe the final stages of Bugeaud's war effort. Lessons Faidherbe learned then he applied in 1851 and 1852, when he campaigned under Saint-Arnaud in the Kabylie. So "well" did Faidherbe acquit himself that Saint-Arnaud recommended him for the Legion of Honor. Faidherbe was convinced that Algerian strategy had relevance elsewhere, and foresaw difficulty in obtaining tribal submissions without initial victories by French arms.[12] Still, he gradually came to perceive the disadvantages of military violence unaccompanied by supplementary strategies. Over time, he became convinced that the threat of force might reap even greater fruits than its employment. Upon his transfer to Senegal in late 1852 as director of France's military engineers there, he had occasion to observe the potential of peaceful French penetration and indirect rule of the backcountry. Senegal, indeed, changed Faidherbe from an unqualified supporter of the rhazzia into one who harshly criticized the violence later employed by Brière de L'Isle and Borgnis-Desbordes against such African rulers as Ahmadou. In Senegal, Faidherbe developed a profound personal respect for Islam as a great world religion. That respect, perhaps, was the primary stimulus to the research he devoted to the languages, history, and ethnology of the populations he ruled as governor-general between 1854 and 1861 and 1863 and 1865. As a humanist and a savant, Faidherbe differed markedly from Bugeaud, and was clearly a precursor of the great scholar-administrators who governed the new French empire in subsequent decades.

During his years in Senegal, Faidherbe organized and led numerous carefully targeted expeditions. The rhazzia was employed, and Senegal was not spared at least some of the smoking native hamlets which had recently dotted Algeria. The impact on Senegalese society, however, of Faidherbe's campaigns was limited, certainly far milder than that of Bugeaud's military efforts in the Regency. As frequently as possible, Faidherbe strove to combine compulsion with conservation and manipulation of native society. Constantly, he attempted to demonstrate to Muslims the advantages of a flourishing commerce, an end to slavery, and a halt to intertribal warfare and exploitation. Fundamentally, he endeavored to extend French authority with the assistance of the native population. Above all, Faidherbe insisted that he "wished to make [French] domination acceptable to the blacks through persuasion." Therefore, he stressed that "care should be taken not to send [as administrators]...individuals who hate or scorn them."[13] Unlike Bugeaud and many later Parisian colonial theorists, he had little patience with the doctrine of assimilation, or with attempts at rule through constant or generalized terror.

Along with several of his successors overseas and in contrast to the marshal, Faidherbe had a scholar's curiosity about the peoples he governed. He learned Arabic, and became sufficiently proficient to correct inaccurate translations from that language.[14] He mastered the Berber dialect spoken in the Senegal basin and published a treatise entitled *Le Zenaga des tribus sénégalaises: Contribution à l'étude de la langue berbère* (1877). Eight other short studies flowed from Faidherbe's pen on Arabic, Berber, Poular, Sarakholé, Serrer, and Woloff. He maintained a substantial correspondence with native chiefs, and became an authority on the history and anthropology of the Senegalese interior. In all this, he drew on little from Algeria but made himself a model for such later colonial administrators as Louis Binger, Maurice Delafosse, and Robert Delavignette. Faidherbe's interests and competence, of course, made a policy of divide and rule possible, and enhanced the precision with which military force might be used on those occasions when circumstances demanded it.

This new approach to colonial rule by the mature Faidherbe was accepted and greatly expanded by Gallieni and Lyautey. Gallieni received his original colonial training in Senegal during the late 1870s, and observed with admiration the results of Faidherbe's approach to empire building there. When he arrived in Southeast Asia in 1892, it was as a committed disciple of the Senegalese governor-general. In 1894, near the Chinese frontier, he first met the future Marshal Lyautey. Lyautey quickly became one of Gallieni's staunchest supporters, and an eloquent spokesman for the philosophy of Faidherbe. He worked closely with Gallieni in both Indochina and Madagascar on military and administrative problems. With great brilliance, Lyautey later applied principles that were first demonstrated in West Africa to the governance of Morocco. Clearly, strategy developed in Senegal, rather than in Algeria, facilitated extension of France's colonial empire after 1880.

Only a few observations concerning application by Gallieni and Lyautey of the methods of Faidherbe are possible here. Neither succeeded in obtaining as profound an understanding of indigenous society as Faidherbe had. Both, however, recognized the importance of such comprehension, and became rather more conversant in native affairs than had Bugeaud. Neither had any sympathy with the marshal's Arab Bureaus, believing that they had abused their power, exploited the population they governed, and created a dualism in France's ruling establishment.[15] Both, following Faidherbe, were strong believers in a policy of divide and rule, and in restraint in the exercise of military power. Both wished to conquer with indigenous assistance, and to preserve, rather than to destroy, native society. On May 22, 1898, Gallieni summarized the strategy they followed: "One must remember that in colonial wars destruction should be avoided except in situations of extreme emergency. Even in such cases, one should destroy only with the intent to better rebuild.... Every time that incidents of war oblige one of our colonial officers to act against a village or inhabited area, care should be taken not to forget that the primary objective, once submission has been obtained, will be the reconstruction of the village, and the creation within it of a market and a school."[16] Both of them repeatedly denounced tribal slaveholding practices, and sought to end internecine tribal warfare. The empathy each manifested with native society surely had roots in aspects of Faidherbe's work in Senegal, and links them with such other Africains as William Ponty and Robert Delavignette, rather than with Bugeaud.

In Madagascar after 1900 and in Morocco after 1912, Lyautey implemented Gallieni's belief in expansion with assistance from the native population. For Lyautey, the fundamental purpose of colonial warfare was that "instead of bringing death to the theater of operations, life should be created within it."[17] If, in attacking a redoubt, one always kept in mind the "market to be established there on the morrow," one would "not take it in the traditional fashion."[18] In the new colonial strategy, Bugeaud's column was replaced by a military, political, and commercial "organization on the march," which, like an inexorably outward-seeping stain of ink, gradually persuaded the conquered to grant France an authority which untrammeled violence had never achieved in Algeria. Constantly, Lyautey urged his colonial subordinates to avoid discrimination against indigenous peoples, and to demonstrate sensitivity to native concerns. For Lyautey, as for Gallieni and Faidherbe, this policy was at least as important in contacts with tribes which had not formally surrendered as in relations with those which had. Thus, the strategy adopted by three of France's most prominent colonial figures was almost the antithesis of that once pursued by Bugeaud in North Africa.

The attitudes of Gallieni and Lyautey concerning assimilation only highlighted their repudiation of the long-range objectives of the marshal. For Bugeaud, as for other supporters of assimilation, that doctrine meant that colonies were to become integral, if noncontiguous, parts of France, with society and population remade in a Gallic image. This was the essence of that *mission civilisatrice* which came to constitute the French version of the white man's burden. Nothing could be further from an emphasis on partnership between natives and Frenchmen, and on nourishment of indigenous institutions and on-going administration and development through them. Fraternity and mutuality, which at least in theory informed the policies of Gallieni and Lyautey toward the populations they ruled, had little in common with the militaristic and culturally absorptive orientation of Bugeaud toward native society. What later was known as "association" was based on ideas that had first been tried in Senegal, and subsequently proven generally applicable. Faidherbe, rather than Bugeaud, was the model for later French empire builders, and the original validator of those associationist policies which won increasing support in Paris after 1890.

In Algeria, Bugeaud left a legacy of corporatism which survived the nineteenth century. "I must say that some of the criticisms which are made of the Algériens," Jules Cambon wrote in 1918, "are perhaps occasioned by certain attitudes which they have imbibed from the personal ideas of Marshal Bugeaud. The Algériens are criticized for relying too much on the government and on the state, of not calling individual initiative sufficiently into play, of practicing a kind of implicit socialism which leads them to expect the state to provide their wealth and to extract them from difficulties. One can say that, if this tendency has not gone beyond all bounds, it is not to Marshal Bugeaud that such a result is owed."[19] However thoroughly Bugeaud himself repudiated collectivism during the last years of his life, it was too late to undo the corporatist heritage which he had already bequeathed to French Algeria.

Happily, his campaign against Algerian Jewry was without similar resonance. For both political and economic reasons, Bugeaud believed that North African Jews constituted an important obstacle to extension of French control over the Algerian interior. Without subtlety or compromise, he denounced them on that basis. However, there is no evidence that he shared the religious anti-Semitism of his friend Louis Veuillot.[20] Rather, his strictures against Algerian Jewry seem based on what he considered to be pressing geo-strategic necessity. No "Jewish problem" preoccupied Bugeaud before his arrival in Algeria, or after his resignation of the governor-generalship.

The anti-Dreyfusards made no use of Bugeaud at century's end, and Vichyites failed to include anti-Semitism among the admirable qualities which they believed Bugeaud to have possessed in abundance.[21]

In France, the question of the scope and duration of Bugeaud's agricultural reforms remains. Clearly, none of his innovations in the Dordogne increased the prosperity or enlightenment of the Department as a whole. Throughout the nineteenth and early twentieth centuries, the Dordogne remained one of the poorest and most ignorant departments in the country. In the late 1820s, only nine of France's eighty-eight other departments contributed military recruits so unlettered as those from Perigord. In 1833, the Dordogne had fewer primary schools than all but eight other departments. Popular belief in witchcraft flourished. Certainly, the Perigordin peasantry around 1830 generally was "ignorant, badly nourished, poorly clothed, always toiling and moiling, counting for nothing...."[22] Most sharecroppers in the Dordogne remained "very poor" in 1848.[23] In fact, through at least 1850 more than 90 percent of the Dordogne's population struggled to eke a livelihood from the land. This percentage of rural inhabitants was equaled by only four other departments. In 1857, the Dordogne was in the bottom quarter of French departments in the payment of taxes both per hectare and per capita. In 1864, the *État de l'instruction* reported patois still in general use, and that rural dialects remained "as indestructible as the air breathed in each locality."[24] Wolves continued to roam the Dordogne, and indeed did so until after World War I.[25] As late as the 1930s, tales of ghosts and werewolves "failed to make the peasants of Perigord smile broadly."[26] Still, within a circle perhaps twenty miles wide centered on La Durantie, Bugeaud did achieve signal success in improving agriculture and lessening rural poverty.

First, of course, he radically transformed farming methods and increased harvests on his own extensive holdings. In 1840, the report of a visit to La Durantie by members of Lanouaille's comice agricole reflected his achievement. "Woods which [once] pressed in close around the buildings have been cleared," the delegation stated. "Wasteland has been converted into superb fields of wheat, clover, and oats, and pasturelands into forage or farmland. This constitutes a veritable colonization, a conquest which Bugeaud has achieved over the cold, damp, and rocky soil of Limousin."[27] By then, "all of the region around his country seat at La Durantie was imitating his methods of rational agriculture, thus becoming prosperous."[28] "What contemporary visitor would ever guess," an observer emphasized in 1842, "that in so little time the appearance of the countryside could have been so transformed by the efforts of a single man? While admiring these neatly plowed fields, thick with wheat, these lush, rich fertilized meadowlands, these macadamized roads, these cheerful, comfortable farmhouses, these healthy, well-clothed country folk, [the visitor] would be unable to believe that this abundance, this prosperity dates from only some twenty years ago. And how should it be otherwise? The region's inhabitants themselves, quite accustomed to this miracle, now only dimly remember the past."[29] Appropriately enough, an agricultural station and experimental farm is located today between Lanouaille and Excideuil, in the heart of that region which Bugeaud first altered so long ago.

All the same, the geographical boundaries of Bugeaud's success are obvious. The same visitors who praised the marshal's accomplishments were quick to note their limits. Beyond Excideuil, they reported in 1840, few agricultural reforms had begun, and farming remained "extremely primitive."[30] Bugeaud himself had no illusions concerning adoption of his innovations. The same year, he complained that proprietors outside Lanouaille continued to resist the planting of clover and other forage, and had done little to increase their livestock. Consequently, many continued to purchase foreign cattle, and still lacked sufficient manure to fertilize their fields properly.[31] However, in subsequent years the region's new comices did help to disseminate techniques used at La Durantie somewhat more broadly. Nevertheless, by 1850 the Dordogne boasted only one small garden set in a surrounding wasteland. By then, Bugeaud's "green revolution," so striking in contrast to what lay around it, reached to Excideuil, Thiviers, Jumilhac-le-Grand, and smaller villages to the east and southeast of Lanouaille. His reforms had created an island of scientific agriculture, but it remained a local, rather than a Departmental, phenomenon.

Sadly, even that island did not endure. After Bugeaud's death, his agricultural principles soon were abandoned by the region's farmers, and the garden which he had created reverted to the backward condition of the rest of Perigord. Without the energizing contributions of Bugeaud himself, neither the Dordogne's Agricultural Society, its comices agricoles, or its local notables possessed the will to continue the techniques extolled by the master of La Durantie. By 1870, the countryside between Excideuil and Lanouaille differed little from what it had been in 1820. Only half a century was required to complete the cycle from agricultural revolution to reaction. Bugeaud was fundamentally responsible for Perigord's brief efflorescence, and with his demise rural progress was radically reversed. Certainly, the very transitoriness of his accomplishments highlights the importance of his personal contributions.

Since at least 1815, France has boasted a peasantist tradition which strongly emphasizes the nation's agrarian roots. In the popular mind, the countryside has represented that untarnished, *vielle France* comfortably immune to most currents of modernization and social change. Peasantism, or the belief that "peasant life possesses unique moral qualities, and that the strength of any society comes from its broad small-peasant base,"[32] has assumed an importance probably unrivaled in other Western countries. Indeed, when traditional French agrarianism began rapidly to disappear after World War II, a cult of rural localism won adherents at an unprecedented rate. Today, the cult of *mon village* probably affects most urban Frenchmen to some degree, and provides a new market for scholarly and popular regional studies. Without doubt, the French peasantry is still perceived as the "sheet anchor, the keel, of the ship of France." To many, the peasant remains "essential for [France's] wealth, her genius and her destiny."[33] Surely, Bugeaud must be accorded major responsibility for the depth of this conviction. In fact, peasantism was greatly strengthened by the marshal, and his figure has bulked large in agrarian imagery and debate throughout the century after his death.

Echoes of Bugeaud's ruralism are many. In later years, specific peasantist proposals of the marshal were reactivated and seriously debated. For example, Bugeaud's insistence on the desirability of repopulating the countryside with city dwellers proved especially attractive. In 1905, former premier and minister of agriculture Jules Méline advocated transfer of population from urban to rural areas in terms almost identical to those of Bugeaud. In his book, *Le Retour à la terre, et la surproduction industrielle*,[34] Méline argued that the great contemporary social question was "how to lead back to the land those surplus workers who can find no employment in the cities." Like Bugeaud, he believed that rural France offered

exciting opportunities for urban colonization. "[France] has many
regions still lying uncultivated," Méline insisted, "moors and poor
grazing grounds the greater part of which might still be turned to
account." Unfortunately, many such lands were reverting to forest
"because owners can find no occupants for them." In his conviction
that there were "great openings for labor in farming regions,"[35] Méline
sounded precisely the note struck by Bugeaud some seventy years
earlier. Of course, he proved no more successful than had the marshal; nor would the Vichy regime, four decades hence, achieve any
significant relocation of population.

Méline's agrarianism and anti-urbanism are striking. "The land
has been thrown into the shade by the manufacturing industries
which have fascinated all eyes, absorbed all minds, given rise to all
kinds of hopes," he wrote. "Until quite recently, our country districts were entirely and shamefully neglected.... 'Everything for
the towns' seems to have been the order of the day, the program of
all our ministries and all our parliaments." Towns were nothing but
the "abysses of the human race." Méline charged urban France
with long refusing to permit increases in tariffs on foreign wheat
and livestock, and with maintaining exorbitant taxes on domestic
agriculture. He also denounced bourgeois newspapers as demagogic,
power-hungry, and responsible, along with urban politicians, for
intimidating the government.[36] At the start of the twentieth century,
several of Bugeaud's major concerns remained those of one of France's most prominent political elder statesmen.

Holistic antimodernism bulked as large in Méline's peasantism
as it had in Bugeaud's. Méline condemned the "parasitic middlemen" who battened on the nation's economy, and denounced the
"degenerate," commercial civilization of early twentieth-century
France. For him, contemporary competitive society was "unnatu-
ral" and debilitating, undermining both health and strength. Life
had become marked by irregularity, disturbances, and contention,
and quite lacked that "tranquillity" which he argued characterized
rural existence.[37] Méline extolled the country's agricultural societies
and comices agricoles, while condemning socialism and defending
private property. Like Bugeaud in the late 1840s, he found no
difficulty combining societal holism and antimodernism with opposition to economic collectivism.

In addition, paternalism and moralism laced Méline's thought as they had that of Bugeaud. Méline extolled the traditional family, and denounced the "somber cafes [which] drive their patrons to drink." In Méline's view, the "cause of morality" would be served if only urbanites could be made to understand "how easily a man goes to his ruin if he runs after money, and is not content with the life of modest comfort and security which the land provides for those who cling to it."[38] Together, Méline and Bugeaud encapsulate the French peasant tradition. Certainly, the marshal could not have asked for a more faithful acolyte.

Other peasantist voices were common in fin-de-siècle and twentieth-century France. As a group, they prepared the ground for Vichy's final attempt to impose an agrarian traditionalism on the French body politic. No theme was more popular than that of the transfer of urban inhabitants to rural districts. As early as 1887, Fernand Maurice echoed Bugeaud in proposing resettlement of rural France as the only solution to the contemporary social crisis.[39] And as recently as 1941, Albert Dauzat called for a "return to the land," a resettlement of agricultural regions.[40] Of course, agrarianism permeated all such works. In 1899, Eugène Le Roy well expressed the bucolic ideal in his delightful *Jacquou le Croquant*. "You see, Jacquou," Le Roy wrote, "man is born for work; it is a law of nature; and since that is so, there is no work more healthy and good for the soul than work on the soil. The more one comes in contact with it the more one has to be grateful for, from the point of view of both bodily and spiritual health."[41] Anti-urbanism was generally shared. Maurice, for example, deplored the "frightful labor, continual misery, and alienation" characteristic of town and city life. Hundreds of thousands of individuals packed together in fetid, unhealthy quarters filled him with horror. He, like other peasantist spokesmen, was strongly antimodernist, and viewed rationalist, industrializing society as a false idol.[42] For such writers, an end to conflict and class struggle could only be achieved by reconstitution of an organic society. When the Vichy government attempted to transform peasantism from a reflexive tradition into a political program, it aptly extolled Père Bugeaud as father and symbol of the good society.

Repopulation of the countryside, not surprisingly, was as important to Vichy as it had been to almost all peasantist spokesmen beginning with Bugeaud. With the new regime, return to the soil became official policy. Marshal Pétain and others repeatedly extolled the family farm as essential to societal health. Vichy offered subsidies to those wishing to restore abandoned lands and undertake agricultural careers. Some fifteen hundred families actually applied for and received such subsidies, although little more than a thousand ever succeeded as farmers. Vichy gave particular attention to settlement of urban craftsmen in rural areas, and by 1942 had moved about two hundred artisans to the provinces. Nevertheless, the long-term effects of its campaign were minuscule. The effort ended with Vichy's collapse, and abandonment of the countryside accelerated after World War II. Still, Vichy's attempt to reshape France in a peasantist mould suggests the enduring appeal of that ruralist tradition to which Bugeaud had contributed so significantly.

Vichy's agrarianism and anti-urbanism made peasantism the regime's official creed. For Pétain, the "soil [did] not lie." In his opinion, it was the "motherland itself." A "field that goes out of cultivation," he proclaimed, "is a bit of France that dies. A field restored to cultivation is a bit of France reborn."[43] Urban culture was denounced as decadent, abstract, and rootless, and cities criticized as enemies of national security. Above all, modern metropolises were seen as centers of class antagonism, that ancient enemy of societal holism.[44] In General Weygand's words, urban class struggle had "divided the country, blocked all profitable enterprise, and permitted every demagogic excess." National restoration, he informed Pétain in June 1940, could only be achieved by cooperation between workers and proprietors.[45] For Vichyites, "liberal disorder" and ideological strife were inimical to an organic society, and "artificial" class groupings needed to be replaced by corporatist economic units. In their view, a natural harmony of interests, long obscured by bourgeois society, might thus once again assert itself. Clearly, most of this echoed arguments made by Bugeaud more than a century earlier.

Like their Perigordin precursor, most Vichyites desired to reestablish the "healthier" France of pre-industrial days. Antimodernism animated their ideas. Thus, they "declared war on the world of money," and sought to revive an earlier order in which "fields were plowed, sown and harvested . . . [by] one single community."[46] Some advocated total abolition of the factory system. Unlimited progress, they agreed with Bugeaud, was a will-o'-the-wisp. Almost to a man, they applauded the conqueror of Algeria as epitomizing those values which they held dear.

In fact, a Bugeaud cult was created by Vichy, and the marshal's qualities were regularly praised in the media. Only under Pétain was "every aspect of his career extolled," and only then were his "private virtues publicly exalted."[47] The Pétainistes renewed with "enhanced authority" the philosophy of Bugeaud.[48] In radio broadcasts, newspapers, and handouts, Vichy publicized Bugeaud as the exemplar after which the new France proposed to model itself. With official encouragement, a number of hack biographies were published, one as far away as Hanoi.[49] Each biography sought to depict Bugeaud as a national and patriotic hero. The ideology of agrarian antimodernism and societal holism, as articulated by Vichy and its supporters, portrayed Bugeaud as the ultimate symbol of French peasantism.

In a sense, Vichy completed what events in the rue Transnonain had begun. Together, Vichy and Transnonain obscured Bugeaud's long-standing opposition to extremism and his support of the juste milieu. Both contributed to Bugeaud's reputation as an eternal enemy of moderation and proto-Fascist demagogue. Both also enhanced the marshal's renown as an inveterate and consistent Rightist. In recent years, French intellectuals have displayed their own ideological allegiances through their treatment of this Bugeaud. For example, Patrick Kessel's attack on Bugeaud, published in 1958, is colored by his Marxist convictions.[50] Charles-André Julien, writing as an opponent of French policy in Algeria during that decade, depicts Bugeaud unfavorably. Indeed, Julien goes out of his way to criticize some of Bugeaud's more conservative scholarly defenders.[51] And in 1960 Pierre Boyer and Gabriel Esquer, supporters of the French effort in North Africa, treat the marshal with sympathy without directly attacking the established stereotype.[52] After World War II, discussion of Bugeaud itself became a political act, and came to serve as a touchstone of political commitment. Given the marshal's dislike of ideological strife and his support of an apolitical society, this surely constitutes no small irony.

Notes

Introduction

1. William L. Langer, *Political and Social Upheaval, 1832-1852*, p. 329.

2. See Dominique Bagge, *Les idées politiques en France sous la Restauration*, and Vincent Starzinger, *Middlingness: Juste Milieu Political Theory in France and England, 1815-1848.*

Chapter 1

1. Bugeaud to Phillis de la Piconnerie, 11 Thermidor 1804 and to same from Fontainebleau, 1804 (otherwise undated), in Henri d'Ideville, *Le maréchal Bugeaud d'après sa correspondance intime et des documents inédits, 1784-1849*, vol. 1, pp. 24-25 and 38.

2. Bugeaud to Phillis, 18 Vendémiaire 1805, in Ideville, vol. 1, p. 71.

3. Bugeaud to Phillis, 16 Brumaire 1805, in ibid., pp. 74-75.

4. Bugeaud to Phillis, 19 Frimaire 1805, in ibid., pp. 79-80.

5. Bugeaud to Phillis, August 6, 1806, in ibid., p. 90.

6. Bugeaud to Phillis, February 12, 1809, in ibid., pp. 111-12.

7. Ibid., p. 111.

8. Bugeaud to Antoinette de la Piconnerie, June 4, 1810, in ibid., p. 126.

9. As quoted in Pierre Boyer and Gabriel Esquer, "Bugeaud en 1840," *Revue Africaine* 1-2 (1960): 68.

10. Bugeaud to Phillis, July 1810, in Ideville, vol. 1, p. 131.

11. Boyer and Esquer, pp. 68-69.

12. Ideville, ibid., p. 153, n. 1.

13. See especially his letter to Phillis of July 12, 1814, in ibid., pp. 151-52.

14. Bugeaud to Bellune, October 30, 1815, in Eugène Tattet, *Lettres inédites du maréchal Bugeaud, duc d'Isly, 1808-1849*, pp. 44-45.

15. Ibid.

16. Bugeaud to d'Esclaibes d'Hust, November 23, 1816, in ibid., p. 62.

17. Ideville, vol. 1, p. 172.

18. See particularly his letter to Bellune of October 30, 1815, in Tattet, p. 46.

19. *Circulaire à tous les déserteurs du 14ᵉ regiment d'infanterie de Ligne*, July 28, 1815, in the Archives nationales (here cited as AN), F⁷ 9082 dossier 33893.

20. Bugeaud to d'Esclaibes, March 3, 1816, in Tattet, p. 54.

21. Bugeaud to Phillis, August 26, 1815, in Ideville, vol. 1, p. 171.

22. Bugeaud to d'Esclaibes, February 20, 1820, in Tattet, p. 81.

23. See the report of the Prefect of the Dordogne to the minister of the *Police Générale*, February 4, 1816, in AN⁷ 9082 dossier 33893.

24. The Minister of the Police Générale to the Minister of War, and same to the Prefect of the Dordogne, February 15 and March 3, 1816, in ibid.

25. Bugeaud to d'Esclaibes, February 13 and March 3, 1816, in Tattet, pp. 51 and 54.

26. Bugeaud to d'Esclaibes, October 11, 1817, in ibid., pp. 57-58.

27. Bugeaud to Phillis, August 3, 1815, in Ideville, vol. 1, p. 167.

28. Bugeaud to d'Esclaibes, October 11, 1816, in Tattet, pp. 57-58.

29. Bugeaud to d'Esclaibes, August 16, 1819, in ibid., p. 78.

30. Bugeaud to d'Esclaibes, October 11, 1816, in ibid., pp. 57-58.

31. Joseph Durieux, *Le Ministre Pierre Magne, 1806-1879. D'après ses lettres et ses souvenirs*, vol. 1, p. 45.

32. Bugeaud to d'Esclaibes, August 16, 1819, in Tattet, pp. 76-77.

33. Bugeaud to d'Esclaibes, June 12, 1819, in ibid., pp. 70-72.

34. Ibid.

35. Procès-verbal du comice agricole du canton de Lanouaille, May 29, 1836, in *Les Annales agricoles et littéraires de la Dordogne. Journal des comices agricoles* (hereafter cited as *Annales agricoles*), 1825-26, p. 40.

36. Bugeaud to d'Esclaibes, June 4, 1830, in Tattet, p. 149.

37. Purchasing power of this windfall is suggested by the fact that the average annual salary of laborers was then about 400 francs. Elementary school teachers earned some 600 francs a year.

38. Procès-verbal du comice agricole du canton de Lanouaille, June 3, 1832, in *Annales agricoles*, 1832, p. 323.

39. Bugeaud to d'Esclaibes, December 27, 1821, in Tattet, p. 82.

40. "Le transport des terres," in *Annales agricoles*, 1821, p. 270.

41. See the *Annales agricoles*, 1821, pp. 266-67.

42. As quoted in Maurice Andrieux, *Le Père Bugeaud, 1784-1849*, p. 110.

43. Société agricole de la Dordogne, April 24, 1821, in *Annales agricoles*, 1821, p. 68.

44. "De la suppression de la jachère...," in ibid., 1822, p. 357.

45. "Du trefle," in ibid., pp. 55-56.

46. "De la suppression de la jachère...," in ibid., p. 359.

47. See his "Considérations générales sur la prairie artificielle" and "Avis aux cultivateurs," in *ibid.*, 1823-24, 1829, pp. 338, 353.

48. Acte de société, in ibid., 1830, p. 14.

49. Procès-verbal de la séance tenue le 29 avril 1823, in ibid., 1823-24, p. 98.

50. Bugeaud to d'Esclaibes, October 26, 1823, in Tattet, p. 88.

51. Procès-verbal du comice agricole du canton de Lanouaille, June 3, 1832, in *Annales agricoles*, 1832, p. 334.

52. Procès-verbal de la première séance du comice agricole du canton de Lanouaille..., in ibid., 1823-24, p. 225.

53. See ibid., pp. 229-30.

54. Procès-verbal de la séance ordinaire de la société d'agriculture de la Dordogne, November 6, 1826, in *Annales agricoles*, 1825-26, p. 322.

55. *Annales agricoles*, 1825-26, pp. 258-64.

56. See the minutes of the Lanouaille comice of January 30, 1828, and May 10, 1829, in ibid., 1828, 1829, pp. 97-98, 250-51.

57. Bugeaud to d'Esclaibes, October 26, 1823, in Tattet, p. 88.

58. Ibid.

Chapter 2

1. Throughout his years in Algeria, Bugeaud retained his seat in the chamber. From December 1848 to May 1849, he served as representative of the Charente-Inférieure in the Legislative Assembly.

2. Léon Michel, "Bugeaud député d'Excideuil," *Perigord actualités*, November 8, 1969, p. 3.

3. *Annales agricoles*, 1832, p. 304.

4. Bugeaud to the editor of the *Mémorial de la Dordogne*, in *Annales agricoles*, 1834, p. 189. At the time, the *Mémorial*'s editor was Louis Veuillot, later to become prominent as an ultramontane Catholic and editor-in-chief of *L'Univers* after 1842. Veuillot became a close friend of Bugeaud, and served as one of Bugeaud's secretaries in Algeria in 1841. A substantial collection of correspondence between the two men was destroyed by fire in the 1850s.

5. *Annales agricoles*, 1831, p. 345.

6. Bugeaud to the comices agricoles of Excideuil, September 1, 1839, in Ideville, vol. 2, p. 170.

7. See his letter to the editor of the *Mémorial de la Dordogne*, in *Annales agricoles*, 1834, pp. 185-90.

8. Archives parlementaires (hereafter cited as AP), V. 75, February 28, 1832, pp. 622-23.

9. For Bugeaud's discussion of this matter and various responses thereto, see ibid., pp. 622-27.

10. Ibid., V. 72, December 10, 1831, pp. 401-5.

11. Ibid., V. 75, February 28, 1832, p. 623.

12. Ibid., p. 630.

13. See ibid., pp. 624-31.

14. Ibid., V. 90, May 6, 1834, p. 12.

15. Ibid.

16. Ibid., V. 95, May 13, 1835, p. 751.

17. *Annales agricoles*, 1832, pp. 97-102.

18. Procès-verbal du comice agricole du canton de Lanouaille, June 3, 1832, in ibid., pp. 322-323.

19. See ibid., p. 336.

20. Georges Rocal, *Croquants du Perigord*, p. 287, n. 1. By 1836 there were more than 12,000 mulberry trees in Lanouaille and Excideuil, of which some 7,400 were on land owned by Bugeaud. The Ministry delegated a specialist to offer advice, and after 1840 the silk industry constituted a modest part of the Dordogne's economy.

21. AP, V. 90, May 6, 1834, p. 10.

22. Ideville, vol. 1, p. 185.

23. For Bugeaud's behavior as commander of the Citadel of Blaye in which the Duchesse was imprisoned from December 1832 through May 1833, and the background and outcome of his duel with Dulong, see ibid., pp. 227-387 and 394-400 respectively.

24. As quoted in Michel, December 13, 1969, p. 3.

25. Bugeaud to Romieu, August 10, 1833, in Archives départementales (Dordogne) (hereafter cited as ADD), J 1368.

26. Bugeaud to Romieu, February 13, 1834, in ibid.

27. AP, V. 79, January 18, 1833, p. 19.

28. Ibid., V. 78, January 15, 1833, p. 706.

29. Ibid., V. 92, February 7, 1835, p. 369.

30. Ibid., V. 79, January 18, 1833, p. 19.

31. Ibid., V. 92, February 7, 1835, pp. 368-69.

32. Ibid., V. 79, January 18, 1833, p. 20.

33. Bugeaud to Gardère, August 3, 1833, in Ideville, vol. 1, pp. 388-89.

34. See Ideville, vol. 2, pp. 194-195.

35. Bugeaud to the Editor of the *Mémorial de la Dordogne*, in *Annales agricoles*, 1834, p. 190.

36. AP, V. 88, March 24, 1834, p. 4.

37. Bugeaud to Romieu, April 17, 1835, in ADD, J 1368.

38. AP, V. 96, May 23, 1835, p. 391.

39. When difficulties arose or Bugeaud had reason to complain, it was "to me that he addressed himself to pour out his discontent and his worries and to request that I help him with his problems," Guizot recalled years later. "Not that there was profound intimacy between us; our backgrounds and tastes, plus our general orientation and life-style were not sufficiently similar to allow this. But. . . [Bugeaud] counted on my goodwill and my willingness to support him within the Ministry, in the Chambers, and before the public. In his general political posture he certainly was. . . one of my firmest adherents" (François Guizot, *Mémoires pour servir à l'histoire de mon temps*, vol. 7, p. 121).

40. Bugeaud to Guizot, July 4, 1835, in AN 42 AP 202 dossier 81A.

41. Ibid.

42. Bugeaud to Gardère, August 3, 1833, in Ideville, vol. 1, p. 389.

43. Bugeaud to Romieu, October 18, 1834, in ADD J 1368.

44. Bugeaud to Guizot, July 4, 1835, in AN 42 AP 202 dossier 81A.

45. Irene Collins, *The Government and the Newspaper Press in France, 1814-1881*, p. 81.

46. Bugeaud to the minister of justice, June 30, 1835, in AN BB[17] A 89 dossier 16.

47. Bugeaud to Guizot, July 4, 1835, in AN 42 AP 202 dossier 81A.

48. For a detailed description of this *attentat* see Louis Blanc, *The History of Ten Years, 1830-1840*, vol. 2, p. 370.

49. Bugeaud to Guizot, October 30, 1835, in AN 42 AP 202 dossier 81A.

50. Bugeaud to d'Esclaibes, March 23, 1836, in Tattet, p. 164.

51. Bugeaud to Genty de Bussy, July 27, 1839, in ibid., p. 195.

52. Ibid.

53. Ibid.

54. Bugeaud to Genty de Bussy, August 25, 1840, in ibid., p. 222.

Chapter 3

1. AP, V. 70, September 22, 1831, p. 84.

2. See ibid., V. 85, January 9, 1834, p. 528, and V. 79, January 28, 1832, p. 219.

3. Ibid., V. 85, January 6, 1834, p. 458.

4. Ibid., V. 70, September 22, 1831, p. 84.

5. Ibid., V. 69, August 12, 1831, p. 165.

6. Ibid., V. 85, January 9, 1834, p. 528.

7. Ibid., January 6, 1834, p. 457.

8. See his letter to Gardère of July 7, 1832, in Ideville, vol. 1, p. 195.

9. AP, V. 85, January 6, 1834, p. 457.

10. Bugeaud to Genty de Bussy, February 3, 1839, in Tattet, p. 187.

11. Bugeaud to Genty de Bussy, February 9, 1839, in ibid., p. 190.

12. Bugeaud to Gardère, February 10, 1839, in Ideville, vol. 2, p. 115.

13. Ibid., p. 114.

14. Bugeaud to Genty de Bussy, August 16, 1839, in Tattet, pp. 202-3.

15. Ibid., p. 202.

16. Bugeaud to Genty de Bussy, July 27, 1839, in ibid., p. 196.

17. See, for example, Bugeaud's comments to Genty de Bussy of August 28, 1840, in ibid., p. 224.

18. Bugeaud to Genty de Bussy, July 4, 1839, in ibid., p. 193.

19. Bugeaud to Genty de Bussy, August 16, 1839, in ibid., p. 203.

20. Bugeaud to Genty de Bussy, July 4, 1839, in ibid., p. 193.

21. Bugeaud to Genty de Bussy, August 16, 1839, in ibid., p. 201.

22. Ibid.

23. Ibid., pp. 201-2.

24. Bugeaud to Genty de Bussy, August 28, 1840, in ibid., p. 224.
25. Bugeaud to the Chamber of Deputies, November 30, 1840, in Ideville, vol. 2, pp. 239-43.
26. Bugeaud to Genty de Bussy, August 28, 1840, in Tattet, p. 224.
27. Bugeaud to Genty de Bussy, October 10, 1840, in ibid., p. 229.
28. AP, V. 121, June 12, 1838, p. 379.
29. See Bugeaud's address to the Chamber of Deputies of January 27, 1841, in Ideville, vol. 2, p. 223.
30. Bugeaud to Genty de Bussy, September 23, 1840, in Tattet, p. 226.
31. See his parliamentary addresses of January 27 and 28, 1841, as reported in the *Moniteur* on the following two days.
32. Édouard de Lamaze, *Bugeaud*, p. 286.
33. Ideville, vol. 2, p. 222.
34. AP, V. 90, May 12, 1834, p. 228.
35. Bugeaud to Guizot, October 5 (?), 1836, in AN 42 AP 202 dossier 81A, letter no. 11.
36. Bugeaud to Thiers, December 25, 1836, as quoted in Charles-André Julien, *Histoire de l'Algérie contemporaine. La Conquête et les débuts de la colonisation, 1827-1871*, p. 171.
37. AP, V. 106, January 19, 1837, p. 510.
38. Bugeaud to Guizot, October 5 (?), 1836, in AN 42 AP 202 dossier 81A, letter no. 11.
39. Bugeaud to Guizot, November 10, 1836, in ibid.
40. See his "Mémoire sur notre établissement dans la province d'Oran par suite de la paix (July, 1837)," in Paul Azan, *Par l'Épée et par la Charrue: écrits et discours de Bugeaud*, pp. 34 and 37.
41. Bugeaud to d'Esclaibes, May 26, 1838, in Tattet, p. 182.
42. Bugeaud to Gentry de Bussy, January 14, 1841, in ibid., pp. 232-33.
43. Bugeaud to Victor Hugo, January, 1841, as quoted in Boyer and Esquer, 3-4 (1960): 284. We reject the unsubstantiated assertion by these authors that Bugeaud's comments were motivated by a desire to depict the conquest of Algeria as nearly impossible and thereby win maximum renown when he accomplished it.
44. As quoted in Pierre Guiral, *Marseille et l'Algérie, 1830-1841*, p. 196.
45. Ibid.
46. Bugeaud to Guizot, October 5 (?), 1836, in AN 42 AP 202 dossier 81A, letter no. 11.
47. AP, V. 106, January 19, 1837, p. 510.
48. Bugeaud to the minister of war, May 5, (1837), in Georges Yver, *Documents relatifs au traité de la Tafna, 1837*, pp. 39-40.
49. Bugeaud to the minister of war, June 4, 1837, in ibid., p. 110.
50. *Annales agricoles*, 1830, p. 13.
51. Bugeaud to Romieu, July 20, 1834, in ADD J 1368.

52. See "Langlade" in the *Courrier français*, September 9, 1838, as quoted in Ideville, vol. 2, p. 180. Bugeaud's generosity had been distributed as follows: road from Excideuil to Perigueux—1,200 fr.; road no. 6—500 fr.; from Thenon—600 fr.; from Excideuil to Brives—600 fr.; from Lanouaille to Thiviers—1,200 fr.; from Excideuil to Jumilhac—1,200 fr.; from Angoulème to Aurillac—3,000 fr.; from Jumilhac—2,000 fr.; from Excideuil to Montignac—2,000 fr.; from Saint-Pierre de Chignac—2,000 fr.

53. As quoted in Boyer and Esquer, 3-4 (1960): 290.

54. Ésprit Victor Castellane, *Journal du maréchal de Castellane, 1804-1862*, vol. 3, p. 178.

55. AP, V. 123, January 17, 1839, p. 423.

56. See Bugeaud's letters to the minister of war of May 28, 1837, and to Molé of May 29, 1837, in Yver, *Documents*, pp. 91 ad 96.

57. Bugeaud to Romieu, October 31, 1837, in ADD J 1368.

58. Boyer and Esquer, 3-4 (1960): 291.

59. Bugeaud to Genty de Bussy, February 3, 1839, in Tattet, p. 188.

60. Bugeaud to Genty de Bussy, July 27, 1839, in ibid., pp. 196-97.

61. Bugeaud to Genty de Bussy, September 7, 1839, in ibid., p. 207.

62. See Sylvain Charles Valée, *Correspondance du maréchal Valée*, vol. 3, pp. 263-64.

63. Bugeaud to Genty de Bussy, July 1, 1840, in Tattet, p. 219.

64. Ibid.

65. Bugeaud to Genty de Bussy, September 23, 1840, in ibid., p. 226.

66. Ideville, vol. 2, pp. 134-35.

67. Ibid., pp. 136-37.

68. Ibid., p. 248, n. 1.

69. Bugeaud to the Chamber of Deputies, May 14, 1840, in ibid., pp. 143-44.

70. AP, V. 121, June 8, 1838, pp. 229 and 231.

71. Bugeaud to the Chamber of Deputies, May 14, 1840, in Ideville, vol. 2, pp. 144-45.

72. Bugeaud to the Minister of War, January 12, 1841, in the Archives nationales, Algérie, Aix (hereafter cited as AGGA), IE liasse 152.

73. The governor-general to the minister of war, August 1, 1841, in ibid., 11 MI 6.

74. See p. 9 of Bugeaud's report entitled *Colonisation* and dated November 27, 1841, in AN 42 AP 202 dossier 81A.

Chapter 4

1. See AP, V. 76, March 20, 1832, pp. 569-70.

2. "De l'enlèvement des corps détachés," in *Aperçus sur quelques détails de la guerre avec des planches explicatives* (hereafter cited as AQDG), pp. 35-36, n. 2.

3. Bugeaud to the minister of war, August 23, 1830, in Tattet, p. 153.

4. "D'un nouveau système d'avant-postes ayant pour objet d'éviter le plus grand danger pour les corps détachés, qui est l'occupation des routes de retraite" (hereafter cited as "D'un nouveau système d'avant-postes"), in *AQDG*, pp. 42-43.

5. Ibid., p. 50.

6. Bugeaud to the minister of war, August 23, 1830, in Tattet, p. 153.

7. "Réponse du Colonel Bugeaud à la réfutation de son système sur le service des avant-postes," in *AQDG*, pp. 117-19. These observations were written in Excideuil and dated July 29, 1829.

8. "D'un nouveau système d'avant-postes," in ibid., p. 42.

9. Ibid., p. 60.

10. Ibid., p. 57, n. 1.

11. "Essai sur quelques manoeuvres d'infanterie," in Weil, *Oeuvres militaires de Bugeaud*, p. 18 and passim.

12. "De l'application des manoeuvres de l'infanterie au combat," in ibid., p. 65.

13. "Essai sur quelques manoeuvres d'infanterie," in ibid., pp. 19-23.

14. "Observations sur un article du *Spectateur* du 15 septembre 1833 intitulé 'Mémoire sur de nouvelles manoeuvres d'infanterie,' " in ibid., p. 36.

15. "Principes physiques et moraux du combat de l'infanterie," in *AQDG*, pp. 147-53.

16. "Mémoire sur la guerre d'Oran," in Bertrand Clauzel, *Correspondance du maréchal Clauzel, Gouverneur général des possessions françaises dans le nord de l'Afrique, 1835-1837* (hereafter cited as *Correspondance du maréchal Clauzel*), vol. 2, p. 584.

17. Ibid., p. 571.

18. Bugeaud to the minister of war, June 16, 1836, in ibid., p. 525.

19. General Voirol to General Desmichels, July 22, 1833, in Théophile Voirol, *Correspondance du général Voirol, Commandant par interim du corps d'occupation d'Afrique, 1833-1834*, p. 157.

20. *La Guerre d'Afrique: Lettre d'un lieutenant de l'armée d'Afrique à son oncle, vieux soldat de la Révolution et de l'Empire* (hereafter cited as *Lettre à son oncle*), in *Mélanges militaires*, p. 11.

21. Ideville, vol. 2, pp. 16-17.

22. Bugeaud to the minister of war, June 16, 1836, in Clauzel, *Correspondance du maréchal Clauzel*, vol. 2, p. 526.

23. See Guizot, vol. 7, p. 130.

24. *Lettre à son oncle*, in *Mélanges militaires*, pp. 16-17, 23-24.

25. See his letter to Adolphe Thiers of August 10, 1836, in Azan, *Par l'Épée et par la Charrue*, p. 24.

26. *Lettre à son oncle*, in *Mélanges militaires*, p. 13.

27. Ibid., pp. 14-15.

28. Combes to Castellane, June 18, 1836, as quoted in Boyer and Esquer, 1-2 (1960): 92, n. 153.

29. "Mémoire sur la guerre d'Oran," in Clauzel, *Correspondance du maréchal Clauzel*, vol. 2, p. 525.

30. Bugeaud to d'Esclaibes, May 26, 1838, in Tattet, p. 182.

31. Bugeaud to Thiers, August 10, 1836, in Azan, *Par l'Épée et par la Charrue*, p. 24.

32. Bugeaud to Guizot, February 18, 1841, in AN 42 AP 202 dossier 81A.

33. Bugeaud to the minister of war, March 7, 1841, in AGGA 18 MI 2EE 1.

34. Bugeaud to the minister of war, August 1, 1841, in ibid.

35. "Proclamation du Général Bugeaud aux tribus insoumises de la province d'Oran," April 29, 1837, in Yver, *Documents*, p. 563.

36. "Mémoire sur la guerre d'Oran," in Clauzel, *Correspondance du maréchal Clauzel*, vol. 2, p. 578.

37. AP, V. 121, June 12, 1838, p. 379.

38. The governor-general to the minister of war, November 14, 1834, in Jean Baptiste Drouet d'Erlon, *Correspondance du général Drouet d'Erlon, Gouverneur général des possessions françaises dans le nord de l'Afrique, 1834-1835*, p. 109.

39. Bugeaud to the minister of war, March 7, 1841, in AGGA 18 M1 2EE 1.

40. "Mémoire sur la guerre d'Oran" in Clauzel, *Correspondance du maréchal Clauzel*, vol. 2, p. 587.

41. For example, see his letter to the minister of war of July 4, 1841, in AGGA 18 M1 2EE 1.

42. Clemens Lamping, *The Soldier of the Foreign Legion*, p. 77.

43. Julien, *Histoire de l'Algérie contemporaine*, p. 175.

44. Lamping, p. 36.

45. A. Bussière, "Le maréchal Bugeaud et la colonisation de l'Algérie: souvenirs et récits de la vie coloniale en Afrique," *Revue des deux mondes* 4 (November 1853): 451-52.

46. As quoted in E. Pélissier de Reynaud, *Annales algériennes*, vol. 3, p. 7.

47. General Canrobert, as quoted in Julien, *Histoire de l'Algérie contemporaine*, p. 175.

Chapter 5

1. Azan, *Par l'Épée et par la Charrue*, p. 136.

2. As quoted in Julien, *Histoire de l'Algérie contemporaine*, pp. 188-89.

3. Bugeaud to the Minister of War, August 1, 1841, in AGGA 11 M1 6.

4. Bugeaud to his *chefs de corps*, December 14, 1841, in Ideville, vol. 3, pp. 262-63.

5. Bugeaud to the Minister of War, August 1, 1841, in AGGA 11 M1 6.

6. Lamping, p. 73.

7. August 1, 1841, in AGGA 11 M1 6.

8. Bugeaud to the Minister of War, November 30, 1841, in ibid.

9. *Rapport Général sur la Guerre, la Colonisation, et les Travaux de tout genre à partir du 22 février 1841, jour de mon entrée au Commandement, jusqu'au 10 janvier 1842*, p. 56, in AN F⁸⁰ 1674.

10. See his letter to the minister of war of January 13, 1842, in AGGA 11 M1 11.

11. Bugeaud to the minister of war, November 30, 1841, in AGGA 11 M1 6.

12. *L'Algérie: des moyens de conserver et d'utiliser notre conquête*, p. 6.

13. Bugeaud to the minister of war, September 20, 1842, in AGGA 18 M1 2EE 3.

14. For the complete text of this edict, see the *Bulletin officiel des actes du gouvernement*, vol. 2, pp. 249-52.

15. Bugeaud to Thiers, August 10, 1836, in Azan, *Par l'Épée et par la Charrue*, p. 24.

16. Bugeaud to the minister of war, April 26, 1841, in AGGA 1E liasse 152.

17. Bugeaud to the minister of war, April 17, 1841, in AGGA 18 M1 2EE 1.

18. Bugeaud to the minister of war, April 26, 1841, in AGGA 1E liasse 152.

19. Bugeaud to Colonel Comman, October 28, 1842, in AGGA 18 M1 2EE 9.

20. See Bugeaud's circular of September 17, 1844, in Azan, *Par l'Épée et par la Charrue*, pp. 183-84.

21. *Quelques réflexions sur trois questions fondamentales de notre établissement en Algérie*, p. 18.

22. As quoted in Roger Germain, *La Politique indigène de Bugeaud*, p. 23.

23. See AGGA 18 M1 2EE 8.

24. Germain, p. 22.

25. AGGA 18 M1 2EE 3.

26. Bugeaud to the minister of war, September 15, 1843, in AGGA 18 M1 2EE 4.

27. See Bugeaud's proclamation in the *Moniteur algérien* of July 29, 1843, as quoted in Ideville, vol. 3, pp. 220-21.

28. Ideville, ibid., p. 221.

29. As quoted in Andrieux, *Le Père Bugeaud*, p. 234.

30. See Bugeaud's circular of September 17, 1844, in Ideville, vol. 3, pp. 223-24.

31. Same circular, as quoted in Azan, *Par l'Épée et par la Charrue*, p. 182.

32. Bugeaud to Thiers, August 10, 1836, in ibid., p. 24.

33. See Bugeaud's letters to the minister of war of July 23, 1847, and to the consul general in Tangiers of April 8, 1847, in Germain, p. 272.

34. Bugeaud to the minister of war, October 28, 1843, in AGGA 18 M1 2EE 5.

35. Circular of September 17, 1844, in Ideville, vol. 3, p. 216.

36. Bugeaud to the Arab chiefs of the province of Algiers, September 21, 1844, in ibid., vol. 2, p. 555.

37. Ibid., p. 556.

38. Bugeaud to the minister of war, August 10, 1843, in AGGA 18 M1 2EE 4.

39. Circular of September 17, 1844, as quoted in Ideville, vol. 3, p. 216.

40. *Quelques réflexions sur trois questions fondamentales de notre établissement en Algérie*, p. 31.

41. For example, see his letter to the minister of war of March 19, 1842, in AGGA 18 M1 2EE 2.

42. *L'Algérie, des moyens de conserver et d'utiliser notre conquête*, pp. 110-12.

43. *Between East and West: A History of the Jews of North Africa*, pp. 53-55. On the normally friendly relations between Jews and Arabs before the French conquest see also Michel Ansky, *Les Juifs d'Algérie: du Décret Crémieux à la libération*, pp. 6-7 and 21.

44. *Tableau de la situation des établissements français dans l'Algérie*, 1838, pp. 129-30.

45. Moritz Wagner, *The Tricolor on the Atlas*, p. 21.

46. Ansky, p. 23.

47. Marc Baroli, *La vie quotidienne des français en Algérie, 1830-1914*, pp. 90-91.

48. Ali ben Baza, Sheikh of the Babor, to the General-in-Chief (*sic*), September 1, 1832, in Anne Jean-Marie René Savary Rovigo, *Correspondance du duc de Rovigo*, vol. 3, p. 465.

49. Ibrahim Bey to the Governor-General, September 15, 1835, in Clauzel, *Correspondance du maréchal Clauzel*, vol. 1, p. 121.

50. "Mémoire sur notre établissement dans la province d'Oran par suite de la paix," in Azan, *Par l'Épée et par la Charrue*, p. 46.

51. Bugeaud to the minister of war, November 19, 1843, in AGGA 18 M1 2EE 5.

52. Bugeaud to Colonel Feray, July 23, 1848, in Ideville, vol. 3, p. 363.

53. Wagner, p. 51.

54. *Tableau de la situation des établissements français dans l'Algérie*, 1838, p. 129.

55. Bugeaud to the minister of war, May 13, 1842, in AGGA 18 M1 2EE 2.

56. "Mémoire sur notre établissement dans la province d'Oran par suite de la paix," in Azan, *Par l'Épée et par la Charrue*, pp. 46-47.

57. Bugeaud to General Bedeau, May 5, 1842, in AGGA 18 M1 2EE 15.

58. Bugeaud to the minister of war, May 13, 1842, in AGGA 18 M1 2EE 2.

59. Bugeaud to the colonel in supreme command in Medea, and to

Lieutenant Colonel Saint-Arnaud, commander-in-chief in Miliana, July 9, 1842, in AGGA 18 M1 2EE 8.

60. Bugeaud to Lamoricière, July 16, 1842, in AGGA 11 M1 10.

61. Bugeaud to the minister of war, May 13, 1842, in AGGA 18 M1 2EE 2.

62. See his "Mémoire sur notre établissement dans la province d'Oran par suite de la paix," in Azan, *Par l'Épée et par la Charrue,* p. 48.

63. Bugeaud to the minister of war, November 19, 1843, in AGGA 18 M1 2EE 5.

64. Bugeaud to the minister of war, May 13, 1842, in AGGA 18 M1 2EE 2.

65. "Mémoire sur notre établissement dans la province d'Oran par suite de la paix," in Azan, *Par l'Épée et par la Charrue,* p. 47.

66. The minister of war to Bugeaud, December 2, 1843, in AGGA 1E liasse 169.

67. See below, chapter 6.

68. Bugeaud to the minister of war, July 19, 1836, in Clauzel, *Correspondance du maréchal Clauzel,* vol. 2, pp. 565-66.

69. Bugeaud to Abdel Qadir, October 1836, in Marcel Émerit, *L'Algérie à l'époque d'Abd el Kader,* p. 156.

70. Bugeaud to Thiers, August 5, 1836, in Azan, *Par l'Épée et par la Charrue,* pp. 19-20.

71. Bugeaud to Guizot, October 5(?), 1836, in AN 42 AP 202 dossier 81A, letter no. 11.

72. AP, V. 106, January 19, 1837, p. 511.

73. "Mémoire sur notre établissement dans la province d'Oran par suite de la paix," in Azan, *Par l'Épée et par la Charrue,* p. 44.

74. See p. 21 of Bugeaud's monograph entitled *Colonisation* and dated November 27, 1841, in AN 42 AP 202 dossier 81A.

75. Bugeaud to the minister of the interior, April 17, 1843, in AGGA 18 M1 2EE 9.

76. Bugeaud to Adolphe Blanqui, November 28, 1843, in Daniel Maze, "Lettres sur l'Algérie à Adolphe Blanqui," *Revue de Paris* 3 (May-June 1898): 773.

77. Circular of July 5, 1845, as quoted in Xavier Yacono, *Les Bureaux Arabes et l'évolution des genres de vie indigène dans l'ouest du Tell Algérois,* pp. 233-34.

78. *Quelques réflexions sur trois questions fondamentales de notre établissement en Algérie,* pp. 20, 32.

79. See Yacono, pp. 233-35, 276-77.

80. Wagner, p. 149.

Chapter 6

1. Bugeaud to Genty de Bussy, February 3, 1839, in Tattet, p. 187.

2. See AP, V. 85, January 9, 1834, p. 528, and Ideville, vol. 2, p. 241.

3. Bugeaud to the Chamber of Deputies, May 8, 1839, in Ideville, ibid., p. 153.

4. AP, V. 76, March 12, 1832, p. 346.

5. "De l'organisation unitaire de l'armée, avec l'infanterie partie détachée et partie cantonée" (hereinafter referred to as "De l'organisation unitaire de l'armée"), in Weil, pp. 145-48.

6. See AP, V. 69, August 12, 1831, p. 165, and "De l'établissement des troupes à cheval dans de grandes fermes" in Weil, ibid., p. 163.

7. AP, V. 85, January 9, 1834, p. 528.

8. Bugeaud to Genty de Bussy, July 27, 1839, in Tattet, p. 196.

9. AP, V. 73, January 3, 1832, p. 548. See also AP, V. 95, May 11, 1835, p. 647.

10. "De l'organisation unitaire de l'armée," in Weil, pp. 146, 148.

11. See AP, V. 96, May 14, 1835, p. 59.

12. Ibid., V. 76, March 12, 1832, p. 346.

13. Ibid., V. 75, February 28, 1832, p. 623.

14. Ibid., V. 76, March 12, 1832, p. 346. On this topic see also his remarks to the Chamber of Deputies on January 19, 1837, in ibid., V. 106, p. 510.

15. "De l'établissement des troupes à cheval dans de grandes fermes," in Weil, pp. 166-70.

16. AP, V. 95, May 11, 1835, p. 647.

17. Bugeaud to Genty de Bussy, August 25, 1840, in Tattet, p. 222.

18. Bugeaud to Genty de Bussy, October 10, 1840, in ibid., p. 229.

19. Bugeaud to the Chamber of Deputies, November 30, 1840, in Ideville, vol. 2, pp. 239-40.

20. Pélissier de Reynaud, vol. 3, p. 471, n. 1.

21. Philip Kearney, Service with the French Troops in Africa, p. 17.

22. Lamping, pp. 68-69.

23. Ibid., pp. 2, 70-72.

24. François Certain Canrobert, Le maréchal Canrobert: souvenirs d'un siècle, by Germain Bapst, vol. 1, p. 393.

25. Bugeaud to the minister of war, April 14, 1842, in AGGA 18 M1 2EE 2.

26. Saint-Arnaud to Leroy de Saint-Arnaud, April 5, 1842, in Arnaud Jacques Leroy de Saint-Arnaud, Lettres du maréchal Saint-Arnaud, vol. 1, p. 379.

27. Montagnac to Bernard de Montagnac, March 8, 1842, and to Elize de Montagnac, April 3-7, 1842, in Lucien-François de Montagnac, Lettres d'un soldat: neuf années de campagnes en Afrique, pp. 206, 230.

28. Saint-Arnaud to Leroy de Saint-Arnaud, October 5, 1842, in Saint-Arnaud, vol. 1, pp. 431-32.

29. Saint-Arnaud to Leroy de Saint-Arnaud, October 11, 1842, in ibid., p. 433.

30. Saint-Arnaud to Leroy de Saint-Arnaud, January 18, 1843, in ibid., p. 465.

31. Saint-Arnaud to Leroy de Saint-Arnaud, February 8, 1843, in ibid., pp. 472-74.

32. Bugeaud to the minister of war, April 10, 1843, in AGGA 1E liasse 156.

33. Montagnac to de Leuglay, January 24, 1843, and to Celestine de Montagnac, May 2, 1843, in Montagnac, pp. 308, 334.

34. Bugeaud to the minister of war, August 30, 1843, in AGGA 1E liasse 157.

35. A participant in the Spanish campaign of 1823, Montagnac commanded the French column which was ambushed and almost totally destroyed near the Muslim shrine of Sidi-Brahim in September 1845.

36. Montagnac to Bernard de Montagnac, March 15, 1843, in Montagnac, p. 299.

37. Montagnac to de Leuglay, January 24, 1843, in ibid., pp. 335-36.

38. Montagnac to Elize de Montagnac, December 5, 1843, in ibid., p. 345.

39. Count d'Herisson, as quoted in Pierre Guiral, "Observations et réflexions sur les sévices dans l'armée d'Afrique," *Revue de l'occident musulman et de la Méditerranée* 15-16 (1973): 15, n. 4.

40. Azan, *Par l'Épée et par la Charrue*, p. 158. Additional portions of Bugeaud's article, signed "A Tourist" and written as a dialogue between a tourist and an officer, are available in Ideville, vol. 2, pp. 434-39.

41. Ideville, vol. 2, pp. 434, 436-37.

42. Azan, *Par l'Épée et par la Charrue*, p. 158.

43. Montagnac to Bernard de Montagnac, March 31, 1842, in Montagnac, p. 222.

44. Bugeaud to General Bourjolly, April 22, 1845, in AGGA 18 M1 2EE 17.

45. Bapst, *op cit.*, pp. 421-22.

46. For one description by Bugeaud of his standing order to so act, see the *Moniteur algérien* of July 15, 1845, in AN 42 AP 202 dossier 81A, document no. 41.

47. Bugeaud to the minister of war, June 29, 1845, in AGGA 1E liasse 160.

48. Bugeaud to Soult, January 5, 1846, in Bapst, *op cit.*, 444-45.

49. Ibid., p. 422.

50. AGGA 1E liasse 160.

51. Bugeaud to the minister of war, July 18, 1845, in AGGA 18 M1 2EE 6.

52. Bugeaud to Thiers, July 20, 1845, in Azan, *Par l'Épée et par la Charrue*, p. 212.

53. Bugeaud to the minister of war, July 18, 1845, in AGGA 18 M1 2EE 6.

54. *Moniteur algérien*, July 15, 1845, in AN 42 AP 202 dossier 81A, document no. 41.

55. Bugeaud to the minister of war, July 18, 1845, in AGGA 18 M1 2EE 6.

56. Saint-Arnaud to Leroy de Saint-Arnaud, July 26, 1845, in Saint-Arnaud, vol. 2, p. 35.

57. Montagnac to Bernard de Montagnac, August 21, 1845, in Montagnac, p. 499.

58. Melvin Richter, "Tocqueville on Algeria," *Review of Politics* 25 (July 1963): 371.

59. *Moniteur algérien*, July 15, 1845, in AN 42 AP 202 dossier 81A, document no. 41.

60. Bugeaud to the minister of war, July 18, 1845, in AGGA 18 M1 2EE 6.

61. Bugeaud to Thiers, July 20, 1845, in Azan, *Par l'Épée et par la Charrue*, pp. 212-13.

62. AGGA 18 M1 2EE 11.

63. Saint-Arnaud to Leroy de Saint-Arnaud, July 19, 1845, in Saint-Arnaud, vol. 2, p. 33.

64. Saint-Arnaud to Leroy de Saint-Arnaud, August 15, 1845, in ibid., p. 37.

65. Bussière, p. 471.

66. Richter, p. 377.

67. See Michel, January 3, 1970, p. 3.

68. Bugeaud to Thiers, June 11, 1847, in Azan, *Par l'Épée et par la Charrue*, p. 306.

69. Saint-Arnaud to Leroy de Saint-Arnaud, July 27, 1846, in Saint-Arnaud, vol. 2, p. 100.

70. As quoted in Georges Rocal, *1848 en Dordogne*, vol. 1, p. 5.

71. Albert Crémieux, *La révolution de février: étude critique sur les journées des 21, 22, 23 et 24 février 1848*, p. 164.

72. Azan, "1848: Le maréchal Bugeaud," *Revue historique de l'armée*, January-March 1948, p. 18.

73. Ibid., p. 19.

74. As quoted in Crémieux, p. 217.

75. Ibid., pp. 214-15.

76. Joseph Rébillot, *Souvenirs de révolution et de guerre*, pp. 11-12.

77. Crémieux, p. 218.

78. Bugeaud to Léonce de Lavergne, October 19, 1848, in Louis Véron, *Mémoires d'un bourgeois de Paris*, vol. 5, p. 14.

79. Rébillot, p. 12.

80. Bugeaud to Léonce de Lavergne, October 19, 1848, in Véron, pp. 15, 22.

81. Ibid., p. 15.

82. As quoted in Rocal, *1848 en Dordogne*, vol. 1, pp. 6-7.

83. As quoted in Azan, "1848", p. 17.

84. Rébillot, p. 14.

85. Bugeaud to General Pélissier, April 3, 1848, in Azan, "1848," p. 20.

86. Rocal, *1848 en Dordogne*, vol. 1, pp. 105-6.

87. Andrieux, pp. 280-81.

88. Bugeaud to Colonel Jamin, in Ideville, vol. 3, p. 361.
89. Bugeaud to Genty de Bussy, August 10, 1848, in Tattet, p. 320.
90. Ibid., p. 334.
91. Rocal, *1848 en Dordogne*, vol. 1, pp. 171-73.
92. Bugeaud to officers of the National Guard and army, in Ideville, vol. 3, pp. 398-99.
93. Bugeaud to an "unknown correspondent," February 13, 1849, in ADD J 118.
94. Bugeaud on March 2, 1849, as quoted in Lanzac de Laborie, "Le maréchal Bugeaud et sa correspondance, d'après une récente publication et des lettres inédites," *Le Correspondant*, September 10, 1923, p. 886.
95. Bugeaud to Genty de Bussy, May 7, 1849, in Tattet, p. 391.
96. Bugeaud had begun this essay while guarding the Duchesse de Berry at Blaye in the early 1830s. He revised and considerably expanded it after his return from Algeria. Only in 1849 did he demonstrate great enthusiasm for its contents, or advocate that his prescriptions be adopted as national policy.
97. Julien, *Histoire de l'Algérie contemporaine*, p. 167.
98. Bugeaud to Genty de Bussy, February 13, 1849, in Tattet, p. 352.
99. Bugeaud to Genty de Bussy, January 31, 1849, in ibid., pp. 346-47.
100. See Saint-Arnaud's letters to Leroy de Saint-Arnaud of October 15, 1847, July 1, 1848 and July 8, 1848, and to Adolphe de Forçade of February 1, 1849, in Saint-Arnaud, vol. 2, pp. 160, 181-82, 197.
101. Saint-Arnaud to Adolphe de Forçade, June 15, 1849, in ibid., p. 212.
102. Wagner, p. 362.
103. Richter, p. 371.

Chapter 7

1. *Moniteur algérien*, August 25, 1845, as quoted in Ideville, vol. 3, pp. 274-75.
2. Ibid., pp. 282-83.
3. Bugeaud to Genty de Bussy, April 27, 1847, in Tattet, pp. 307-8.
4. Bugeaud to the minister of war, January 23, 1842, in AGGA 18 M1 2EE 2.
5. Bugeaud to Genty de Bussy, April 27, 1847, in Tattet, p. 307.
6. Victor Demontès, *La Colonisation militaire sous Bugeaud*, pp. 353, 364-66. For a more detailed exposition of Enfantin's ideas, see Enfantin's book entitled *La Colonisation de l'Algérie*, published in 1843.
7. Bugeaud to the minister of war, January 12, 1841, in AGGA 1E liasse 152.
8. Demontès, p. 353.
9. *Bulletin officiel des actes du Gouvernement*, vol. 2, pp. 291-95.
10. Augustin Bernard, *L'Algérie*, p. 264.

11. *Moniteur algérien*, August 25, 1845, as quoted in Ideville, vol. 3, pp. 275-76.

12. *Quelques réflexions sur trois questions fondamentales de notre établissement en Algérie*, pp. 26-27.

13. See Bugeaud's proclamation of February 23, 1841, in Ideville, vol. 2, p. 251.

14. *Moniteur algérien*, August 25, 1845, as quoted in ibid., vol. 3, p. 276.

15. Bugeaud to the minister of war, November 19, 1843, in AGGA 18 M1 2EE 5.

16. Ministère de la Guerre, *Tableau de la situation des établissements français dans l'Algérie*, 1840, 1841, pp. 96, 73.

17. Bugeaud to the minister of war, November 19, 1843, in AGGA 18 M1 2EE 5.

18. Report of General Staff Attaché Lapasset, as quoted in Andrieux, pp. 204-5.

19. Ideville, vol. 2, p. 323.

20. Bugeaud to the minister of war, November 19, 1843, in AGGA 18 M1 2EE 5.

21. As quoted in Julien, *Histoire de l'Algérie contemporaine*, p. 235.

22. Bugeaud to the minister of war, January 19, 1843, in AGGA 1E liasse 156. Reality was less promising. Only two petty officers knew anything about farming, and few of the former infantrymen had ever handled a plow. One officer, who had actually studied agronomy and who volunteered for the settlement, was initially rejected and finally permitted to participate only after considerable personal sacrifice. Such early agricultural success as the village did achieve was due to his direction.

23. Julien, *Histoire de l'Algérie contemporaine*, p. 237.

24. Clemens Lamping's observations in 1842 were validated by events. "At Kolea they have begun to form a colony of old worn out soldiers," he wrote then, "but I have great doubts of its success. These veterans, it is true, have the double advantage of being tolerably well used to the climate and of knowing how to conduct themselves with prudence and coolness when attacked by the enemy; on the other hand, an old soldier generally makes a very bad peasant, and is ten times more patient of the dangers and hardships of war than of daily work with spade and plough. He usually takes unto himself some profligate woman not at all likely to attach him to his home, and then of course, neglects his farm, and soon dissipates the small sum allowed him by the Government, and the end of it all is, that he sells his oxen and his plough, turns off his female companion and enlists for a few years more. And now the old fellow who used to curse the service heartily, finds it quite a decent and comfortable way of life, and it is amusing to hear with what indignation he speaks of the life of a colonist" (p. 74).

25. Demontès, p. 318.

26. Demontès maintains that the governor-general erred in his recollection of this date, and suggests September 1844 as a more likely time.

27. "Les Socialistes et le travail en commun," *Revue des deux mondes* 23 (July 1848): 252-53.
28. Ibid., p. 254.
29. Bussière, p. 461.
30. Demontès, pp. 314-15.
31. Bugeaud to General Charon, June 5, 1849, in Ideville, vol. 3, p. 422.
32. "Des Travailleurs dans nos grandes villes," *Revue des deux mondes* (June 1848): 793.
33. *Veillées d'une chaumière de la Vendée*, pp. 61-62.
34. Bugeaud to General Charon, June 5, 1849, in Ideville, vol. 3, pp. 422-23.
35. "Les Socialistes et le travail en commun," p. 255.
36. *Veillées d'une chaumière de la Vendée*, p. 52.
37. Ibid., pp. 28, 55-57. In his opinion, pension plans might make revolutions rare. Then "Proudhon and the other socialists would preach in the desert, because the workers would understand very well that a revolution would cause the cash on which they planned to live during their old age to disappear."
38. "Les Socialistes et le travail en commun," pp. 245, 247.
39. *Veillées d'une chaumière de la Vendée*, pp. 23, 25, 38, 45, 47-48.
40. "Les Socialistes et le travail en commun," p. 246.
41. Ibid., p. 251.
42. Ibid., pp. 256-57.
43. Ibid., pp. 245, 251.
44. *Veillées d'une chaumière de la Vendée*, pp. 25-26.
45. Bugeaud to Thiers, July 14, 1848, in Azan, *Par l'Épée et par la Charrue*, pp. 326-27.
46. "Les Socialistes et le travail en commun," p. 248.
47. *Veillées d'une chaumière de la Vendée*, pp. 53, 60.
48. "Les Socialistes et le travail en commun," p. 248.
49. *Veillées d'une chaumière de la Vendée*, pp. 6-7.
50. *Moniteur*, April 19, 1840.
51. Lanzac de Laborie, August 25, 1923, p. 629.
52. *Veillées d'une chaumière de la Vendée*, p. 5.

Chapter 8

1. See AP, V. 88, March 24, 1834, pp. 4-5.
2. AP, V. 92, February 7, 1835, pp. 369-71.
3. As quoted in Starzinger, p. 109.
4. On this point see ibid., pp. 58-59, and Bagge, p. 100.
5. Patricia O'Brien, "*L'Embastillement de Paris:* The Fortification of Paris during the July Monarchy," *French Historical Studies* 9 (Spring 1975): 64.
6. *Oeuvres posthumes*, vol. 1, pp. 224-25.
7. See Rovigo's letter to the minister of war, February 12, 1832, in Rovigo, *Correspondance du duc de Rovigo*, vol. 1, pp. 221-22.

8. Pélissier de Reynaud, vol. 3, p. 295.

9. See Gottmann's "Bugeaud, Gallieni, Lyautey: The Development of French Colonial Warfare," in Edward Mead Earle, ed. *Makers of Modern Strategy: Military Thought from Machiavelli to Hitler*, pp. 234-59.

10. In his "Du rôle colonial de l'armée," *Revue des deux mondes* 157 (January 15, 1900): 311.

11. Huré, "Stratégie et tactique marocaine," *Revue des questions de défense nationale* vol. 1, no. 3 (July 1939): 397-412.

12. Leland C. Barrows, "Louis Léon César Faidherbe (1818-1889)," in L. H. Gann and Peter Duignan, eds. *African Proconsuls: European Governors in Africa*, pp. 57-58.

13. Faidherbe to the minister of war, October 14, 1859, in Oumar Ba, *La pénétration française au Cayor*, vol. 1, p. 197.

14. Ibid., p. 23.

15. See Lyautey, p. 311.

16. As quoted in ibid., p. 316.

17. Gottman, p. 246.

18. Lyautey, p. 315.

19. Jules Cambon, *Le gouvernement-général de l'Algérie, 1891-1897*, pp. 146-47.

20. Interestingly, religion in general was a matter almost never discussed by Bugeaud. He certainly did not share the perfervid Catholicism of Veuillot, or Veuillot's dream of reclaiming North Africa for the Roman Church. At most, the Church probably appeared useful to Bugeaud as a potential bulwark of traditional society in France.

21. For a discussion of Bugeaud in the pantheon of Vichy, pp. 175-77.

22. Eugène Le Roy, *Jacquou le Croquant*, p. 304. This and other quotations and citations are from Eleanor Stimson Brooks's translation (*Jacquou the Rebel*) of 1919.

23. Georges Rocal, *Croquants du Périgord*, p. 192.

24. As quoted in Eugen Weber, *Peasants into Frenchmen: The Modernization of Rural France, 1870-1914*, p. 67.

25. Jacques Crouzy, personal communication, August 7, 1979.

26. Andrieux, pp. 19-20.

27. July 19, 1840, in *Annales agricoles*, 1840, p. 225.

28. Rocal, *1848 en Dordogne*, vol. 1, p. 105.

29. de Bezancenetz, as quoted in Ideville, vol. 1, p. 180.

30. July 19, 1840, in *Annales agricoles*, 1840, p. 226.

31. Ibid., p. 222.

32. Gordon Wright, *Rural Revolution in France: The Peasantry in the Twentieth Century*, p. 1, n. 1.

33. Ibid., p. 2.

34. This was translated into English and published in 1906 under the title *The Return to the Land*. Quotations are from the English edition. Méline expanded his arguments years later in his *Le Salut par la terre et le programme économique de l'avenir*.

35. Jules Méline, *The Return to the Land*, pp. xvi-xix, 208-09.

36. Ibid., pp. 87-88, 96-97, 131, 159.

37. Ibid., pp. 110, 157-158.

38. Ibid., pp. 148, 156-57.

39. Fernand Maurice, *La Réforme Agraire et la Misère en France*, passim.

40. Albert Dauzat, *Le Village et le paysan de France*, pp. 208-9.

41. Le Roy, p. 235.

42. Maurice, pp. 128-30.

43. As quoted in Wright, p. 76.

44. See Robert O. Paxton, *Vichy France: Old Guard and New Order, 1940-1944*, pp. 200, 270.

45. Weygand to Pétain, June 28, 1940, in Jacques de Launay, *Le Dossier de Vichy*, p. 264.

46. As quoted in Paxton, p. 141.

47. Patrick Kessel, *Moi, maréchal Bugeaud: un soldat de l'ordre*, p. 10.

48. Lamaze, p. 273.

49. In 1942, Jean Maubourguet's *Bugeaud, laboureur périgourdin* appeared. There followed within a year or two Edouard de Lamaze's *Bugeaud*; Paul Lesourd's *Bugeaud: le soldat laboureur*; and Claire Petit-Colin's *Bugeaud*.

50. See Kessel, p. 10.

51. See Julien, *Histoire d l'Algérie contemporaine*, especially pp. 165-66.

52. See Boyer and Esquer, *loc. cit.*

Bibliographical Essay

This book is based primarily on archival and published primary sources, and this essay has been prepared accordingly. Included are only materials of significant assistance to research and writing of this study. No attempt has been made to itemize all of the literature on France and North Africa which was consulted during preparation of this work.

1. Archival Sources

The Dépôt des archives d'Outre-Mer, a constituent part of the Archives nationales located in Aix-en-Provence, now has the most extensive collection of unpublished primary materials on French colonialism in the nineteenth and twentieth centuries of any research institution in the world. It is the repository in which any serious study of France in North Africa should begin. Working conditions are excellent and the staff cooperative. As of early 1982, discussions continued between the French and Algerian governments concerning return of all or part of the post-1830 holdings to Algeria with no final decision yet taken. Most of Bugeaud's correspondence while governor-general is available in the Dépôt.

The Dépôt's Archives du Gouvernement Général de l'Algérie (denoted AGGA above) contain letters written by Bugeaud to the minister of war during the 1841-47 period. The originals of series AGGA 18 M1 2EE 1 to 2EE 19, the most voluminous single file of Bugeaud correspondence, are not open for direct examination because of concern over possible damage to the documents. However, they may be examined on nine reels of microfilm. A complete copyflow run of this series has been donated by the author to the Hoover Institution, Stanford University. Despite the enhanced readability provided by this reproduction, decipherment remains a challenge because of the generally poor handwriting of secretaries to whom Bugeaud dictated his communications while overseas.

Originals of letters by Bugeaud in AGGA 1E 152-210, also mainly addressed to the minister of war, are (or were) available to researchers in a series of *liasses*, or folders. At such time as their microfilming was complete they too were to be removed from the dangers of direct examination. AGGA 18 M1 2EE 1 to 2EE 19 and AGGA 1E 152-210 together constitute the bulk of Bugeaud's correspondence on politico-strategic subjects while governor-general.

The several reels of Dépôt microfilm denoted 11 M1 5-15 (prefixed AGGA above) reproduce letters by Bugeaud to the minister of war and to his fellow Algerian commanders which remain deposited in the Ministry of War in Vincennes. This microfilm also includes correspondence between Bugeaud and Enfantin (11 M1 8) which is still in the Bibliothèque de l'Arsenal in Paris. Material in this series proved of somewhat lesser value to the present study.

The most important collection of unpublished documentation on Bugeaud in the Archives nationales in Paris is his extensive correspondence with Guizot, primarily during the 1830s, designated AN 42 AP 202 in this book. Bugeaud's own handwriting was even worse than that of his secretaries, and considerable portions of these letters are unreadable. These private (Guizot) archives require special permission to consult but are basic to an understanding of Bugeaud's political views in the decade before his governor-generalship. In addition, the following Archives nationales collections contain information provided by or relevant to Bugeaud and pertinent either to metropolitan or overseas aspects of his career: 225 AP; F[80] 1672, 1674-1676; F[7] 6780 dossier 1 and 9082 dossier 33893; BB[17 A] 89 dossier 16, 18 1477 dossier 7379, and 24 361-368 dossier S 4.382.

J 1368 (denoted ADD above) in the Archives Départementales de la Dordogne in Perigueux contains numerous letters from Bugeaud to the Prefect Romieu between 1833 and 1844. It is particularly valuable for the light it throws on local politics and on Bugeaud as a budding *grand notable*. Also in the Archives Départementales, in J 118, are letters written by Bugeaud from Lyons to an unknown correspondent in February and March of 1849.

2. Published Primary Sources on Bugeaud

The principal documentary collections are:

Azan, Paul. *Par l'Épée et par la Charrue: écrits et discours de Bugeaud*. Paris: Presses universitaires de France, 1948.

Ideville, Henri Amédée Le Lorgne, comte d'. *Le maréchal Bugeaud d'après sa correspondance intime et des documents inédits, 1784-1849*. 3 vols. Paris: Librarie de Firmin-Didot et Cie, 1882.

Tattet, Eugène. *Lettres inédites du maréchal Bugeaud, duc d'Isly, 1808-1849*. Publiées par Mademoiselle Feray-Bugeaud d'Isly. Paris: Émile-Paul Frères, 1922.

Weil, [?]. *Oeuvres militaires du maréchal Bugeaud, duc d'Isly, réunies et mises en ordre*. Paris: Librairie Militaire de L. Baudoin et Cie, 1883.

Lesser but useful collections include:

Lanzac de Laborie, [?]. "Le maréchal Bugeaud et sa correspondance, d'après une récente publication et des lettres inédites." *Le Correspondant*, August 25 and September 10, 1923, 620-43, 870-90.

Maze, Daniel. "Lettres sur l'Algérie à Adolphe Blanqui." *Revue de Paris*, 3 (May-June 1898): 765-95.

Reyniers, François. "Treize lettres inédites du maréchal Bugeaud au colonel Rivet." *Revue africaine* 434-35 (1953): 165-95.

Other letters of interest by Bugeaud are available in:

Bourgin, Georges. "Deux hommes de 1848." *Revue politique et parlementaire* 659 (June 1956): 303-6.

Jardel, E. "Une lettre inédite de Bugeaud (20 fevrier 1820)." *Bulletin de la société historique et archéologique du Périgord*, bk. 103, no. 2 (1976): 148-9.

Reyniers, François. "Bugeaud et le père Enfantin." *Actes du 90e congrès national des sociétés savantes* (section d'histoire moderne et contemporaine) 3 (1965-66): 148-58.

———. "Bugeaud et le père Enfantin. Nouveaux documents inédits (1844)." *Actes du 91e congrès national des sociétés savantes* (section d'histoire moderne et contemporaine) 1 (1966): 341-54.

————. "Bugeaud et le père Enfantin. 3: documents inédits (1845)."
Actes du 92ᵉ congrès national des sociétés savantes (section
d'histoire moderne et contemporaine), 3 (1967): 261-73.

————. "Une lettre inédite du maréchal Bugeaud à M. Merilhou,
pair de France (1847)." *Actes du 93ᵉ congrès national des
sociétés savantes* (section d'histoire moderne et contemporaine)
3 (1968): 229-38.

With the exception of Ideville's pioneering effort, which mixes
primary sources with advocacy, these publications maintain consistently high scholarly standards.

For Bugeaud's parliamentary addresses in the 1831-39 period,
see

Chambres françaises. *Archives parlementaires de 1787 à 1860; recueil
complet des débats législatif et politique*. Paris: Paul Dupont,
1879-1913.

For the 1839-47 years, consult *Le Moniteur universel, Journal
officiel*. Most of his few parliamentary speeches during the latter
period are also available in Ideville.

3. *Published Primary Sources Pertaining to*
Bugeaud and the Dordogne

Easily the most important items in this category are the *Annales
agricoles et littéraires de la Dordogne. Journal des comices agricoles*,
published in Périgueux under the aegis of the Department's *Société
d'Agriculture, Sciences et Arts* between 1820 and 1890. Volumes
covering the 1820-40 period provide a wealth of information on
Bugeaud and agricultural reform in Perigord. Speeches by Bugeaud,
minutes of meetings of the Department's various comices, extracts
from farm journals and the local press, and commentaries on agricultural implements and techniques abound. Indeed, the *Annales
agricoles* constitute a fundamental source for any study of farming
in the Dordogne during the nineteenth century.

Also helpful to an understanding of Bugeaud, agriculture, and
local politics under the Restoration and July Monarchy are the
Department's various newspapers. Particularly interesting are the
*Mémorial de la Dordogne, organe ministeriel, administratif, politique,
littéraire, commercial et agricole*, and the *Écho de Vésone*. Under

the influence of Louis Veuillot and Pierre Magne, the *Mémorial de la Dordogne* was consistently friendly to Bugeaud and his political philosophy. The *Écho de Vésone*, on the other hand, attacked Bugeaud regularly from the Left for almost two decades. The *Écho* became particularly strident against the marshal in 1848 and 1849. Both papers are informative on local economics and elites, and mirror the shifting alliances and power centers of the time.

4. *Publications by Bugeaud*

A list of all essays Bugeaud wrote, and of articles or addresses whose republication he secured in booklet form, is available in Ideville, vol. 3, pp. 264-65, nn. 1-28. The most important of these are:

Bugeaud, Thomas-Robert. *L'Algérie: des moyens de conserver et d'utiliser notre conquête.* Paris: Dentu, 1842.

———. *Aperçus sur quelques détails de la guerre avec des planches explicatives.* Paris: Leneveu, 1832, 1846, 1860, 1873.

———. *De l'établissement des troupes à cheval dans de grandes fermes.* Paris: E. Brière, 1840.

———. "Des Travailleurs dans nos grandes villes," *Revue des deux mondes,* 22 (June 1848): 790-99.

———. *La Guerre d'Afrique. Lettre d'un lieutenant de l'armée d'Afrique à son oncle, vieux soldat de la Révolution et de l'Empire.* Paris: Gaultier-Laguionie, 1839. This pamphlet is included with twenty-nine others by various authors in an undated volume, with no collator or place of publication indicated, entitled simply *Mélanges militaires.*

———. "Les Socialistes et le travail en commun," *Revue des deux mondes* 23 (July 1848): 244-59.

———. *Mémoire sur notre établissement dans la province d'Oran par suite de la paix.* Paris: Gaultier-Laguionie, 1838.

———. *Quelques réflexions sur trois questions fondamentales de notre établissement en Algérie.* Paris: A. Guyot et Scribe, 1846.

———. *Veillées d'une chaumière de la Vendée.* Lyons: Guyot frères, 1849.

All or parts of several of these works, and of most of the other essays, are included in one or another of the four major documentary collections, or in the published correspondence of the Algerian governors-general between 1830 and 1840.

5. General Works on Bugeaud

No analytical, full-length biography of Bugeaud has yet been published. Most articles and books on Bugeaud are unscholarly, polemical, and tend to underemphasize his metropolitan in favor of his Algerian career. An important exception is:

Boyer, Pierre, and Esquer, Gabriel. "Bugeaud en 1840." *Revue africaine* 1-2, 3-4 (1960): 57-98, 283-321.

Also of use are:

Azan, Paul. "1848: Le maréchal Bugeaud." *Revue historique de l'armée* 4 (January-March 1948): 17-24.

Cossé-Brissac and Foucart, [?]. "Les grands hommes de guerre, vus par les Saint-Cyriens: le maréchal Bugeaud, duc d'Isly." *Revue historique de l'armée* 1 (February 1960): 104-24.

Dutacq, F. "Le dernier commandement du maréchal Bugeaud." *La Révolution de 1848* 23 (June 1926): 829-49.

Henon, Marcel. "Bugeaud, soldat de l'empereur (Napoleon 1er)." *Technique art science. Revue de l'enseignement technique* a. 30, trimester 4 (1977): 35-38.

Michel, Léon. "Bugeaud député d'Excideuil." *Périgord actualités* (September 1969-March 1970): 3 (each issue).

Reyniers, François. "Le Caméléon, navire à roues au service du maréchal Bugeaud (1844-1847)." *Revue maritime* 246 (August-September 1967): 1004-22.

Apart from these articles, however, the quality of publications which focus on Bugeaud is generally poor.

The most complete biography of Bugeaud is Maurice Andrieux's *Le Père Bugeaud, 1784-1849* (Paris: Librairie Plon, 1951). This book, however, is anecdotal, excessively laudatory, and lacks any significant basis in archival research. Additional biographies of Bugeaud include:

Azan, Paul. *Bugeaud et l'Algérie.* Paris: Le Petit Parisien, 1931.

Birr, Georges. *Un gentilhomme terrien: Thomas-Robert Bugeaud de la Piconnerie, maréchal de France, duc d'Isly.* Limoges: La Cour d'Appel, 1970.

Esperey, Franchet de, Louis Félix Marie François. *Bugeaud.* Paris: Hachette, 1938.

Kessel, Patrick. *Moi, maréchal Bugeaud: un soldat de l'ordre.* Paris: Petite Bibliothèque Républicaine, 1958.

Lamaze, Édouard de. *Bugeaud.* Paris: H. Lardanchet, 1943.

Lesourd, Paul. *Bugeaud: le soldat laboureur.* Paris: Les Éditions de Loisirs, 1943.

Lichtenberger, André. *Bugeaud.* Paris: Librairie Plon, 1931.

Lucas-Dubreton, Jean. *Bugeaud, le soldat—le député—le colonisateur; portraits et documents inédits.* Paris: Albin Michel, 1931.

Maubourguet, Jean. *Bugeaud, laboureur périgourdin.* Paris: Les Éditions de la France Nouvelle, 1942.

Morard, Louis. *Bugeaud.* Paris: Editions de l'Encyclopédie de l'Empire Français, 1947.

Petit-Colin, Claire. *Bugeaud.* Hanoi: Éditions de la Direction de l'Instruction Publique en Indochine, 1943 (?).

Poullin, Marcel. *Le maréchal Bugeaud: soldat et agriculteur.* Limoges: E. Ardant, 1887.

Generally, these works repeat each other and ignore most of the relevant archival sources.

6. *Works on Bugeaud in Algeria*

The best and broadest study of Bugeaud's Algerian career is available on pp. 164-387 of:

Julien, Charles-André. *Histoire de l'Algérie contemporaine. La Conquête et les débuts de la colonisation, 1827-1871.* Paris: Presses universitaires de France, 1964.

This magisterial history incorporates and expands upon Julien's essay "Bugeaud" in *Les Techniciens de la colonisation* (Paris: Presses universitaires de France, 1947) which he edited, and constitutes a point of departure for further study. Also instructive are:

Bussière, A. "Le maréchal Bugeaud et la colonisation de l'Algérie: souvenirs et récits de la vie coloniale en Afrique." *Revue des deux mondes* 4 (November 1853): 449-506.

Cochut, A. "De la colonisation de l'Algérie: les essais et les systèmes." *Revue des deux mondes* 17 (February 1847): 498-537.

Cossu, Pier Paolo. *I "bureaux arabes" e il Bugeaud.* Milan: Guiffrè, 1974.

Demontès, Victor. *La Colonisation militaire sous Bugeaud*. Paris: Larose, 1918.

Germain, Roger. *La Politique indigène de Bugeaud*. Paris: Larose, 1955.

Hugonnet, Ferdinand. *Bugeaud, duc d'Isly, maréchal de France, le conquerant de l'Algérie*. Paris: Leneveu, 1859.

————. *Français et Arabes en Algérie*. Paris: Challamel, 1860.

Ridley, Jack B. *Marshal Bugeaud, the July Monarchy and the Question of Algeria*. Ph.D. dissertation. University of Oklahoma: 1970.

The value of the last work, which summarizes political developments, the process of colonization and military progress in Algeria between 1841 and 1847, may be judged by its minimal primary documentation and failure to utilize Ideville's work except in an abridged English translation.

7. *Memoirs of Soldiers Who Campaigned in Algeria*

Helpful for analysis of Bugeaud and the colonial military are memoirs by the following soldiers who served in Algeria:

Canrobert, François Certain. *Le maréchal Canrobert: souvenirs d'un siècle*. Ed. Germain Bapst. 6 vols. Paris: Plon, 1899.

Lamping, Clemens. *The Soldier of the Foreign Legion*. Translated by Lady Duff Gordon. London: John Murray, 1845.

Montagnac, Lucien-François de. *Lettres d'un soldat: neuf années de campagnes en Afrique*. Paris: Plon, 1885.

Saint-Arnaud, Arnaud Jacques Leroy de. *Lettres du maréchal Saint-Arnaud*. 2 vols. Paris: Michel Levy, 1855.

8. *Correspondence of Algerian Governors-General, 1830-1840*

Publication by the *Gouvernement Général de l'Algérie* in the half century after 1914 of the correspondence of each of the Algerian governors-general (or their equivalent) during the first decade of the conquest, under the general title *Collection de documents inédits sur l'histoire de l'Algérie depuis 1830*, has made available an historical source of the highest importance to students of Bugeaud, colonial military policies, and Franco-Algerian relations in general. Individual titles in this series are:

Clauzel, maréchal comte Bertrand. *Correspondance du maréchal Clauzel, Gouverneur général des possessions françaises dans le nord de l'Afrique, 1835-1837.* Edited by Gabriel Esquer. 2 vols. Paris: Larose, 1948.

Damrémont, Lieutenant-général comte Charles Marie de. *Correspondance du général Damrémont, Gouverneur général des possessions françaises dans le Nord de l'Afrique 1837.* Edited by Georges Yver. Paris: Champion, 1927.

Erlon, lieutenant-général Jean Baptiste Drouet comte de. *Correspondance du général Drouet d'Erlon, Gouverneur général des possessions françaises dans le Nord de l'Afrique, 1834-1835.* Edited by Gabriel Esquer. Paris: Champion, 1926.

Rovigo, Anne Jean-Marie René Savary, duc de. *Correspondance du duc de Rovigo, Commandant en Chef du Corps d'Afrique, 1831-1833.* Edited by Gabriel Esquer. 4 vols. Algiers: Adolphe Jourdan, 1914-21.

Valée, maréchal comte Sylvain Charles. *Correspondance du maréchal Valée, Gouverneur general des Possessions françaises dans le Nord de l'Afrique, 1837-1840.* Edited by Georges Yver. 5 vols. Paris: Larose, 1949-57.

Voirol, Baron Théophile. *Correspondance du général Voirol, Commandant par interim du corps d'occupation d'Afrique, 1833-1834.* Edited by Gabriel Esquer. Paris: Champion, 1924.

9. Other Governmental and Official Publications

The two most important official publications relevant to the early years of French Algeria are:

Gouvernement général de l'Algérie. *Bulletin officiel des actes du gouvernement.* Paris: Imprimerie Royale, 1834-44. Algiers: Imprimerie du Gouvernement, 1840-70.

Ministère de la Guerre. *Tableau de la situation des établissements français dans l'Algérie.* Paris: Imprimerie Royale / Imperiale, 1838-58.

These multivolume works include the decrees of the colonial regime and of the metropolitan government concerning Algeria, and provide diverse information on all aspects of efforts by French administrators in Algiers to rule and develop their African colony. Many of the ordinances published in the *Bulletin officiel*, plus other official pronouncements and unofficial notices, are available in the *Moniteur algérien: Journal officiel de la Colonie, annonces légales, judicaires, administratives, commerciales et maritimes*, published under the aegis of the Gouvernement Général from 1832 through 1869.

10. Books, Monographs, Articles, General.

Given our era of high-cost publishing, I have attempted to keep this list as brief as possible. Included are only works specifically cited in the text or footnotes.

Ansky, Michel. *Les Juifs d'Algérie: du Décret Crémieux à la libération.* Paris: Editions du Centre, 1950.

Ba, Oumar. *La pénétration française au Cayor.* Dakar: Archives du Sénégal, 1976.

Bagge, Dominique. *Les idées politiques en France sous la Restauration.* Paris: Presses universitaires de France, 1952.

Baroli, Marc. *La vie quotidienne des français en Algérie, 1830-1914.* Paris: Hachette, 1967.

Barrows, Leland C. "Louis Léon César Faidherbe (1818-1889)." In *African Proconsuls: European Governors in Africa.* Edited by L. H. Gann and Peter Duignan. New York: The Free Press, 1978.

Bernard, Augustin. *L'Algérie.* Vol. 2 of *L'histoire des colonies françaises et de l'expansion de la France dans le monde.* Edited by Gabriel Hanotaux and Alfred Martineau. 3 vols. Paris:·Plon, 1931.

Blanc, Louis. *The History of Ten Years, 1830-1840.* 2 vols. London: Chapman and Hall, 1844-45.

Cambon, Jules. *Le gouvernement-général de l'Algérie, 1891-1897.* Paris: Champion, 1918.

Castellane, Esprit Victor Elisabeth Boniface, comte de. *Journal du maréchal de Castellane, 1804-1862.* 5 vols. Paris: Plon, 1895-1900.

Chouraqui, André N. *Between East and West: A History of the Jews of North Africa.* Philadelphia: Jewish Publication Society of America, 1969.

Collins, Irene. *The Government and the Newspaper Press in France, 1814-1881.* London: Oxford University Press, 1959.

Crémieux, Albert. *La révolution de février: étude critique sur les journées des 21, 22, 23 et 24 février 1848.* Paris: Bibliothèque d'histoire moderne, 1912.

Dauzat, Albert. *Le Village et le paysan de France.* Paris: Gallimard, 1941, 1949.

Durieux, Joseph. *Le Ministre Pierre Magne, 1806-1879. D'après ses lettres et ses souvenirs.* 2 vols. Paris: Librairie Ancienne Honoré Champion, 1929.

Émerit, Marcel. *L'Algérie à l'époque d'Abd el Kader.* Paris: Larose, 1951.

Enfantin, Barthelemy Prosper. *La Colonisation de l'Algérie.* Paris: P. Bertrand, 1843.

Gottman, Jean. "Bugeaud, Gallieni, Lyautey: The Development of French Colonial Warfare." In *Makers of Modern Strategy: Military Thought from Machiavelli to Hitler.* Edited by Edward Mead Earle, pp. 234-59. Princeton: Princeton University Press, 1943.

Guiral, Pierre. *Marseille et l'Algérie, 1830-1841.* Gap: Editions Ophrys, 1957.

———. "Observations et réflexions sur les sévices dans l'armée d'Afrique." *Revue de l'occident musulman et de la Méditerranée* 15-16 (1973): 15-20.

Guizot, François Pierre Guillaume, *Mémoires pour servir à l'histoire de mon temps.* 8 vols. Paris: Michel Levy frères, 1858-67.

Huré, [?]. "Stratégie et tactique marocaine." *Revue des questions de défense nationale,* vol. 1, no. 3 (July 1939): 397-412.

Kearny, Philip. *Service with the French Troops in Africa.* New York: William Abbott, 1913.

Langer, William. *Political and Social Upheaval, 1832-1852.* New York: Harper and Row, 1969.

de Launay, Jacques. *Le Dossier de Vichy.* Paris: Julliard, 1967.

Le Roy, Eugène. *Jacquou the Rebel.* Translated by Eleanor Stimson Brooks. New York: E. P. Dutton and Company, 1919.

Lyautey, Louis Hubert Gonzalve. "Du rôle colonial de l'armée." *Revue des deux mondes* 157 (January 1900): 308-28.

Maurice, Fernand. *La Réforme Agraire et la Misère en France.* Paris: La Terre aux Paysans, 1887.

Méline, Jules. *Le Retour à la terre et la surproduction industrielle.* Paris: Hachette, 1905.

———. *The Return to the Land* with preface by Justin McCarthy. London: Chapman and Hall, 1906.

———. *Le Salut par la terre et le programme économique de l'avenir.* Paris: Hachette, 1919.

O'Brien, Patricia. "*L'Embastillement de Paris*: The Fortification of Paris during the July Monarchy." *French Historical Studies* 9 (Spring 1975): 63-82.

Paxton, Robert O. *Vichy France: Old Guard and New Order, 1940-1944.* New York: Alfred A. Knopf, 1972.

Pélissier de Reynaud, E. *Annales algériennes.* 3 vols. Paris: Librairie Militaire, 1854.

Rébillot, Joseph Paul Alfred. *Souvenirs de révolution et de guerre.* Paris: Berger-Levrault, 1912.

Richter, Melvin. "Tocqueville on Algeria." *Review of Politics* 25 (July 1963): 362-98.

Rocal, Georges. *Croquants du Périgord.* Paris: Librairie Floury, 1934.

———. *1848 en Dordogne.* 2 vols. Paris: Occitania, 1933.

Rogniat, Joseph. *Considérations sur l'art de la guerre.* 2nd edition. Paris: Magimel, Anselin and Pochard, 1817.

———. *De la colonisation de l'Algérie et des fortifications propres à garantir les colons des incursions des tribus africaines.* Paris: Gaultier-Laguionie, 1840.

Starzinger, Vincent E. *Middlingness: Juste Milieu Political Theory in France and England, 1815-1848.* Charlottesville: University Press of Virginia, 1965.

Trochu, Louis Jules. *L'armée française en 1867.* Paris: Amyot, 1867.

———. *Oeuvres posthumes.* 2 vols. Tours: Alfred Mame, 1896.

Véron, Louis Désiré. *Mémoires d'un bourgeois de Paris.* 5 vols. Paris: Librairie nouvelle, 1855-1856.

Wagner, Moritz. *The Tricolor on the Atlas: or, Algeria and the French Conquest.* Translated by Francis Pulszky. New York: T. Nelson and Sons, 1854.

Weber, Eugen. *Peasants into Frenchmen: The Modernization of Rural France, 1870-1914.* Stanford: Stanford University Press, 1976.

Wright, Gordon. *Rural Revolution in France: The Peasantry in the Twentieth Century.* Stanford: Stanford University Press, 1964.

Yacono, Xavier. *Les Bureaux Arabes et l'évolution des genres de vie indigène dans l'ouest du Tell Algérois.* Paris: Larose, 1953.

Yver, Georges. *Documents relatifs au traité de la Tafna (1837).* Algiers: Carbonel, 1924.

Index